ISTORICAL COLLECTION OF THE DETROIT PUBLIC LIBRARY

Rabbi Norbert L. Rosenthal

A million candles have burned themselves out. Still I read on.

—Montresor.

The
BETH EL
Story

with

A HISTORY OF THE JEWS IN MICHIGAN
Before 1850

DEDICATED TO THE MEMORY OF

LEO M. FRANKLIN AND

B. BENEDICT GLAZER

DR. LEO M. FRANKLIN

Rabbi of Temple Beth El *Rabbi Emeritus*

1899 — 1941 *1941 — 1948*

DR. B. BENEDICT GLAZER

Rabbi of Temple Beth El

1941 — 1952

THE BETH EL STORY

with a history of

THE JEWS IN MICHIGAN BEFORE 1850

by IRVING I. KATZ

and

THREE HUNDRED YEARS IN AMERICA

by DR. JACOB R. MARCUS

DETROIT WAYNE UNIVERSITY PRESS 1955

DETROIT 1, MICHIGAN

LIBRARY OF CONGRESS CATALOG CARD NO. 55-7560

A Prefatory Note by the City Historiographer

In a community like Detroit, where peoples from all the world have come to mingle their cultures and traditions, it is extremely important to have an understanding of all the groups making up our common society.

Now we congratulate ourselves on having this new and comprehensive study of the coming of the Jew to Detroit and Michigan. His contributions to our development in trade and commerce has been considerable and to our culture even greater.

Nobody is better qualified to examine the factors in this story and to put them together than Irving I. Katz, executive secretary of Temple Beth El. He is qualified by a scholarly temperament and by a close experience of his subject.

He has been at Temple Beth El a matter of sixteen years and thus was closely associated with the late revered Rabbi Leo M. Franklin. Dr. Franklin had already accumulated a mass of historical data respecting the Jew in Detroit and Michigan, possibly with some idea of bringing it out as a book at some future time.

That future time is now and Mr. Katz has wisely selected the American Jewish Tercentenary Year, now being observed, for this publication.

The non-Jew will find as much excitement in perusing Mr. Katz's story as the Jew. For the familiar names of history are invoked again and we come face to face with those men and women of good will who have made so tremendous an impact on the Detroit story.

GEORGE W. STARK
Historiographer of Detroit
President, The Detroit Historical Society

Foreword

AT LAST the first comprehensive story of the Jews of Michigan has been published for the benefit of posterity—a most gratifying thought.

Knowledge of the past is a valuable means to an understanding of the present. This book, based as it is on years of research, is a veritable gold mine of information and pictorial remembrance.

It is especially fitting that Temple Beth El, which was the first synagogue in Michigan, should also be the one to make possible the publication of the first important Michigan Jewish history. That has long been overdue.

I am happy to report to Nate S. Shapero, president during our centennial year, that the assignment has been completed.

Back in 1950 the president and board of trustees of the Temple approved a history of our Temple's first century as one of the highlights of Beth El's 100th anniversary celebration. Research and preparation were to be by Irving I. Katz, our indefatigable executive secretary, in collaboration with Dr. B. Benedict Glazer. I was given the responsibility of seeing the project completed.

Then, the sudden tragic death of our beloved Rabbi Glazer. . . .

After many months conditions at the Temple returned to normal. Mr. Katz gradually found the time to complete his labor of love.

We of Beth El are grateful that the origin and development of our spiritual institution and its contributions through the years to the welfare of our membership, of the Detroit community and our nation, have been chronicled in these pages.

On behalf of the 1,663 families that are today members of our congregation, I wish to congratulate and thank Irving I. Katz. We are deeply indebted to him. Well done, Irving.

LEONARD N. SIMONS
President, Temple Beth El

Author's Preface

I DEEM IT A rare privilege and a signal honor to dedicate this book as a tribute to the inspired leadership of two "giants of the spirit" who have played an important role in my life—the illustrious rabbis of Beth El, Dr. Leo M. Franklin and Dr. B. Benedict Glazer.

For nearly half a century, Franklin, disciple of Isaac M. Wise, the founder and master builder of Reform Judaism in the United States, was esteemed throughout Detroit and Michigan and the nation as a distinguished leader and rabbi.

I owe my interest in local Jewish historical matters primarily to him. He carefully preserved every historical record he found at Beth El at the time of his arrival in 1899 and he wrote the history of Beth El at the time of its fiftieth anniversary in 1900. He shared with me his recollections of some of the early pioneers of our congregation as well as of his early ministry in Detroit. He made available to me all the important historical documents which he had unearthed during his long residence in Detroit.

When I read his warm letter of welcome on my appointment as Executive Secretary of Beth El, I sensed his spiritual greatness. I soon learned how beloved and revered he was among people of all creeds and what he did for his own people as well as for the community. In a city which has become a world-wide symbol of the machine age, he fought for the dignity and rights of the individual, and it was this philosophy of the individual that he brought into the councils of the many organizations with which he was prominently identified.

In my daily contacts with him I observed his intense love for America and for Judaism. Throughout his rich and varied career, he taught the vital message that the basic premises of American democracy flow from and are reinforced by the insights and teachings of the Prophets of Israel. Thus, he proclaimed constantly that "one became a better American by being a better Jew."

What inspired me most of all in his ministry was his dedication to the tireless service of his congregation. He gave unsparingly of his time, energy and good heart to the troubled, the sick, and the sorrowing. He was greatly beloved by all as the perfect pastor, and his memory is cherished by thousands of men and women whom he served in hours of joy and sorrow.

Dr. B. Benedict Glazer came to Detroit in 1941 to succeed Dr. Franklin after serving with distinction two leading congregations in the country—Temple Rodef Shalom of Pittsburgh and Temple Emanu-El of New York. Despite the fact that under the leadership of his predecessor a pattern of ministrations was set for him that seemed almost impossible of emulation, he found new tasks to perform and new services to render, touching deeply the lives of thousands of persons during the comparatively short time of his sojourn in Detroit.

He possessed the priceless gift of an unusual personality, a personality richly compounded, a personality rare in the variety of its ingredients and rare, also, in its depth and strength. Outstanding among his qualities was his questing intellect, his eager, open and alert mind, a mind quick to perceive and comprehend and as sure to retain not only facts but their significance as well. With such a mind, he was able to bring to bear upon the troubled situations of life the authority of both reason and knowledge. Added to these fine endowments, Dr. Glazer was blessed with an exceedingly sympathetic heart. This is why of all forms of social endeavor and helpfulness he gave the maximum amount of his time and thought to mental health. Then, too, he was always in the forefront as a champion for some righteous cause and as a fearless and forthright spokesman for a better social order based on truth, justice and humanity. There was one other trait with which he was blessed—his fine sense of humor, whose mirthful quality issued from a nature that loved life, loved people, and above all, loved to see them happy and at ease.

He was greatly admired, beloved and respected by all of us. No wonder, then, that he was regarded as one of the leading rabbis in the United States and that shortly before his untimely death he was cited as one of the seven leading citizens of Detroit.

I am indebted to the following faculty members of Wayne University for their suggestions and guidance: Harold A. Basilius, Professor of German and Director of the Humanities Program; Alexander Brede, Associate Professor of English; Sidney Glazer, Associate Professor of History; G. Flint Purdy, Director of Wayne University Libraries and Chairman of the Editorial Board of Wayne University Press; and G. Alden Smith, Associate Professor of Art. I am especially grateful to Louis L. Friedland, Associate Professor of Public Administration and a member of Temple Beth El, for his interest in this book and for his valuable assistance at all times.

To my friend and mentor, Dr. Jacob R. Marcus, America's foremost Jewish historian, I owe more than mere words can express, for he has been my inspiration for many years. He saw the original manuscript through from its very beginning to its publication by the Wayne University Press. I am grateful to him for his unflagging interest in my humble efforts and for permission to use his address "300 Years in America," which he delivered from the pulpit of Temple Beth El on January 15, 1954.

I wish, also, to record my appreciation to the following individuals and institutions who were most helpful in the preparation of this volume: Mrs. Elleine H. Stones, Chief of the Burton Historical Collection of the Detroit Public Library; Francis W. Robinson, Curator of Medieval Art at the Detroit Institute of Arts; Ralph L. Polk, Jr., president of R. L. Polk and Company; the Library of the Hebrew Union College and the American Jewish Archives in Cincinnati; and the William L. Clements Library of the University of Michigan in Ann Arbor.

To my good friend, Nate S. Shapero, president of Temple Beth El during its eventful centennial year, I gratefully acknowledge my indebtedness for his vision in urging the Board of Trustees to undertake and underwrite the publication of the hundred years' history of our congregation. Unfortunately, pressure of duties and the untimely death of Dr. Glazer prevented the publication of the history as originally scheduled. The present volume, which has had the unabated interest of Mr. Shapero, is an enlargement of his original plans. While the historical data and pictorial matter of the volume are the result of painstaking research of many years, it does not purport to be a definitive history either of the Jews in Michigan prior to 1850 or of Temple Beth El of Detroit, Michigan's oldest Jewish congregation.

To Dr. Richard C. Hertz, Rabbi Minard Klein, Dr. Norman Drachler, to the officers and trustees of Temple Beth El, and to the men and women who comprise the warm fellowship of the congregation, I express my sincere thanks for their interest in this book. I am especially grateful to Dr. Hertz for his scholarly introduction to it and his enthusiastic interest in the publication. I want to thank also my secretary, Mrs. Bernice Reisler, for her competent assistance to me.

Finally, I desire to acknowledge my everlasting gratitude to Leonard N. Simons, present president of Temple Beth El. It was he who encouraged me time and again to complete the history manuscript so that it could be published during the American Jewish Tercentenary Year and it is his personal interest and financial support that are largely responsible for the appearance of this book.

IRVING I. KATZ

Detroit, Michigan
December, 1954

Contents

Introduction

RABBI RICHARD C. HERTZ

Introduction

ANYONE WHO HAS ever wandered about the stony trails of Mackinac Island, let us say, or among the gravestones of Detroit's Lafayette Cemetery (originally Champlain Cemetery), Detroit's oldest extant Jewish cemetery, must muse on what long-forgotten memories are held beneath these stones!

In these pages such memories come to life again. Here you will find history in its most interesting sense: biography, controversy, romance, devotion—the stuff out of which pioneer men and women in Michigan created Congregation Beth El.

It is good to be reminded that Jews came to the Michigan territory when it was still a battleground for the French and English, when the Indians regarded all white men, regardless of their national loyalties or creedal beliefs, as predatory interlopers preying upon their precious hunting grounds. Yes, the forbears of Jews in Detroit fought and bled, lived and died, during the early development of Michigan. One can scarcely realize that only a few generations ago pioneering Jews, along with Catholics and Protestants, Frenchmen and Englishmen, pushed back the wilderness of the Great Lakes country and opened a new continent. They may have amassed no fortunes and left few landmarks, but those old-timers performed a useful function for their day. Life was rough and barren in the wilderness. Who knows what simple comforts those Jewish peddlers brought with their needles and threads, their kitchen utensils and buttons and cottons!

Try to visualize what it meant a century or two ago to procure a needle on Mackinac Island, the center of the fur-trading business of the Great Lakes region. The needle made in Great Britain had to be shipped by slow sailing vessel across the Atlantic Ocean to Montreal, there transferred to river cargo on the St. Lawrence, then put in canoes at the edge of the Great Lakes, paddled through Lake Ontario, Lake Erie, the Detroit River, Lake St. Clair and Lake Huron until at long, long last it reached Mackinac Island—that is, barring violent storms, or attacks by Indians, or sickness or disaster along the way. And all for a needle!

* * *

The year 1850, when Temple Beth El was organized, was a year of great decision in the national life of this country. It was the year of the great compromise, expected to settle the irrepressible conflict and set at rest the sectional conflict over slavery. That year ushered in a decade of mounting tensions that saw the anti-alienism of the Know-Nothing movement reach its zenith. Before long, "bleeding Kansas" became a battleground for border ruffians who fought it out with guns even as Stephen A. Douglas was trying to smooth it out with words. Mr. Lincoln of Illinois was coming into his own, soon to challenge Douglas in a series of immortal debates that "this nation cannot remain half-slave, half-free . . . a house divided against itself." The turbulent 1850's were a period of ferment, when reformers of society were boiling over and abolitionists of slavery were seething with indignation. A new era was in the making. Men were trying to chart a new society, and liberals faced hopefully the task of building a new world.

This was the time, then, when a few devout Jews gathered in Detroit during the summer of 1850 to establish a synagogue. The story of Beth El's rise from humble beginnings to the fourth largest Reform Jewish congregation in America is a mirror of Detroit's rise from obscurity to industrial might. As Detroit grew, so grew Beth El. In 1850, twelve families gathered to form the congregation. A half century later, when Rabbi Franklin became spiritual leader in 1899, the congregation numbered 136 members. When Dr. B. Benedict Glazer, his successor, died prematurely in 1952, the congregation had grown to 1,524 members. Today, in 1954, 1,663 families are affiliated—a community of nearly 6,000 men, women and children. Truly a stalwart host!

Temple Beth El was formed in 1850 as a strictly traditional synagogue. But just as the 1850's were a decade of ferment in political affairs, so were those years a time of change in Jewish religious affairs as well. During this period, reforms were being adopted in congregations all over the land. Boston, New York, Chicago, Baltimore, Cleveland, Cincinnati —everywhere the trend was towards reform in ritual: mixed choirs, men and women sitting together in family pews, prayers offered in the vernacular, the prayer book revised, abolition of the *talis* and covered heads for men during worship, introduction of confirmation for boys and girls. These reforms were adopted in Detroit's new synagogue during the first years, so that before long it had put aside its orthodox ways.

In 1854, just one hundred years ago this year, Isaac M. Wise left his post in Albany to become rabbi of Cincinnati's Congregation B'nai Yeshurun. He brought with him the idea of reform, a plan to change not alone his own congregation but all others in the land as well. Almost immediately after his arrival he established *The Israelite,* a weekly journal that found its way into the homes of Jews in nearly every state of the Union. Just a few years before, in 1843, Isaac Leeser, spiritual leader of Philadelphia's Mikveh Israel Congregation, had established the national Jewish periodical *The Occident.* Leeser and Wise, each a titan, seldom saw eye to eye on Jewish issues. Leeser was a conservative, Wise a reformer. Between Philadelphia and Cincinnati there developed an East-West conflict over the pattern of Jewish life in America. For a time it seemed that Detroit hesitated, yet it was soon clear that Detroit's Beth El was siding with Wise and Reform. The defection of seventeen Beth El members over the issue of music and a mixed choir at worship, a split which resulted in the forming of Shaarey Zedek in 1861, cast the die irrevocably. Temple Beth El had become a Reform congregation!

During this same period, the public school movement of Horace Mann was gaining popular acceptance. Local communities were at last recognizing their responsibilities to provide free, tax-supported, nonsectarian public schools for children. The need, therefore, disappeared almost at once for a synagogue to maintain a parochial day school. Instead, the Sunday School movement grew in its place and became the standard method of providing religious instruction to the young. Gradually, English replaced German as the tongue of teaching and the language of the sermon. The Americanization of immigrant Jews was hastened beyond calculation when their children went to public school and mastered the three R's not as Jews but as Americans; the language of the younger generation ceased to be German and became English.

The Americanization of early Reform Jewish leaders became their abiding passion. They looked upon Reform Judaism as the Americanized version of the Jewish religion. The liberal Pittsburgh platform of 1885 crystallized the classic position of Beth El and other Reform congregations of the day.

In the 1870's Isaac M. Wise's dream of an alliance of all Reform congregations was realized. The year 1873 saw the formation of the Union of American Hebrew Congregations, in which delegates from Temple Beth El served as charter representatives. Two years later came the realization of another of Wise's dreams—the Hebrew Union College, established in 1875 so that rabbis could be trained in an American environment and with American standards of pedagogy. Nine different European-trained rabbis were to serve Beth El, however, before the tenth, Dr. Louis Grossmann, became the congregation's first rabbi to have been ordained in the United States at the Hebrew Union College. From his time on, in 1884, no rabbi ever served Temple Beth El who was not a graduate of the Hebrew Union College.

Rabbi Grossmann ushered in a new era for Temple Beth El. The Orthodox *Machzor* was replaced with Wise's *Minhag America* prayer book for the High Holidays; emphasis on teaching the young was accelerated; Sunday morning services were instituted; and ultimately, late Friday evening services were reintroduced. The congregation was on a solid and substantial foundation when Rabbi Grossmann left in 1898 to become Associate Rabbi to Isaac M. Wise himself and, two years later, on Wise's death, to succeed him in Cincinnati.

Thus, when that remarkable man, Rabbi Leo M. Franklin, arrived from Omaha in January, 1899, the time had come when a gifted organizer and energetic leader could convert Temple Beth El from one of many small synagogues scattered throughout the land into one of America's largest, most prominent and influential congregations in the entire Reform Jewish movement.

The pages that follow speak for themselves. Line by line, they detail Dr. Franklin's great contribution to Beth El and those which his distinguished and beloved successor, Dr. B. Benedict Glazer, added to its glory.

INTRODUCTION

This year 1954 marks the 300th anniversary since twenty-three Jews, seeking a chance to live freely and happily, landed on Manhattan Island. They had no right to citizenship; they had to work for it. They had no right to worship; they had to fight for it. But from their time on, Jews came to these shores with hope in their hearts, "with ideas in their heads, with muscles in their arms." The spiritual birthday party which American Jewry is celebrating this year calls for something else besides self-congratulations. The tercentenary is a call for each community in America to "remember the days of old," to dig deeply into the records of the past, to emulate the spiritual heroism of our founding fathers.

Back in 1892, when Oscar S. Straus served as first president of the American Jewish Historical Society, he uttered these prophetic words: "Every nation, race and creed which contributed towards building up this great continent and country, should, from motives of patriotism, gather up its records and chronicles, so that our historians may be able to examine and describe the forces that our national and political existence have amalgamated."

This is what Irving I. Katz has done here; this is what other Jewish communities elsewhere ought to do. For this we owe our country: to tell the story of our years. It is a chronicle that will make our hearts glow with pride!

RICHARD C. HERTZ

Jews in MICHIGAN before 1850

IRVING I. KATZ

Diorama of the arrival of 23 Jews at New Amsterdam, 1654. Courtesy of the American Jewish Archives

Jews in Michigan Before 1850

THREE CENTURIES AGO, in 1654, a group of twenty-three Jews who had fled Brazil in the face of threatened persecution, arrived in New Amsterdam. There, in the town that was later to become New York City, these twenty-three refugees founded the first Jewish community in what is now the United States. This year, 1954, marks the tercentenary of organized Jewish life on the North American continent.

The Northern Hemisphere had seen the arrival of individual Jews even before 1654 in Virginia, Maryland, and Massachusetts, where they were among the earliest pioneers. There are records of the first Jews in Pennsylvania in 1656, Rhode Island in 1658, Connecticut in 1659 and South Carolina in 1695. Hardly had the new colony of Georgia been founded when the first Jews arrived there in 1733. By the time of the American Revolution, the number of Jews living in the Thirteen Colonies has been estimated at from 1,000 to 2,500. Almost all of them were merchants and traders and the majority settled in the major towns along the Atlantic seaboard.

It is doubtful whether any professing Jews lived as permanent settlers in New France (Canada) during its occupancy by the French. The Jewish settlement in Canada, of which present day Michigan was a part, began following the conquest by the English of Quebec (September, 1759) and Montreal (September, 1760). During the eighteenth century, the area that constitutes modern Michigan was physically and politically part of a sprawling Canadian wilderness. The fur traders who early exploited the vast territory had access to the East only by way of the river and lake routes. As a consequence, Michigan and Canadian history are for practical purposes of a single fabric until 1796. Only then did an international boundary effectively sever the unity of Michigan and Canada.

The Peace of 1763 brought an end to the Seven Years' War (French and Indian War) and to French rule in the New World. Canada, including what is now Michigan, passed into British hands. As early as 1760, however, Major Robert Rogers and an English garrison had captured control of Detroit, the French trading post and village established fifty-nine years before by Antoine de la Mothe Cadillac. But formal British rule from 1763 to 1774 was to differ little from the original policies established by the French in the Canada-Michigan area. With passage of the Quebec Act in 1774, Michigan was officially attached to Canada by the English Crown.

In 1783, however, the treaty of peace, marking the end of the Revolutionary War, stipulated a new disposition for Michigan, that it be ceded to the new-born American republic. Yet, it was not until 1796 that the British relinquished their hold on American Northwest forts. For thirteen years, the Union Jack flew "illegally" over Michigan and during those years Canadian and Michigan history remained knit as one.

British inroads into Canada brought in their wake the first Jewish immigrants. Jewish migrants followed close on the heels of the British seizure of Quebec, Montreal, and Detroit. After 1760, Montreal was to become the commercial headquarters of Jewish traders. Detroit, established as Fort Pontchartrain du Détroit, was predominantly French Catholic when the British wrested it from French control. Fort Pontchartrain du Détroit simply became Fort Detroit. It was still the center of the Indian trade in the Northwest. But the stockade and village which to the Indians had symbolized French mastery over the territory now became the sign of British power. The infiltration of Anglo-Saxon influences into the heretofore French Catholic domain brought also the earliest Jewish settlers and commercial pioneers.

Among the first Jewish merchants who came to Montreal at the time of the English occupation were Ezekiel Solomon, Chapman Abraham, Levi Solomons, Benjamin Lyon, and Gershon Levi. They were business partners, engaged as commissaries of the English armies during the French and Indian War, the final contest between England and France for supremacy on the American continent, and the subsequent Indian

War of 1763 led by Chief Pontiac. They probably came together directly from England with the troops themselves and may have learned their trade as supply men to the armies of Europe. Quartermaster work was a common Jewish occupation on the European continent in the eighteenth century; an arduous but often lucrative trade. The partners had their own limited resources, some financial support back in England, and possibly the help of Hayman Levy, the well-known colonial trader of New York. After the conquest of Canada the partners branched out into the expanding fur trade.

Ezekiel Solomon

The story of earliest Michigan is one of the explorer, the missionary, and the trader—the men who followed the Great Lakes waterways to the frontiers of Michigan and beyond. Along these waterways the traders established trading posts and so contributed greatly to the settlement and growth of Michigan.

Fort Michilimackinac (Mackinac) was one of the most important of the early posts on the Great Lakes. Located on the sandy south side of the straits near the tip of Michigan's lower peninsula, it was the principal fort north of Detroit. It oversaw the commerce of three lakes and served as a meeting place for the nearby Chippewa and Ottawa Indian tribes. The French occupied the fort until the autumn of 1760, when its commandant, Captain Louis de Beaujeu, abandoned it to the victorious British. English troops did not arrive to take possession of their prize until a year later, on September 28, 1761. During that year, the fort was occupied by bush-ranging French traders, most of them half-breeds.

Ezekiel Solomon and a few hardy traders came to Mackinac in the summer of 1761 in advance of the English troops, in order to pre-empt some of the rich northern fur trade. So that they might win over the Chippewa Indians to their side, the English traders distributed presents to them and succeeded in winning their friendship. But no sooner had they become friendly with the Chippewas than a band of nearby Ottawas presented demands and threatened destruction of the group. Fortunately Captain Henry Balfour, Lieutenant William Leslye and a garrison of English soldiers arrived in time to rescue the traders, including Ezekiel Solomon, from the impending peril. Solomon continued his trading business in Mackinac and so became the first known Jewish settler in Michigan. A native of Berlin, Germany, he was the brother of Esther Solomon, who married Moses Hart, a brother of Aaron Hart, the foremost Jewish settler in Canada at the time of the English occupation in 1760 and the founder of the prominent Jewish Canadian family of that name. He was also the cousin of Levi Solomons, his business partner.

Ezekiel Solomon and three of his partners went through the horrors of the general Indian uprising of 1763, known as Pontiac's Conspiracy, and shared the common experience of an Indian captivity with its imminent threat of death by torture. Most of the Indian leaders realized that once the English settlers began pouring across the Allegheny Mountains, hunting and trapping would be threatened and the Indians themselves would have to move out.

Indian resentment of English officials and unscrupulous traders was further heightened by the incitements of a bitter French population. The Indians rose in a great effort to end the influx of English settlers and soldiery. Significantly enough, Pontiac's Conspiracy was not directed against the French. The Indians were quite aware of many of the advantages offered to them by the fur trade with white settlers.

According to Chief Pontiac's plan, a simultaneous attack was to have been launched on all the forts in the possession of the English and the garrisons annihilated in one stroke. At Mackinac, the scheme was to engage in a game of ball, at the exciting stage of which the ball was to be tossed, presumably by accident, within the fort, whither the warriors were to rush after it, only to seize the weapons which their squaws, by prearrangement, had taken into the fort, hidden under their blankets. The scheme was carried out successfully on June 2, 1763.

Among the traders who witnessed the horrible massacre by the Indians of the English soldiers and traders was Ezekiel Solomon. This appears from his affidavit taken in Montreal for use before the Military Court of Inquiry held later by Major Henry Gladwin at Detroit. It reads as follows:

> I Ezekiel Solomon, Resident in the Fort of Michilimackinac at the time it was surprised by the Savages, declare that on the 2d day of June a Frenchman, Mons. Cote, entered my House several Times and carried from thence several Parcels of Goods, my Property. And also an Indian named Sanpear carried the Peltry from my House to the House of Amiable Deniviere in whose Garret I

> was concealed. I owed Monsr Ariek a sum of money, but at the time He demanded it the payment was not become due, and I refused to pay Him till the Time I contracted for; but he told me if I did not pay it he would take it by force; I told him, the Commanding Officer would prevent that, & he replyed that the Commanding Officer was nothing, and that he Himself was Commanding Officer. Sworn, &c., 14th Aug., 1763, before me.
>
> Danl Disney, Town Major

Solomon was taken prisoner by the Indians and was one of the few Englishmen, military or civilian, to remain alive. According to Alexander Henry, traveler and trader, he was later taken to Montreal by the Ottawas and ransomed.

The fur trade was a hazardous industry. Most of the Indian goods had to be transported all the way from London to the warehouses on the St. Lawrence River. Marine insurance was expensive and not always easy to secure. Once the trade supplies arrived, the canoes were loaded and sent to the Upper Country, risking the dangers of pioneer travel, rivers, rapids and difficult portages. Frequently the Indians had to be "carried on the books" for a season or two before the furs came in. Then came the arduous task of carrying the skins back to settlements and of transporting them to the European market. It was not unusal for a merchant in England to wait two, if not three, years for the arrival of the bale of furs which was to compensate him for his advances. When the furs finally arrived he was never certain that the public wanted his merchandise or that they could afford his luxury product at that particular time. Added to these normal difficulties was the looting, in 1763, of the merchants' stocks. Outstanding debts owed by Indians for preceding seasons were hardly collectable. The Pontiac War ravaged the frontier for over a year and it was not until July, 1766 that a peace treaty was finally signed between the English and the Indians.

Despite the obstacles which stood between the commercial pioneer and the realization of profit, competition among merchants grew sharper as American traders from New York and Pennsylvania began to invade the western frontiers. Working out of Lancaster and Philadelphia, these eastern traders, a number of whom were Jews, penetrated the Ohio and Mississippi river basins as far west as the Illinois country. There, with increasing frequency, they began to cross paths with their competitors, the Canadian fur packs inching north toward the trading posts and ports of the Great Lakes. American and Canadian traders bore similar difficulties in the struggle against distance, nature, and Indians, but the Canadian merchants labored under several additional burdens—the 3 per cent tariff on imports and another 3 per cent on furs exported. Not until 1769 were these taxes lifted. American traders in these years held an advantage in their freedom from any such tax load. Even the new licenses issued to Canadian fur traders after 1769 preserved a number of severe restrictions. But until 1769, Montreal and Quebec merchants were particularly hard-pressed.

Solomon and his partners were no exceptions, and in 1768 they confessed they were unable to meet their financial obligations. They offered to make a settlement, surrendering all their property, and most of the creditors were willing even though the assets would not have yielded more than seven shillings in the pound. However, when other creditors would entertain no thought of such an arrangement, the debtors, on the advice of Attorney General Francis Maseres, presented a joint petition to Governor Guy Carleton asking for some sort of financial arrangement, or the appointment of a commission of bankruptcy which would be authorized to divide the remaining assets equally among the creditors.

They did not want to expose themselves to the danger of court action by individual creditors and of imprisonment for debt. Once they were jailed, their hopes of making a living for their families and getting back on their feet would have been slim indeed. Isaac Levi, one of the creditors, whom the firm owed £1,000, joined in the following memorial:

> The memorial of Isaac Levi of Quebec, merchant, and Levi Solomons, Benjamin Lyon, Gershon Levy, Ezekiel Solomon, and Chapman Abraham of Quebec, late merchants and copartners, to the Honourable Guy Carleton, Esquire, Lieutenant-Governor and Commander-in-Chief of the province of Quebec, and the Honourable Council of said province, humbly sheweth unto your Excellency and Honours:
>
> That your petitioners Levi Solomons, Benjamin Lyon, Gershon Levy, Ezekiel Solomon, and Chapman Abraham were for many years together merchants and copartners in trade in North America, and more especially during the time of the late war with France and the subsequent Indian War in the year 1763;

And that they were employed during part of the time of the said wars to furnish divers necessaries to his Majesty's armies in North America, in which employment they behaved with diligence and honesty and gave general satisfaction to the commanders and other officers of his Majesty's armies aforesaid, as is well known and may be easily proved to the satisfaction of your Excellency and Honours by divers respectable persons now in this province;

And that during the aforesaid Indian War four of your five petitioners last mentioned were made prisoners by the Indians near the forts of Detroit and Michilimackinac and despoiled by them at the same time of a great quantity of goods, which they were carrying to the said forts, of the value of eighteen thousand pounds of lawful money of this province;

And that by this and other unavoidable losses and misfortunes in the said war, no ways owing to any misconduct in your petitioners, your petitioners became utterly unable to pay their creditors the full amount of their just debts;

And further that your said last mentioned petitioners having preserved another considerable part of their effects were and still are earnestly desirous of surrendering the same into the hands of proper persons for the general satisfaction of all their creditors in proportion to their several just debts and demands, without any undue preference of some of their said creditors above the rest, in making which surrender they conceive they should act both according to the rules of equity and good conscience, and according to the true intent and meaning of the last clause of a certain ordinance of this province dated on the ninth day of March in the year of Christ, 1765;

And that they were at the same time in hopes of obtaining from their creditors a release and discharge from the said debts, after they should have given them all the satisfaction in their power by making the said general surrender, and that they should afterwards by such reasonable indulgence of their said creditors have been at liberty to exercise their industry in some new pursuit in order to gain a livelihood....

And for these and other reasons, which may occur to your Excellency and Honours in this behalf, your memorialists humbly hope that your Excellency and Honours will be graciously pleased to pass a particular ordinance, in the nature of a private act of Parliament, directing, that for the settling of the affairs of the said bankrupts, a commission of bankruptcy shall be passed under the public seal of the province, by his Excellency the Lieutenant-Governor, as keeper of the public seal thereof, to such three or more wise, honest, and discreet persons as his Excellency shall think fit to appoint, to execute the law and statutes of England relating to bankrupts with respect to the said bankrupts, your memorialists. Or if this method of relieving your memorialists doth not seem expedient to this Honourable Board, to give such other relief to your memorialists touching the premisses, as to your Excellency and Honours shall seem meet.

And your memorialists, as in duty bound, shall ever pray for the welfare of your Excellency and Honours.

Isaac Levy

Levi Solomons, Benjamin Lyon, Gershon Levy, Ezekiel Solomon, Chapman Abraham.

Evidently their petition was not without effect; there is no record that they were confined for debt. On the contrary, we meet them again as active, if not successful, merchants.

On July 23, 1769 Ezekiel Solomon was married in Montreal to Louise Dubois, a French-Canadian girl. Despite his marriage to a Christian girl, Solomon was an active member of the Sephardic[1] Congregation Shearith Israel, Canada's first Jewish congregation founded in Montreal in 1768. In the minutes of this congregation of the 25th of Elul, 5538 (September, 1778) it is recorded that Ezekiel Solomon and Levy Michaels were selected for the high religious honors of *Hatan Torah*[2] and *Hatan Breshit*,[3] respectively, during the forthcoming Festival of *Simchas Torah*.[4] The following year, Solomon was elected a member of the *Mahamad*.[5]

Despite the Indian disturbances of 1761 and 1763, Solomon decided

[1] A congregation using the Spanish-Portuguese ritual of worship.
[2] Bridegroom of the Law.
[3] Bridegroom of the Beginning.
[4] Last day of the Feast of Tabernacles.
[5] Board of directors in Sephardic congregations.

93

The Memorial of Isaac Levi of Quebec Merchant, and Levi Solomons Benjamin Lyon, Gershon Levi, Ezekiel Solomons and Chapman Abraham of Quebec late Merchants and Copartners, to the Honourable Guy Carleton Esquire, — Lieutenant-Governor and Commander in Chief of the Province of Quebec and the Honourable Council of the said Province;

Humbly sheweth unto your Excellency and Honours

That your Petitioners Levi Solomons, Benjamin Lyon, Gershon Levi, Ezekiel Solomons and Chapman Abraham were for many Years together Merchants and Copartners in Trade in North America and more especially during the Time of the late War with France and the subsequent Indian War in the Year 1763, and that they were employed during part of the Time of the said Wars to furnish divers Necessaries to his Majesty's Armies in North America, in which Employment they behaved — with Diligence and Honesty and gave general Satisfaction to the Commanders and other Officers of his — Majesty's Armies aforesaid, as is well known and may be easily proved to the Satisfaction of your Excellency and Honours by divers respectable Persons now in this Province; And that during the aforesaid — Indian War four of your said five Petitioners last mentioned were made Prisoners by the Indians near the Forts of Detroit and Michalimakinac and despoiled by them at the same Time of a great Quantity of Goods which they were carrying to the said Forts of the Value of Eighteen Thousand Pounds of lawful Money of this Province: And that by this and other unavoidable Losses and Misfortunes in the said War, no ways owing to any Misconduct in your Petitioners, your Petitioners became utterly unable to pay their Creditors the full Amount of their just Debts: And further that your said last mentioned Petitioners having preserved another considerable Part of their Effects were and still are earnestly desirous of surrendering the same into the Hands of proper persons for the general Satisfaction of all their Creditors in proportion to their several just Debts and Demands without any undue Preference of some of their said Creditors above the Rest; in making which Surrender they [illegible] according to the Rules of Equity and good Conscience And according to the true Intent and Meaning of the last Clause of a certain Ordinance of this Province dated on the Ninth Day of March in the Year of Christ 1765; And that they were at the same Time in hopes of obtaining from their Creditors a Release and Discharge from the said Debts after they should have given them all the Satisfaction in their Power by making the said general Surrender, and that they should afterwards by such reasonable Indulgence of their said Creditors have been at Liberty to exercise their — Industry in some new Pursuit in order to gain a Livelihood; And that thereupon they did apply to a Counsellor at Law to advise them concerning the best Method of carrying their said Intention of making this Surrender of all their Effects for the general Benefit of their Creditors into Execution; And for these and other Reasons, which may occur to your Excellency and Honours in this Behalf, your Memorialists humbly hope that your Excellency and Honours will be graciously pleased to pass a particular Ordinance, in the Nature of a private Act of Parliament, directing, that for the settling the Affairs of the said Bankrupts, a Commission of Bankruptcy shall be passed under the public Seal of the Province, by his Excellency the Lieutenant Governor, as Keeper of the — public Seal thereof, to such three or more wise, honest, and discreet Persons as his Excellency shall think fit to appoint, to execute the Laws and Statutes of England relating to Bankrupts with respect to the said Bankrupts your Memorialists. — Or if this Method of relieving your Memorialists doth not seem expedient to this Honourable Board, to give such other Relief to your Memorialists touching the Premisses, as to your Excellency and Honours shall seem meet.

And your Memorialists, as in Duty bound shall ever pray for the Wellfare of your Excellency and Honours —

Isaac Levy

Levy Solomons
Benjemen Lyons
Gershon Levy
Ezekiel Solomons
Chapmon abarham

Memorial of LEVI SOLOMONS, BENJAMIN LYON, GERSHON LEVY, EZEKIEL SOLOMON *and* CHAPMAN ABRAHAM, *1768. Courtesy of the Public Archives of Canada, Lower Canada S. 13*

to resume his trading enterprises in the Northwest. Mackinac became his center of operations. It is of some interest to note what Solomon brought with him from Montreal and Quebec to Mackinac. From an invoice of one of his expeditions, in 1770, we are in a position to know in detail the nature of his cargo. On this particular trip he came up with two "canoes." There were sixteen French Canadians in his crew; he was the only literate man among them. There were in the cargo 28 bales of dry goods: blankets, cotton goods, linens, and the like; 2 sacks of flour; 4 bales and 1 "role" of tobacco; 4 boxes of iron ware containing brass and copper kettles, and, no doubt, an assortment of knives, needles, axes, etc.; 24 Indian guns, 600 pounds of gunpowder and 1,000 pounds of shot and ball. So much of the solids. In addition, there were 256 gallons of rum and brandy, and 64 gallons of wine. The whole cargo, an 18 months' supply of "sundry goods," was valued at £750.

Before the men who took this load west to Mackinac set forth, all seventeen were called in by an officer of the Crown and asked to take an oath of loyalty to King George and to promise most solemnly that they would engage in no political intrigue with the Indians. Solomon was also required to post bond of almost double the value of his wares as assurance that he would scrupulously observe all prohibitions governing relations with the Indians.

This rigid supervision of the Indian trade by the Crown authorities after 1763 was in part a justified reaction to the abuses of individual traders who had taken advantage of the rather naive savages. In its large sense, the detailed control of the fur trade by the British authorities was part of the new colonial policy to integrate governmental activities in all North America, to tie the colonies closer to the mother country, both commercially and administratively, and to compel the American provinces to accept a fair share of the financial burdens incurred on their behalf.

In 1773 and 1774, Solomon's name appears on a petition of the residents of Montreal and Quebec to the King of England for a house of assembly for Canada. This action reflects the desire for greater "home rule in Canada" which was to flare up shortly in rebellion directed against the Crown by the thirteen American colonies to the south.

Solomon's business activities were quite extensive. In 1770, he was among the fourteen English traders who were granted licenses to exploit the fur trade in what is now the state of Wisconsin. In 1777 he went up to Mackinac with a passport from the military authorities at Quebec, which, said the letter of transmittal, "was granted him in consideration of his creditors." Some of his furs must have come from as far west as the foothills of the Rockies, for in 1778 he and his partner, Grant, sent a load of supplies to strategic Lake Nipigon, west of Lake Superior. There they could siphon out furs from the backyard of the Hudson's Bay Company to the east, and at the same time barter for the beaver that came down the Saskatchewan River from the distant west.

More and more, as Solomon and his friends reached out for furs, it became evident that this could not be a simple or one-man enterprise. As early as 1761, some of the traders, dealing in Saskatchewan River furs, had made an agreement to work co-operatively. They pooled their stocks and divided the profits, the furs. Co-operation was desirable and necessary because of the heavy expense of doing business, because of the dangers of competition and price-cutting, and because of the obvious advantages of monopolistic control and price-fixing. When the Revolutionary War broke out in 1775, the British authorities encouraged the creation of a "general store" or co-operative centralized enterprise. It was easier to watch one company than twenty-five or thirty and thus to cut down the smuggling of much needed supplies into the United States, where there was a ready market for English manufacture and consumer goods.

Accordingly, the commandant at Mackinac, in June and July, 1779, encouraged a group of about thirty traders and companies, operating in that area, to form a loose trading partnership, something like the usual shipping "adventure" in which several persons were "concerned." Under the terms of the twenty-article agreement, which was to run for about a year, the traders created a single store, forebore to trade privately, and agreed to split the profits in proportion to the stock thrown into the common pot. Ezekiel Solomon was a member of this Mackinac Company, believed to be the first example of a department store operation in the United States.

Mackinac was a French Catholic town, and in 1778, the people there wanted a missionary priest. But a missionary required money to live. Accordingly, a subscription list was sent around and some time later Ezekiel Solomon obligated himself for the sum of 50 livres, a generous amount in those days.

In 1784, Solomon joined other traders in creating a committee of eight to regulate the trade of Mackinac and "dependencies," the first "Board of Trade" in Michigan formally organized of which there is any record. The reason for the formation of this Board of Trade was the resumption of hostilities between the Chippewa Indians of Lake Superior and the Fox and Nadowessioux Indians in the Menominee region. In wartime the Indians were restricted in hunting, and the supply of furs was reduced to the smallest proportions. The traders had, therefore, incentive enough to work in concert and promote peace. This was a year after the close of the Revolution, the treaty of peace having been signed in Paris, September 3, 1783. But the English did not evacuate Mackinac until 1796.

In 1786, Solomon's name appeared among a list of "traders to the Upper Country, trading to the Grand Portage," which was located at the northwest end of Lake Superior, about thirty miles west of the Kaministiquia River. It was selected by the English as early as 1765 because of its easy access to the Indians of the Northwest with whom a most profitable trade arose. Out of this early trade grew the famous North West Company.

In 1789, Solomon is listed as a resident of Detroit, where he was engaged in business with John Askin, one of the most important merchants at that time. In 1798, two years after the occupation of Mackinac by the Americans, Solomon was still listed as a resident of that place.

In the hearings on land claims in Michigan Territory, conducted in Detroit on April 13, 1808, there is presented a "claim to the widow and heirs of the late Ezekiel Solomon to a lot of ground at Michilimackinac which had been entered with the former commissioner of the land office at Detroit in Volume 1, page 464, under date of December 24, 1805." From this entry it would appear that Solomon died between 1805 and 1808, after a residence in Mackinac for at least forty-five years.

Chapman Abraham

Chapman Abraham has the distinction of being the first known Jewish settler in Detroit. Early in the spring of 1761, English traders began to arrive, and in 1762 the name of Chapman Abraham appears in the Detroit records, doing business with James Sterling, a well known early merchant of Detroit, and, in subsequent years, with the other early merchants of Detroit.

Chapman Abraham, like Ezekiel Solomon, experienced captivity by the Indians, near Detroit, during the Pontiac uprising. As is well known, Pontiac's plan at Detroit contemplated a formal parley within the fort with Major Henry Gladwin, the English commandant, where, at a signal from Pontiac, the Indian warriors were to bring into action their guns, with barrels sawed off, which were hidden beneath their blankets. But Major Gladwin, informed of the plot, held the entire garrison under arms in instant readiness for combat. The baffled chieftain dared not give the signal for the massacre to begin. There ensued a siege for months, the memorable siege of Detroit, which was unprecedented in Indian annals; but in the end Pontiac failed.

In May, 1763, Chapman Abraham sought to bring up five boats of merchandise from Niagara apparently totally unaware of the Indian uprising. According to the trader John Porteous, in his narrative of the siege of Detroit, Abraham was captured with his cargo on the Detroit River on May 12th and made a prisoner of the Indians. After a harrowing experience of two months, he was finally exchanged by the Indians for a Potawatomi chief.

Abraham's capture by the Indians appears in his own affidavit taken before a Military Court of Inquiry held by Major Henry Gladwin in Detroit. The affidavit, dated August 9, 1763, is as follows:

> Mr. Chapman Abraham being sworn informs the Court that in coming up Detroit River, having put on shore at the place of Monsieur St. Lewis, he acquainted this Deponant that the Fort was besieged by the Indians & Capt. Robertson, Sir Robert Daviss [Sir Robert Davers, British tourist] and a great many more English were killed, & that they intended to kill all the English that would come up the Detroit River. This Deponant immediately told his men to go back with him; but the before mentioned soldiers told his men if they returned they would be all killed, as the Indians were round the whole lake and at Niagara, upon which they absolutely refused to return with him. In consequence of which this Deponant put all his goods in said St. Lewis's house, who told him he would do his best to save them from the Indians; Then this Deponant asked him where he should go to hide himself to save his life. He and Madam Esperame (who was present) answered him

he should go to her home & hide himself in her cellar; where he continued about ten minutes and then was told by said Madam Esperame to go out of the house; which he obeyed and in going out she perceived his watch chain & told him to give it to her that she was certain the Indians would kill him; upon which this Deponant told her he would make her a present of it, if she would let him stay in the cellar to save him from the Indians. She answered he should stay no longer in the house; upon which he endeavored to gain the woods; she followed him, demanding the watch a second time, which he again refused. By this time the Indians discovered him, took him prisoner and carried him to St. Lewis's house, where he found some of his goods were put in his canoe. This Deponant says further that one Pero Barth told him that Major Gladwin was the occasion of this Indian War; That if Capt. Campble [Captain Donald Campbell, first appointed English Commandant of the Post of Detroit, 1760–1762] had commanded this would not have happened; That the aforesaid Major would not give the Indians presents nor suffer their guns to be mended as Capt. Campble did; This Deponant replied that perhaps it was the General's orders not to do so, upon which he immediately said that the General did not order the Major to call them Dogs, Hogs & bid them go out of his house. This Deponant one Day saw Batist Devuiere and a great many other Frenchmen going to a Council with the Indians, he asked them what was the matter, they would not tell him anything. This Deponant has daily seen some of the Frenchmen trading with the Indians giving them bread, tobacco and fish for English Merchants Goods that were taken from the Prisoners. That Piero & Hyacinth Reaume have traded with the Indians for his effects some of which he had seen worn by said Hyacinth's Daughters since his arrival in the Fort. That Piero LaBute [Pierre La Butte, Frenchman who served as Indian interpreter to Gladwin] told him he bought of his effects. That Madam La Jenness being indebted to Monsieur Labadie & knowing him to owe this Deponant upward of twelve hundred louis, asked him if he had occasion for a quarter of veal & she would send it to him & discount it, which was proposed to said Labadie, who absolutely refused it. This Deponant says further that Batist Devuiere had bought of his effects.

The Reverend John Heckewelder of Bethlehem, Pennsylvania, the missionary of the United Brethren, preserved for us an account about

Abraham which is somewhat at variance with the story of the above capture but which is said to have been confirmed in later years by Abraham himself. It reads as follows:

> About the commencement of the Indian War in 1763, a trading Jew, named Chapman, who was going up the Detroit River with a batteau-load of goods which he had brought from Albany, was taken by some Indians of the Chippewa nation, and destined to be put to death. A Frenchman impelled by motives of friendship and humanity, found means to steal the prisoner, and kept him so concealed for some time, that although the most diligent search was made, the place of his confinement could not be discovered. At last, however, the unfortunate man was betrayed by some false friend, and again fell into the power of the Indians who took him across the river to be burned and tortured. Tied to the stake and the fire burning by his side, his thirst from the great heat became intolerable, and he begged that some drink might be given to him. It is a custom with the Indians, previous to a prisoner being put to death, to give him what they call his last meal; a bowl of pottage or broth was therefore brought to him for that purpose. Eager to quench his thirst, he put the bowl immediately to his lips, and the liquor being very hot, he was dreadfully scalded. Being a man of very quick temper, the moment he felt his mouth burned, he threw the bowl with its contents full in the face of the man who handed it to him. "He is mad! He is mad!" resounded from all quarters. The bystanders considered his conduct as an act of insanity and immediately untied the cords with which he was bound, and let him go where he pleased.
>
> This fact was well known to all the inhabitants of Detroit from whom I first heard it, and it was afterwards confirmed to me by Mr. Chapman [1] himself, who was established as a merchant at that place.

[1] Mr. Chapman and Chapman Abraham are one and the same person. In the "James Sterling Letter Book" he is mentioned as "Chapman Abraham" as well as "Mr. Chapman." In the *Diary of the Siege of Detroit,* written by Lieutenant Jehu Hay, and in a letter by Lieutenant James McDonald to Colonel Henry Bouquet ("Bouquet Papers," in *Michigan Pioneer and Historical Collections,* Vol. 19) he is mentioned as "Mr. Chapman." In *Robert Navarre's Journal of the Conspiracy of Pontiac,* he is referred to as "Chapman Abraham," and in John Porteous' account of the siege of Detroit he is mentioned as "Chapman Abram." Dr. Howard H. Peckham, author of the widely acclaimed book, *Pontiac and the Indian Uprising,* mentions the capture and release of Chapman Abraham and refers to him as a Jewish trader. In a letter to the present writer, Dr. Peckham states that "Chapman Abraham" and "Abraham Chapman" are one and the same person.

Stephen Vincent Benet, the well-known American poet and novelist, used this incident in *Tales Before Midnight,* in a story of a Jewish fur trader, "Jacob and the Indians."

Abraham's capture in 1763 may have been his second captivity by the Indians. In November, 1759, General Jeffery Amherst, Commander-in-Chief of the English forces in North America, sent a scouting party from Crown Point, New York, into Canada to establish communications with General James Wolfe, then closing in on Quebec. It was expected that bribery would allay the enmity of any Indians encountered and that the Indians would lead them to Wolfe. Indians did appear, but their hostility made them immune to persuasion, and the entire party was taken prisoner. Among the captives was a man named Abraham, who may possibly have been Chapman Abraham.

Abraham came to Canada from England, though he was probably a native of Germany. He was a professing Jew and a member of the Montreal synagogue. Affiliation with the synagogue in those days, even though a voluntary one, was a "must." In order to make sure that every newcomer would unite with it, the democratically created organic statutes of the organized congregation grimly informed him that if he did not join he would be denied the basic religious rites, both in life and in death. The fear of not receiving Jewish burial was a most effective argument.

The reference to Abraham as a baptized Jew in a 1763 letter of the trader James Sterling of Detroit need not be taken literally. In this letter Abraham was addressed facetiously as "damned Jew" and told to start acting like a Christian, now that he was baptized. Frontier wit was anything but delicate. One suspects that the reference was to some carousal, and that the baptism was a secular one of immersion in liquor, rather than a priestly ceremony in water.

When Montreal Jewry wrote its congregational constitution in 1778, it gave all Israelites in town twenty days to sign, under the threat of the loss of synagogue honors. Those fur traders who had gone into the wilderness were given a six-month period of grace. Two of the men, Chapman Abraham and Benjamin Lyon, were on a very long trip. Abraham, no doubt, was at his favorite post, Detroit; Lyon, at Mackinac. These two traders were specially favored; they were given twenty days to sign after their return to town. If a man threatened to resign or actually did

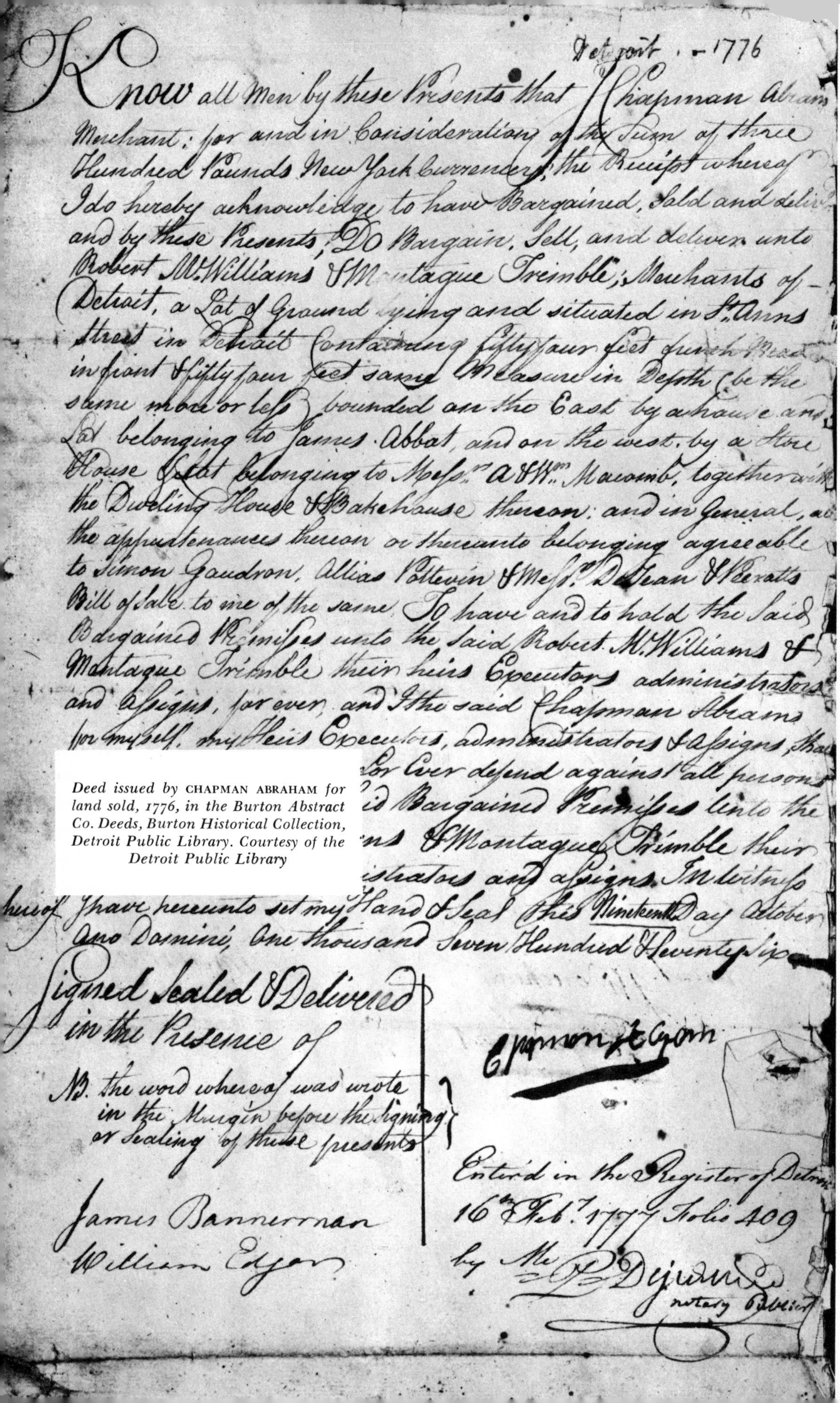

Detroit - 1776

Know all Men by these Presents that I Chapman Abrams Merchant: for and in Consideration of the Sum of three Hundred Pounds New York Currency, the Receipt whereof I do hereby acknowledge to have Bargained, Sold and deliv[ered] and by these Presents, Do Bargain, Sell, and deliver unto Robert McWilliams & Montague Tremble, Merchants of Detroit, a Lot of Ground lying and situated in St. Anns Street in Detroit Containing fifty four feet French Mea[sure] in front & fifty four feet same Measure in Depth (be the same more or less) bounded on the East by a house and Lot belonging to James Abbot, and on the west by a Store House & Lot belonging to Messrs. A & Wm. Macomb, together with the Dwelling House & Bakehouse thereon: and in General, all the appurtenances thereon or thereunto belonging agreeable to Simon Gaudron, Allias Poitevin & Messrs. DeJean & Peratts Bill of Sale to me of the same. To have and to hold the Said Bargained Premisses unto the Said Robert McWilliams & Montague Tremble their heirs Executors administrators and Assigns, for ever, and I the said Chapman Abrams for myself, my Heirs Executors, administrators & Assigns, shall [illegible] for Ever defend against all persons [illegible]id Bargained Premisses unto the [illegible]ms & Montague Tremble their [illegible]istrators and assigns. In witness whereof I have hereunto set my Hand & Seal this Nineteenth Day October Anno Domini, One thousand Seven Hundred & Seventy Six.

Signed Sealed & Delivered in the Presence of

NB. the word whereof was wrote in the Margin before the signing or Sealing of these presents

James Bannerman

William Edgar

Chapman Abraham

Entered in the Register of Detroit 16th Feb. 1777 Folio 409 by Me P. Dejean notary Public

Deed issued by CHAPMAN ABRAHAM *for land sold, 1776, in the Burton Abstract Co. Deeds, Burton Historical Collection, Detroit Public Library. Courtesy of the Detroit Public Library*

resign from the Montreal congregation, he was cut off from all ritual honors and religious privileges till he paid a fine of £40, the maximum fine permitted, a large sum for those days.

Clarence M. Burton, the noted historian of Detroit, lists Chapman Abraham among the early merchants of Detroit and states that following his release by the Indians in 1763, Abraham carried on a successful business in the village.

Of Abraham's residence and activities in Detroit we find many evidences. In 1765, he was selling rum in partnership with a man by the name of Lyons (possibly Benjamin Lyon). In 1767, he owned a lot and house within the fort of Detroit and purchased a piece of additional land adjoining his property. In the same year he did business under the firm name of Chapman Abraham and Company, and in 1768, when Detroit had 678 white inhabitants, exclusive of the garrison, he purchased an additional "tract of land with house and appurtenances." In 1769, he was granted a license by Governor Guy Carleton at Montreal to trade at "Michilimackinac and beyond," and his one canoe of merchandise consisted of "rum and brandy, wine, gunpowder, ball and shot, and fusils." In 1776, he sold a tract of land in Detroit, and the following year he purchased a parcel with a house and appurtenances within the fort of Detroit.

Although Abraham had been trading in the Upper Country, he was not a member of the 1779 co-operative store formed in Mackinac. The year before, he had been elated to hear that Frederick Haldimand, his old commanding officer, was returning to Canada to succeed Guy Carleton as governor. In 1760, he had worked under Haldimand, supplying several regiments. Now with his old chief back, Abraham looked forward to new opportunities, economically speaking, a chance to collect some old debts. The following letter, dated Montreal, August 11, 1778, reflects both the satisfaction which he felt at the appointment and some of the ways in which he had been of service to Sir Guy Carleton.

> To His Excellency, Frederick Haldimand, Esquire, Captain General and Governor in Chief of the Province of Quebec and the territories thereon depending in America, Vice-Admiral and Keeper of the Great-Seal thereof, etc., etc. May it please your Excellency: Impress with a deep and lively sense of those favors I have already experienced under your Excellency's command,

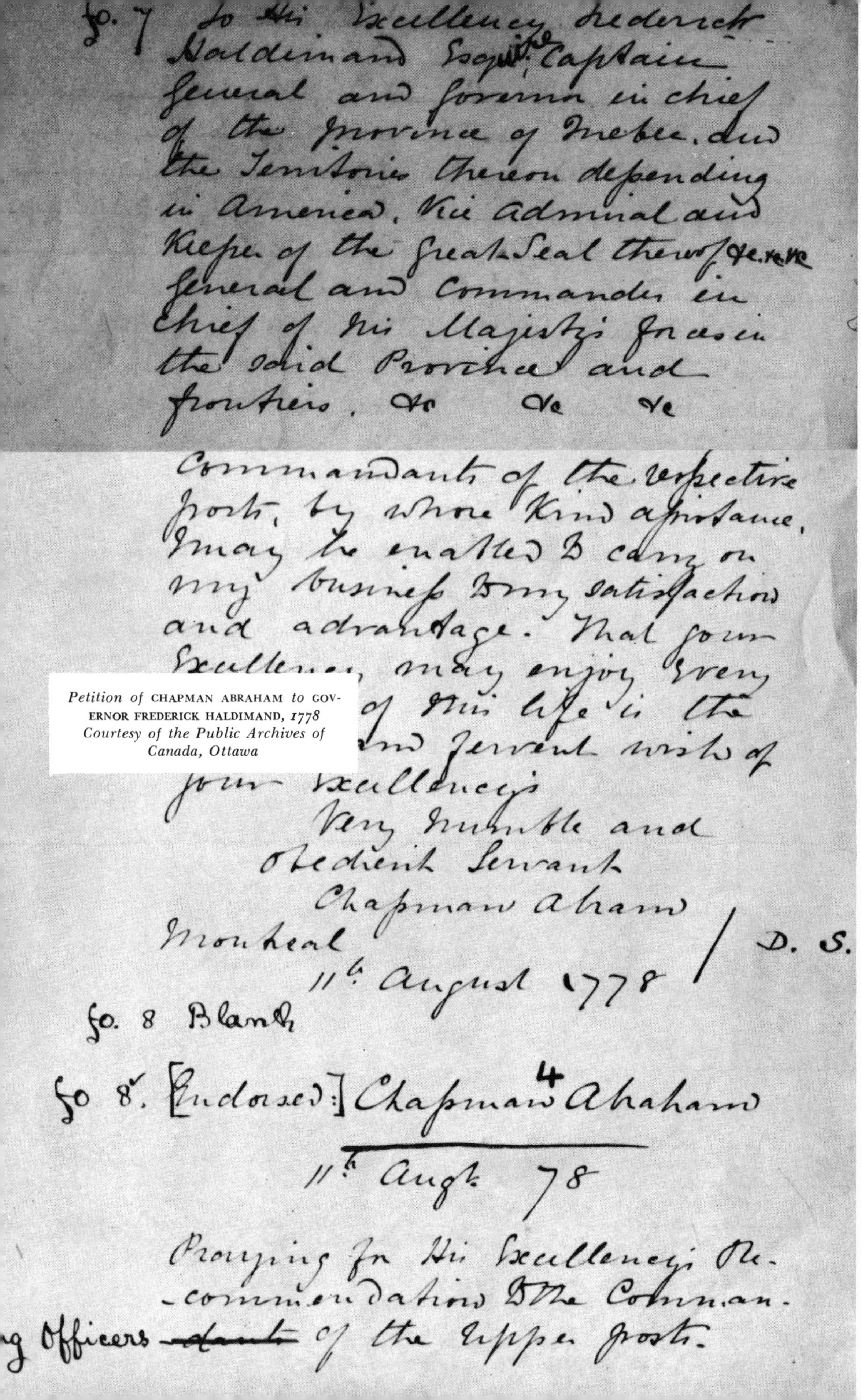
fo. 7 To His Excellency Frederick Haldimand Esqr. Captain General and Governor in chief of the Province of Quebec and the Territories thereon depending in America, Vice Admiral and Keeper of the Great Seal thereof &c &c &c General and Commander in chief of His Majesty's forces in the said Province and frontiers. &c &c &c

Commandants of the respective posts, by whose kind assistance, I may be enabled to carry on my business to my satisfaction and advantage. That your Excellency may enjoy every ... of this life is the ... and fervent wish of your Excellency's

Very humble and
Obedient Servant
Chapman Abram
Montreal
11th August 1778 / D. S.

fo. 8 Blank

fo 8v. [Endorsed:] Chapman Abraham 4

11th Augt. 78

Praying for His Excellency's Recommendation to the Commanding Officers ~~dants~~ of the Upper posts.

Petition of CHAPMAN ABRAHAM *to* GOVERNOR FREDERICK HALDIMAND, *1778*
Courtesy of the Public Archives of Canada, Ottawa

permit me to testify the joy and satisfaction I now feel on your happy arrival in this province. It is so much the more agreeable as I have already experienced your Excellency's kindness to me during the last war [with the French and the Indians to 1763], when I had the honor of supplying several regiments with necessaries under your command.

Permit me likewise to assure your Excellency that neither my loyalty or zeal for his Majesty's service have in the least abated, that during the present unfortunate contest, I flatter myself in having shown new testimonies of my attachment for his Majesty's service under the command of your late worthy predecessor, Sir Guy Carleton, particularly in being one of those who had the honor of repelling the rebels at Long Point [Montreal, September, 1775], who, with an effrontery only peculiar to themselves, had formed the design of taking this city, and likewise in [1775] being one of a party that was detached from Quebec to surprise a party of Mr. [Benedict] Arnold's men just before that town was invested by the rebels; and lastly having turned out a volunteer with the troops when the rebels were defeated at Three Rivers [June, 1776].

This enumeration of my services, I assure your Excellency, proceeds not from a vain misplaced pride. It is only intended to inform your Excellency of my loyal conduct at a time when I am sorry to say that many of my fellow-citizens, unfortunately for them, gave way to those baneful insinuations which a despicable set of seditious men and tools of an unnatural rebellion endeavored to diffuse throughout the whole province. That having been deeply engaged in the trade of the Upper Countries for these many years past, I have unavoidably many considerable outstanding debts due me there. Therefore, relying on your Excellency's past kindness, permit me most humbly to supplicate you may be pleased to recommend me to the care and attention of the commandants of the respective posts, by whose kind assistance I may be enabled to carry on my business to my satisfaction and advantage. That your Excellency may enjoy every blessing of this life is the sincere and fervent wish of your Excellency's

Very humble and obedient servant,
Chapman Abram

Letters of recommendation such as Abraham requested were of real value to a merchant. The post commander, as at Mackinac, followed closely into every detail of the life of the people who came to the fort. He supervised the trading, watched the prices, controlled the Indians, and could be very helpful in the collection of money outstanding. The post commander could almost make or break a man.

In 1778, 1780, and 1781, Abraham was granted licenses to trade at Detroit. In 1779, he was a witness at a sale of land in Detroit. His name is listed on a petition dated January 5, 1780, of the merchants of Detroit to Governor Haldimand, which refers to "the heavy losses which they have sustained since the commencement of the present disturbances, in the transportation of merchandize, liquors, and peltries, on the communication and over the Lakes." He is also listed among the merchants of Detroit who shipped rum on December 25, 1780.

In 1781, he was still doing business as a member of the firm of Chapman Abraham and Company. He is mentioned in the manuscripts of John Askin. On March 28, 1781, he appears on a list of merchants of Detroit who petitioned Major Arent Schuyler De Peyster, then the commanding officer of Detroit, to grant relief from merchants who are able but are unwilling to pay their lawful debts. In the same year, he purchased a "tenement" (a dwelling) on St. Louis Street from William Edgar, the well-known trader.

Under a contract dated October 23, 1781, Abraham sold to Pawling & Burrel all his goods, which included "snuff tobacco, mustard and silver works," and rented them his "house, shop, cellar and room" for a period of six months. In 1782, when the number of inhabitants in the entire Detroit settlement was 2,191, Abraham sold a "tenement" and lot to James May. In 1782 and 1783, he did business with Thomas Williams.

Abraham died in 1783. His recently discovered last will and testament reads as follows:

> The last Will and Testament of Chapman
> Abraham late of Montreal, merch't,
> Deceased, depositted, and proved the
> 11th April, 1783 in the Registor's
> Office, Montreal.
>
> J. B., Cl'k

This Will of the within named Chapman
Abram was opened and read in the pres-
ence of us in Montreal the Seventh day
of April 1783.
Chas. Blake, Surgeon Garrison Montreal
Henry Lowel, Assistant to Mr. Chas Blake

IN THE NAME OF GOD, AMEN.

I, Chapman Abraham, of the City of Montreal, Merchant being in a weak and low State of body, but of sound and disposing Mind and Memory, and being desirous to settle my worldly affairs, do make and publish this my last Will and Testament, thereby revoking and making void all former Wills by me at any time heretofore made; and first and principally, I commit and recommend my Soul to God, and my body to the Earth, to be decently interred in the burial ground of the Jewish Congregation near to the City of Montreal, and I request of My Executors hereinafter to be named that they would invite the Brethren of the Free-Mason Lodge of which I am a Member to accompany my body to the Grave. And as to such worldly Estate wherewith it has pleased God to entrust me I dispose of the same as followeth:

Imprimis, my Will is that all my just debts shall be first paid by my Executors after discharging the Expenses of my funeral.

Item, My Will is that my Executors do as soon as conveniently may be after my decease pay to my beloved Wife Elizabeth the Sum of One thousand pounds lawful money of the Province of Quebec.

Item, I will and bequeath unto my said wife, the Bed, bedstead, Curtains, and Appurtenances together with a small table and six chairs making part of the furniture of her present bed-Chambers.

Item, I will and bequeath to my said Wife all my bed and table linnen.

Item, I will and bequeath unto my Nephew Isaac Abraham of Montreal all my wearing Apparel except my linnen stocking, Shoes and buckles.

Item, I will and bequeath unto Richard Macniel of Montreal, Merchant, the Sum of fifty pounds lawful money of the Province of Quebec, in testimony of my grateful acknowledgment of his kind and friendly attention to me in my weak and low Estate.

Item, I will that all my household furniture, books, plates, linnen,

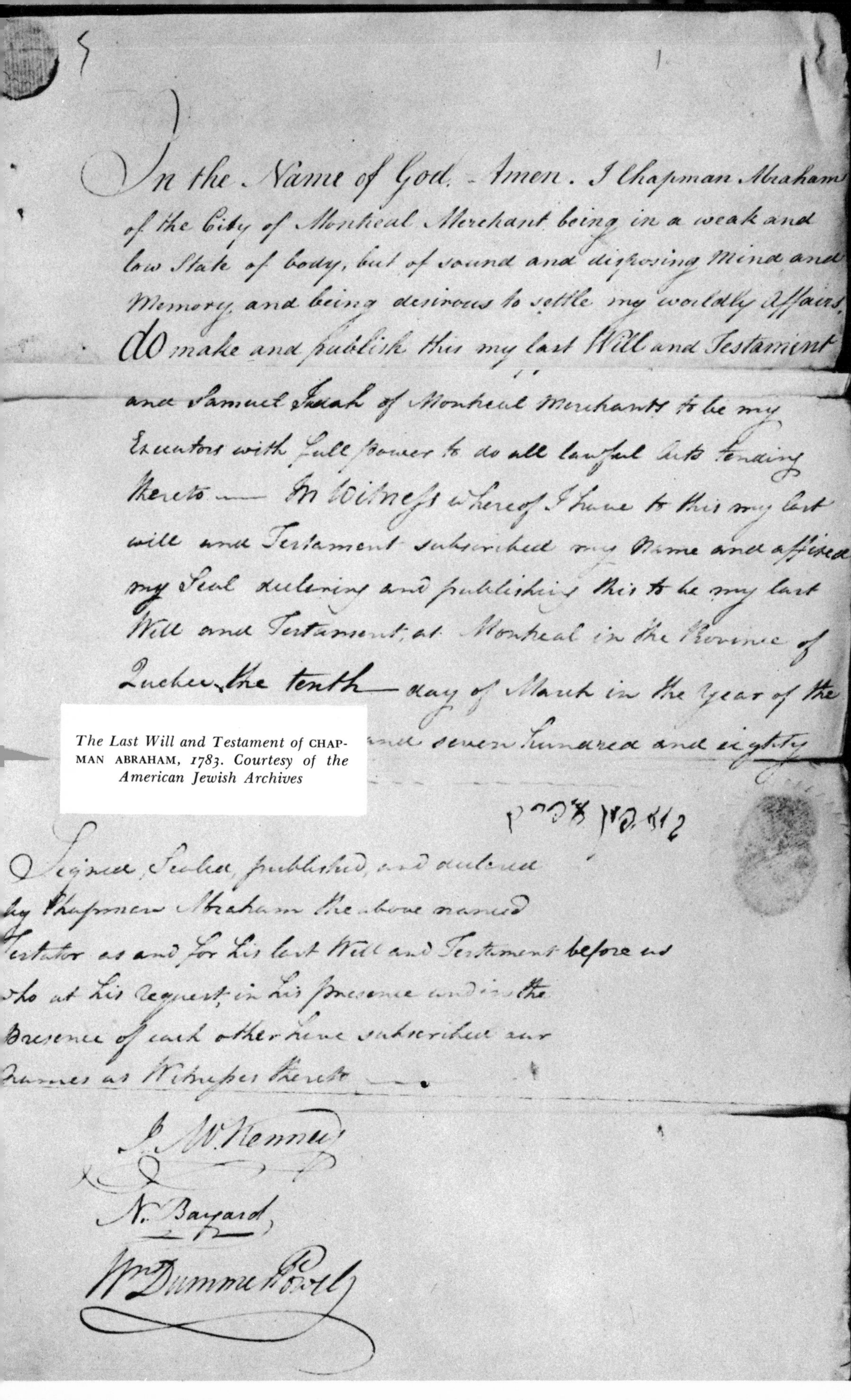

In the Name of God. Amen. I Chapman Abraham of the City of Montreal Merchant being in a weak and low State of body, but of sound and disposing Mind and Memory and being desirous to settle my worldly Affairs, do make and publish this my last Will and Testament

[illegible]

and Samuel Judah of Montreal Merchants to be my Executors with full power to do all lawful Acts tending thereto — In Witness whereof I have to this my last will and Testament subscribed my Name and affixed my Seal declaring and publishing this to be my last Will and Testament, at Montreal in the Province of Quebec the tenth day of March in the Year of the [illegible] one seven hundred and eighty

קלמן בן אברהם

Signed, Sealed, published, and declared by Chapman Abraham the above named Testator as and for his last Will and Testament before us who at his Request, in his presence and in the presence of each other have subscribed our names as Witnesses thereto —

J. McKennet

N. Bayard

Wm Dummer Powell

The Last Will and Testament of CHAPMAN ABRAHAM, 1783. Courtesy of the American Jewish Archives

and all my Moveables, not before especially bequeathed be sold to the highest bidder, and the Moneys arising therefrom, as well as the Moneys due to me, may be disposed of by my Executors in trust for the following purposes:—Whereas my wife is now enceint by me, I do will, give, and bequeath all the residue of my Estate so above described unto Richard Macniel and Samuel Judah, of Montreal, Merchants, in trust to be by them employed for the best use and behalf of the Child whereof my said wife is now enceint if it should be born with life, and my will is that the interest of the said Residue should be added to the Principal and be paid to the said child on the day it shall attain the Age of twenty-one years; and in the event that the said Child shall not be born with life or shall not attain the age of twenty-one years, then I give the said residue and interest thereof to my said Trustees to be by them possessed on this farther trust, that is to say, to pay the same in equal portions to my dear Brothers Solomon Abraham and Hart Abraham of Plimouth in Great Britain, their Executors, administrators or assigns.

And for the due Execution of this my last Will and Testament I do appoint Richard Macniel and Samuel Judah of Montreal, Merchants, to be my Executors with full power to do all lawful acts tending thereto.

In witness whereof I have to this my last Will and Testament subscribed my name and affixed my Seal declaring and publishing this to be my last Will and Testament, at Montreal in the Province of Quebec the tenth day of March in the year of the world five thousand seven hundred and eighty-seven [*sic* 5543].

Signed [in Hebrew script], Sealed, published, and declared by Chapman Abraham the above named Testator as and for his last Will and Testament before us who at his request, in his presence and in the presence of each other have subscribed our names as Witnesses thereto.

I. W. Nenney,
N. Bayard,
Wm. Dummer Powel.

Levi Solomons

Levi Solomons, a cousin and business partner of Ezekiel Solomon, was also captured by the Indians during the Pontiac Conspiracy. Unlike Ezekiel, who supported the English in their struggles with the American colonists, he agreed to serve the American forces which held Montreal for a short period during the Revolution.

LEVI SOLOMONS. *Courtesy of the American Jewish Archives*

Solomons was born in England in 1729. He arrived in Montreal immediately following the capitulation of Montreal to the English in 1760, from Albany, New York, where he had previously lived and where he would return from time to time for business purposes. A trader, whose successful and large-scale enterprises extended from Michilimackinac to the Gulf of St. Lawrence and down the Hudson River, he played a most conspicuous part in Jewish and public affairs. He was one of the founders of Montreal's Congregation Shearith Israel and served as its *parnas* (president) in 1778 when its first by-laws were adopted. He was among the English "free holders, merchants and traders" in the Province of Quebec who in 1773, 1774, and 1784 petitioned the King for a House of Assembly for Canada.

When the American Revolutionary War broke out and General Richard Montgomery, in 1775, invaded the country and captured Montreal, he regarded Solomons as a former American and as such asked him to supply food for the army and to provide hospital facilities for the wounded American soldiers. Solomons furnished a large house for this purpose and later two additional houses for smaller infirmaries and even provided all the necessary supplies for the patients. All of this was done at his own expense, as he later complained in a memorial to the American government. When, after having been defeated, the Revolutionary army was forced to withdraw, he was exposed to the enmity of the English who branded him a traitor for having openly fraternized with the enemy. In addition, the Americans had requisitioned and confiscated all of his possessions prior to their retreat. After the American forces had retired from Montreal, he charged in the same memorial, "General Arnold sent a party from Laprairie who without the consent or privity of your petitioner seized and carried off from La Chine a quantity of Brazil and carrot tobacco with other Indian goods, the property of your memorialist and by him destined for Michilimackinac, for which he never obtained a receipt or any acknowledgement whatever." A few days later, he continued, on the orders of General John Burgoyne, the English commander, he and his family were ejected from his own home on July 4, 1776, by soldiers and turned into the street, exposed to the contempt of all, even of his co-religionists. He was literally driven out of Montreal. After many trials he finally secured permission to return. The American government ignored Solomons' petition and never compensated him for the losses he had sustained or for the help he had rendered the Revolutionary Army.

In 1775, Solomons made Rebecca Franks his second wife. Her father, Abraham Franks, was one of the earliest Jewish settlers in Canada. Her brother, Col. David Salisbury Franks, took a prominent part in the American Revolutionary War. One of his daughters, Mary, married Jacob Franks, who was an important person in the early history of what is now the state of Wisconsin.

A Solomon ben Isaac Halevi is mentioned as a witness in a matrimonial case before the *Beth Din* (Jewish Court) of London, England, and the records state that he lived in Detroit in 1783. This man is probably none other than Levi Solomons.

Solomons died in Montreal on May 18, 1792.

Gershon Levy

The fourth member of the partnership who was captured by the Indians in 1763 was Gershon Levy. He, too, gained his freedom. There

R. Tevele's name soon became well known in the Jewish world. The London Jews had business connexions on the Continent and overseas, and frequently questions and inquiries reached him from relations of London Jews in those parts, especially religious questions relating to marriages and divorce cases. He in turn had occasion to address letters of a similar kind to Rabbis residing on the Continent. Thus we have a letter he wrote to R. Joseph Steinhart of Fürth, inquiring whether the letter of divorce produced by the woman Frumet, daughter of Leb, wife of Lebele Roedelsheim, dated five years previously, was a valid document, and he asks him for confirmation of the same. This letter (App. V, Letter XIII) also contains a request to the same Rabbi to intervene in the case of a certain Gedaliah b. Leb of Maineck, near Burgkundstadt in Bavaria, now living in London. His wife refuses to follow him to this country, and R. Tevele asks the Rabbi of Fürth to persuade her to accept a letter of divorce which the man intends sending to her through a messenger (שליח). Interesting is the story of another woman, the wife of Nathan Harris of London, recorded in a document of testimony (גביית עדות, App. V, XXI), taken up by the Beth Din of London under the presidency of R. Tevele in the year 1783. The husband had left England on board a warship for Jamaica, and died some time afterwards on board another ship, anchored at Port Antonio, on his return journey to England, and was buried in the latter place. As witness figures a certain Solomon **b. Isaac the Levite, who lived in Detroit opposite the house of Admiral Route (or Rowthe ?),[82] whose steward brought him the news of Harris's death.**

From proceedings of Beth Din of London, England, stating that SOLOMON b. ISAAC, the Levite (probably LEVI SOLOMONS), resided in Detroit in 1783.

is little of historical record available to describe Gershon's activities except that his name appears in the accounts of the businessmen with whom he was associated.

Benjamin Lyon

Benjamin Lyon was apparently the only member of the trading firm to elude the Indians in 1763. He may possibly have been the same Lyon who managed to escape General Montcalm's Indian cohorts in the 1757 Fort William Henry massacre, at the head of Lake George, New York.

As early as 1770, Lyon is mentioned as a member of the Mackinac settlement where he apparently established his permanent residence. A merchant and trader, he was active in civic and Jewish community affairs both in Mackinac and Montreal throughout the next thirty years.

He was a correspondent for Aaron Lopez, the well-known merchant-shipper in Newport, Rhode Island. In 1770, Lyon sent a letter to this businessman to be delivered by Hyam Myers, who was making a trip to the south and had scheduled a personal visit with Lopez in Rhode Island. For a time, Lyon was a partner of John Askin at Mackinac; in 1780 the firm name was cited as Askin, Lyon and Bostwick. In 1779 he participated in the formation of the co-operative Mackinac Company and served as a member of its merchandising committee. A year later, he and the other merchants of Mackinac signed a memorial in favor of removing Fort Michilimackinac to the island of Michilimackinac.

On May 12, 1781, Lyon witnessed the formal Treaty of Cession whereby the Indians agreed to transfer Mackinac Island into British hands. Both Arent Schuyler De Peyster and Patrick Sinclair, commandants at Mackinac, had found Lyon useful as an aid to the government Indian Department.

Like Ezekiel Solomon, Lyon made a generous contribution of 50 livres in 1778 to a Mackinac fund for the support of a missionary priest to serve the Catholic community.

Active in the Canadian Jewish community, Lyon was a member of the Montreal synagogue. In 1779, he contributed toward the cost of a Scroll of the Law to be purchased in London. The Scroll was brought to the colony by Joseph Pines, a member of one of Canadian Jewry's earliest pioneer families.

As late as July 28, 1800, Lyon is recorded as a witness in the Mackinac

INDIAN DEED FOR THE ISLAND OF MACKINAC.

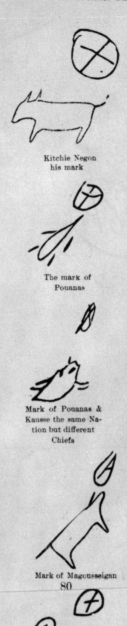

Kitchie Negon
his mark

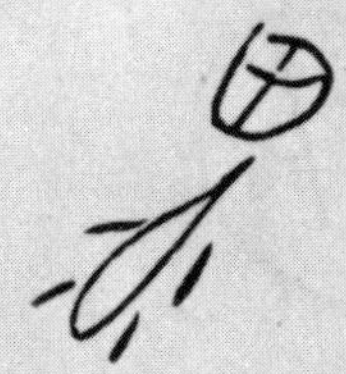

The mark of
Pouanas

Mark of Pouanas &
Kausse the same Nation but different
Chiefs

Mark of Magousseigan

80

Oka

By these Presents we the following Chiefs Kitchie Negon or Grand Sable, Pouanas, Koupe and Magousseihigan in behalf of ourselves and all others of our Nation the Chipiwas who have or can lay claim to the herein mentioned Island, as being their Representatives and Chiefs, by and with mutual consent do surrender and yield up into the hands of Lieut Governor Sinclair for the Behalf and use of His Majesty George the Third of Great Britain France and Ireland King Defender of the Faith &c. &c. &c. His Heirs Executors, Administrators for ever the Island of Michilimackinac or as it is called by the Canadians La Grosse Isle (situate in that Strait which joins the Lakes Huron and Michigan) and we do hereby make for ourselves and our Posterity a Renunciation of all claims in future to said Island; We also acknowledge to have received by command of His Excellency Frederick Haldimand Esqr. Governor of the Province of Quebec, General & Commander in Chief of all His Majesty's Forces in Canada &c. &c. &c. from the said Lieutenant Governor Sinclair on His Majesty's Behalf, the sum of Five Thousand Pounds New York Currency being the adequate & compleat value of the before mentioned Island of Michilimackinac, and have signed two Deeds of this Tenor and Date in the presence of Mathew Lessey, John Macnamara, David Rankin, Henry Bostick, Benjamin Lyons, Etienne Campion, and P. Antoine Tabeau the under written witnesses, one of which Deeds is to remain with the Governor of Canada, and the other to remain at this Post to certify the same, and we promise to preserve in our Village a Belt of Wampum of Seven feet in Length to perpetuate secure and be a lasting memorial of the said Transaction to our Nation for ever hereafter, and that no defect in this Deed from want of Law Forms or any other shall invalidate the same. In witness whereof We the above mentioned Chiefs do set our Hands & Seals this Twelfth day of May in the year of our Lord one thousand seven Hundred and Eighty one and in the twenty First year of His Majesty's Reign.

[signed]

Matthew Lessey	Benjamin Lyon
David Rankin	Ett Campion
Henry Bostick	P. An. Tabeau

Patt Sinclair
Lt. Govr & Commandant.

John Mompesson
Capt. Comg. a Detachment of the King's Reg't

R. B. Brooke
Lieutenant King's or Eighth Regiment

John Robert McDonall
Ensign Kings or Eighth Regiment

Indian Deed for Island of Mackinac, witnessed by BENJAMIN LYON, *1781. From* Michigan Pioneer and Historical Collections, *XIX (1892), 633*

[B 114, p 178]

Register of Marriages. His name also appears in a 1787 merchants' petition to Captain Thomas Scott, Mackinac commandant.

William Solomon

In his youth, William Solomon, one of the sons of Ezekiel Solomon, entered the service of the North West Company and drifted to the Sault and Mackinac. He became expert in the Indian language and worked as an interpreter for the British government for fifty-six years. During the War of 1812, he served as an interpreter at British-occupied Mackinac.

In December, 1814, however, the Treaty of Ghent awarded Mackinac Island and its two forts to the United States. When the news reached the British garrison at Mackinac six months later, they were forced to evacuate to temporary quarters on nearby St. Joseph Island. But what the British now wanted was a "Gibraltar" of the Great Lakes, an island fortress from which they could command the St. Marys River and maintain their trade with the Indians. They believed they had found it in 1815, when a force dispatched from the St. Joseph post took over a nameless island in the chain that extends west from Georgian Bay. They christened it Drummond Island after the British military commander in the Niagara to Detroit river areas, Sir Gordon Drummond. There, they erected Fort Collier and the town of the same name. For thirteen years, the British labored to build and nourish the new settlement.

Then, in 1828, the English learned to their chagrin that an international boundary commission had ruled that Drummond Island was actually American territory—that the British boundary commissioner who had surveyed the area in 1815 had miscalculated. (According to the legend on Drummond Island today, he had been drunk.) The island reverted to the United States. The fort and town became American prizes.

William Solomon had been among those Mackinac evacuees who settled and worked to build a community on Drummond Island only to see it become American property. In 1816, he had been granted a building lot on the island. When the British pulled out and moved to Penetanguishene, Ontario, William went with them. There he remained for the rest of his life.

Today Drummond Island is part of Chippewa County, Michigan.

The British fort and parade grounds are still there for the inspection of the hunting and tourist trade. It is inhabited mainly by Americans of Finnish descent and Indians.

A GROUP OF VOYAGEURS.

LEWIS SOLOMON, (left) *grandson of* EZEKIEL SOLOMON. *Courtesy of* Ontario Historical Society, Papers and Records, *vol. III, 1901*

Lewis Solomon

Lewis Solomon, the youngest son of William Solomon and grandson of Ezekiel Solomon, was born on Drummond Island in 1821. He was groomed by the family to succeed his father in the government service as Indian interpreter and to that end he was sent to French and Indian schools and also for a term to the Detroit Academy. Lewis was looked upon by his townspeople as a man of education, but unlike his father he never entered the government service. He died in Victoria Harbour, Ontario, in 1900.

Sophia Solomon

Sophia Solomon, one of the daughters of Ezekiel Solomon, was married to Isidore Peltier on July 23, 1798. Their son, Ezekiel Peltier, born May 26, 1799, was a resident of Detroit for many years and moved in 1846 to Monroe, Michigan, where he remained for the rest of his life.

James Solomon

Under date of January 17, 1824, a James Solomon of Drummond Island, who was probably related to Ezekiel Solomon, is mentioned as having given to Michael Dousman, a prominent merchant of Mackinac, a mortgage deed for two pieces of property in Mackinac as security on a note. James is also mentioned as a merchant who sold a house, in 1824, at Drummond Island to Isaac Blackburn, assistant commissary general at that place. This James Solomon is probably the "Mr. Solomon, a merchant" who applied in 1818 to Major Thomas Howard of Drummond Island to settle and cultivate land at St. Joseph Island, claiming the right to do so because "he paid a valuable consideration to Mr. Askin of the Indian Department at Amherstburg for a tract of land on that Island." Solomon's claim was refused.

In noting the arrival in Detroit of the steamer *Walk-in-the-Water,* the pioneer steamer on the Great Lakes, the name of J. Solomon—probably James Solomon—appears as one of the ten passengers, who expressed in the columns of the *Gazette* of June 17, 1820, their "satisfaction with arrangements and accommodation." Solomon and the others, principally Americans, were en route to Mackinac. James Solomon died between 1824 and 1829.

Hayman Levy

Hayman Levy of New York, the largest fur trader among the colonists and at one time a partner of Levi Solomons, carried on an extensive business with Detroit merchants during the colonial period as is evidenced in a series of business letters written in 1774 and published in volume 28 of the *Michigan Pioneer and Historical Collections.* The *Michigan Collections* also refers to a trading company named "J. Levy and Richard McCarthy," which was doing business in Mackinac in 1774.

MICHAEL GRATZ. *Courtesy of the American Jewish Archives*

Michael Gratz

Michael Gratz, a famous Jewish merchant and communal leader in Philadelphia in colonial times, and father of Rebecca Gratz, the Rebecca of Scott's immortal novel *Ivanhoe,* helped plan and supply an expedition against the English in Detroit in 1781, during the struggle for independence. Although Michael Gratz did not live in Michigan his interest in the George Rogers Clark Expedition and the Detroit area warrants his inclusion in this account. Gratz, whose all-out sympathies were with the Americans, advanced supplies for the proposed campaign, under the leadership of General Clark, to the value of nearly £1500. The campaign against Detroit did not materialize, however, and Gratz had to wait three years before he was paid in full in tobacco for the equipment he had furnished for the Expedition. The Expedition eventually, however, was in a sense successful, since Clark captured most of the West.

Samuel Judah

Samuel Judah of Montreal, brother-in-law of Aaron Hart of Three Rivers, the wealthiest and most influential Jew in Canada in colonial times, was in Detroit in 1780, trading with Chapman Abraham. He was later designated as one of the executors and trustees of the estate of Abraham. In the spring of 1784, Judah was again in Detroit with a cargo, doing business with Detroit merchants.

Jacob Franks

Jacob Franks, an English Jew, was a resident of Mackinac as early as 1807 and fought on the side of the English during the War of 1812. He figures in the Northwest as a trader and person of prominence. In 1792, the trading establishment of Ogilvie, Gillespie and Company of Montreal sent Franks as their agent to Green Bay (a post in present-day Wisconsin). Two years later the Menominee Indians made Franks a land grant for 999 years and in 1797, he went into business there under his own name, becoming one of the most influential residents of the settlement. That year he established a trading post at Fond du Lac, and in 1804, he sent an agent to do a "summer business" in raw deer skins in Milwaukee, long before the time of Solomon Juneau, the founder of Milwaukee. In 1805, he erected a grist and saw mill on Devil River, three miles east of DePere, the first of its kind in that section of the country. He carried on an extensive trade with the Indians and won a high reputation for his integrity, fair dealing and hospitality. In 1806, he with one other sent to Mackinac not less than 10,000 pounds of deer tallow.

When the English withdrew from Mackinac after the War of 1812, Franks paid for his loyalty to England. His home was "wantonly pillaged" when it was broken into by the Americans. An official report states that "unusual harshness" was shown to all who had supported England in the War of 1812.

In 1814, Franks and three others were appointed to inventory the two schooners *Scorpion* and *Tigress* captured from the Americans and brought to Mackinac. In 1815, his name appears as one of the thirteen signers describing themselves as "Magistrates, merchants, traders and principal inhabitants of Michilimackinac and St. Josephs." In 1816, he was allotted a building plot in the new English post at Drummond Island, but it appears marked in the list as "not occupied." Documents dated 1817 show that he became an army purveyor in that year. He married a half-breed Indian in Green Bay and had a large family. He spent the last years of his life in Montreal, with his second wife, Mary Solomons, daughter of Levi Solomons. He died about 1823.

JOHN LAWE. *Courtesy of* Jewish Community Blue Book of Milwaukee and Wisconsin, *1925*

John Lawe

John Lawe, a nephew of Jacob Franks, served as a lieutenant with the English forces that defended Mackinac against the Americans during the War of 1812. He was born in Montreal on December 6, 1779. His father was a captain in the English army and his mother was a sister of Jacob Franks. Lawe was educated in Quebec and came in 1797 to Green Bay with his uncle, Jacob Franks, who there founded his famous trading post. One early traveler speaks of the two as "Jews extensively embarked in the fur trade here."

At first Lawe worked for his uncle. When Franks returned to Montreal he left his extensive property and the care of his Indian family to Lawe, who became a very successful merchant. He was also a public spirited man who took part in many worth-while activities of his day. He learned the Indian tongue and was commissioned a lieutenant in the Indian Department by the English.

In 1822, Lawe was appointed by Lewis Cass, Governor of the Michigan Territory, as Associate Justice in the first court held in Brown County, which was then a part of Michigan Territory. In 1835, he was elected a member of the first Legislative Council of Wisconsin Territory. He was an organizer and one of the largest stockholders of the Fox River Hydraulic Company, formed in 1836 to build a dam across the Fox River.

There is no evidence of just how conscious Lawe was of his Jewish heritage. If he was, he probably had no way of expressing it, being the only Jew in the territory; but that he had a general religious interest is indicated in the fact that he made possible the establishment of Christ Church, the first Protestant Episcopal Church in Green Bay, incorporated in 1829. He was also the founder, in 1831, of the first Temperance Society west of the Great Lakes. When it is recalled that life in this frontier outpost was rather rough and unrestrained by established law and order, Lawe's activities in establishing religious and temperance institutions as moral influences can well be appreciated.

Lawe married Theresa Rankin, daughter of an English officer and a Chippewa mother, and had several children. He died in Green Bay on February 11, 1846, highly respected and honored by his fellow citizens.

Moses David

Moses David, a Jewish trader from Montreal who is listed as a resident of Sandwich (now Windsor, Ontario) as early as 1794, conducted an extensive trade with Detroit merchants until 1818, the probable year of his death.

Isaac Moses

Under date of November 5, 1798, two years after the occupation of Detroit by the Americans, the name of Isaac Moses appears in the records of Zion Lodge, Detroit's first Masonic lodge. Moses was not only one of the earliest Jews in Detroit but presumably the first Jewish Mason in the city.

Stephen Cohen

The name of Stephen Cohen appears in 1834 in a "Memorial to Congress by the Inhabitants of Southern Michigan" and the document states that he was a resident of Adrian in that year.

W. A. Cohn

In 1835, W. A. Cohn, who is listed as a resident of Huron Township, Wayne County, signed a petition to Congress by the inhabitants of Michigan Territory.

Alex Cohen

Alex Cohen was, according to the Journal of the Common Council of Detroit, on a payroll for grading a street in 1835.

Frederick E. Cohen

Frederick E. Cohen, an English Jew from Woodstock, Ontario, is mentioned as a Detroit resident in 1837. He became a prominent portrait painter, the first Jewish artist in Michigan. Cohen was a handsome, genial, witty and kindly man, well liked by everybody. He was considered quite a dandy, sporting a blue swallowtail coat trimmed with brass buttons, a buff waistcoat and a high white beaver hat, and was rarely seen without a cane. He came to Detroit at the time of the "Patriot" War and being of an adventurous disposition enlisted in the Canadian militia. It was not his nature, however, to take military discipline seriously and he spent most of his time during the war in the jail in Sandwich Township. Imprisonment seems in no way to have dampened his spirits, for the hours spent in his cell were most enjoyably passed in adorning the walls with sketches, comic and serious, with not a few questionable cartoons in which he lampooned his fellow soldiers and the officers most unmercifully. These drawings were a source of merriment to the visitors and inmates for many years.

When peace once more came to the area, Cohen settled in Detroit. The decorating firm of Godfrey, Atkinson and Godfrey, appreciating Cohen's ability, gave him the use of a room for a studio and also employment at painting decorative panels for the passenger boats, this being quite a feature of their business. His talents as a portrait painter were soon recognized and he had many commissions from citizens of prominence. Sometimes these pictures failed to satisfy the sitters and payment for them was long delayed or entirely ignored. Cohen was always equal to the emergency and many are the stories of his practical jokes, not always relished by his victims. One of the stories told about Cohen is of his painting the portraits of a prominent Detroit stone contractor and his popular daughter, who were not satisfied with the work when completed and refused to pay. Cohen said nothing, but took the portraits to his studio, where he painted a huge pair of asses' ears on the man's head, while on the lower part of his daughter's face he painted a beard, giving her the appearance of a bearded woman of the circus. He then hung the portraits in the corridor of the post-office, the general meeting place of all the townspeople. Needless to say, the portraits were quickly paid for and removed from public exhibition.

Cohen was an artist of wide range and versatility, painting portraits, landscapes, historical and biblical scenes, and many other types of work as was usual among early nineteenth century painters. In the late 1840's and early 1850's, the Detroit Fire Department conducted many a parade with many a banner attesting to Cohen's skill as a painter.

He was the teacher of Robert Hopkin, prominent marine painter of Detroit, and Lewis T. Ives, famous portrait painter of Michigan. The Detroit Institute of Arts has a number of paintings by Cohen, including his self-portrait. The Burton Historical Collection of the Detroit Public Library and the Detroit Historical Museum possess several, including the famous "Meeting of the Michigan State Agricultural Society: Reading the Premiums at the First State Fair, 1849" in which every face is a portrait.

Cohen married about 1850 and moved about 1855 to Oberlin, Ohio, the residence of his wife's parents. He also resided at Mansfield, Ohio, and later bought a farm and lived near Fredericktown, Ohio. He also painted at Mt. Vernon, Ohio, and Buffalo, New York. He was in correspondence with the American Art Union of New York in the early

Self-portrait of FREDERICK E. COHEN.
Courtesy of the Detroit Institute of Arts

1850's, attempting to interest that organization in purchasing his pictures.

Cohen died in 1858 of apoplexy while leveling his gun during a hunting trip near Mt. Vernon, Ohio.

GERMAN-JEWISH IMMIGRATION

Mid-century brought a new influx of Jews to American shores immediately before and after the abortive European revolutions of 1848. The revolutionary fire which swept across Europe in the 40's fed on many fuels—nationalism, socialism and liberalism. Within the multi-national Austrian Empire especially, political, social and economic dissent raged high. The Austrian Empire was a hodgepodge of national and ethnic groups—Germans, Slavs, Magyars and Italians. It extended into Bohemia, Hungary, Italy and the Germanies, all spliced together by the Hapsburg monarchs into a motley and loose-jointed empire.

The rising currents of liberal and nationalist sentiment in Europe of the 30's and 40's lifted these peoples to rebellion against the aristocratic government of Prince Metternich and the monarchy. Throughout most of the Germanies, led by independent Prussia, there was a clamor for liberal reform and the formation of a German federation which would exclude Austria. In Germany, it was largely a middle class movement which drew its recruits from the ranks of university professors, students, and literati as well as from merchants and some workers. In 1848, revolutions erupted throughout the Austrian Empire and in almost every continental country but Russia. Liberals and nationalists, often allied, fought for the independence of subject nationalities and for governmental reforms. Socialists also joined in the general revolt.

Within a year, however, those new revolutionary governments which had been formed either failed or were snuffed out by the Hapsburgs as quickly as they were established. The elements of idealism and optimism of the pre-1848 years gave way to those of reaction and bitterness. Nationalism became a militant and aggressive religion. The age of "Blood and Iron" was being ushered in.

During these years, there began the early exodus of many central and southern Europeans to the United States. Among them were Jews from Germany and Hungary, where nationalist and racist feelings were on the rise. A number of these Jews, particularly from Bohemia, Silesia, Bavaria, and Hungary finally settled in Michigan.

Michigan was now attached to the East by a transportation network of water and rail lines. The Michigan Central Railway provided a number of commercial opportunities to merchants and peddlers. Many Jews continued west from the Atlantic seaboard to Buffalo, then on to Michigan, settling in Detroit and those cities linked to Detroit by rail. Many German Jews settled in Ann Arbor, where there was already a large German-speaking population.

Ann Arbor and Ypsilanti were among the first communities where Jews settled in the 1840's. In 1850, the entire population of Washtenaw County totaled 28,567. Ann Arbor counted something less than 5,000 citizens; Ypsilanti, only about 3,000. In the decade from 1840 to 1850 Detroit had increased its population from 9,102 to 21,019. Michigan itself had grown from about 212,000 to almost 400,000 by 1850. Saginaw was a mere village with about 900 citizens. The populations of Grand Rapids and Kalamazoo both ran about 2,500. Adrian had 3,006 inhabitants.

Ann Arbor and Ypsilanti were chosen by the new Jewish immigrants for two principal reasons: first, because in the 1840's Washtenaw County was the best county for farm stock, wool and hides; second, because many of the farmers in this county were recent German immigrants themselves and the Jewish arrivals found here the language of their native land and a place where they could earn a living, mostly as peddlers, until they could establish themselves as merchants, manufacturers or craftsmen.

SOLOMON WEIL

MOSES WEIL

LEOPOLD WEIL

MARCUS WEIL

JACOB WEIL

Among the first to come to Ann Arbor from Bohemia were the five Weil brothers, who arrived as follows: Solomon in 1843, Moses and his wife in 1844, Leopold in 1845, Marcus in 1846 and Jacob in 1848. The Weil brothers formed the nucleus of a colony of Jews and their home

JOSEPH WEIL

became the headquarters of all German-Jewish arrivals. Here the humblest peddler always found a hospitable welcome. The brothers were orthodox in their religious observances, maintained a kosher household, and conducted the first *Minyanim* (services) held in Michigan. The first Sabbath and festival services were held, in 1845, in a house in the lower town of Ann Arbor which was jointly occupied by Leopold Weil and his brother-in-law, Judah Sittig, who came to Ann Arbor about 1845. Later they gathered at the home of Leopold and Moses on Washington Street or at that of Solomon and Marcus on Huron Street. After their parents arrived in 1850, services were held uniformly at the parents' home, a brick house on Washington Street, near their tannery.

For the rites which followed the birth of Solomon Weil's eldest son in 1848, a *mohel* (circumcizer) was brought all the way from Cleveland, Ohio, and it is said that when in 1850, the parents of these brothers were sent for, the father, at their request, purchased a *Sefer Torah* in Prague and piously bore the Scroll of the Law in his arms all the way to Ann Arbor.

MOSES RINDSKOFF

ADAM HERSCH

The Jewish Cemetery at Ann Arbor was acquired in 1848 or 1849.

Leopold Weil and Judah Sittig attempted farming in Lima Township as did Moses Weil, together with one Woodel, a Bohemian Jew, in South Lyons Township, but all gave it up after a year or so because of the wildness of the locality and the rampage of the savage beasts of the forest.

Other German-Jewish immigrants who came to Ann Arbor and Ypsilanti before 1850 were: Charles, Adolph, and Louis Bresler with their father, Leo Bresler; Charles, Henry, and Emanuel Lederer; Moses Rindskoff, Charles Fantle, Solomon Bendit, David Weidenfeld and brother, Adam Hersch, Isaac Altman, Simon Sloman, the Fantes brothers, one Hayman, one Feder, and possibly Alex and Martin Guiterman, Solomon Sondheim and Benjamin Goodkind. Many of these later moved to Detroit, when the city began its commercial rise.

Lewis F. Leopold, whose name was Freudenthaler in his native Baden, Germany, his wife, Babette, who was a member of the Oesterreicher (Austrian) family, their infant son, Lewis' sister, Hannah, and Lewis' brother, Samuel, were located on the Island of Mackinac in 1845. The brothers became the first pioneers in this locality in the fishery business and were soon shipping a thousand barrels of salted fish to Cleveland each season. This business, together with the sale of supplies to fishermen, Indian trading and the purchase of furs, laid the foundation for an extensive business and they became prominent as owners of Lake Michigan vessels and merchants in the ports of the Great Lakes.

Samuel Leopold left Mackinac in 1853 to join his two other brothers and Julian Austrian, who had married Hannah Leopold in 1849, in their recently undertaken business enterprises at La Pointe and Fond du Lac, Wisconsin, where they were among the first white settlers. Lewis Leopold officiated as cantor at the first High Holy Day services held at La Pointe in the fall of 1855. Within a few years after 1850, the Leopolds and Austrians established leading stores in Michigan, at Eagle River, Eagle Harbor, the Cliff Mine, Calumet, and at Hancock, Joseph Austrian having selected the latter place as the site for his first store and warehouse.

EDWARD KANTER

Edward Kanter, a native of Breslau, Germany, who came to Detroit in 1844, was a resident of Mackinac in 1845, where he was employed by the American Fur Company. In 1846, he worked for the Leopolds and Austrians mentioned above. He remained in Mackinac until 1852 when

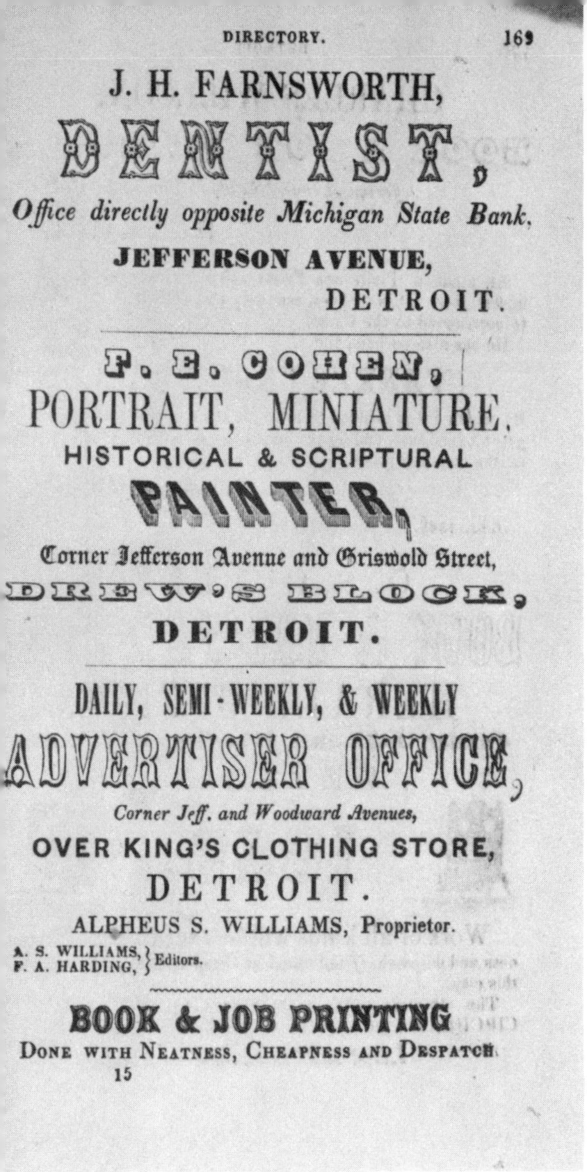

DIRECTORY. 169

J. H. FARNSWORTH,

DENTIST,

Office directly opposite Michigan State Bank,

JEFFERSON AVENUE,

DETROIT.

F. E. COHEN,

PORTRAIT, MINIATURE,

HISTORICAL & SCRIPTURAL

PAINTER,

Corner Jefferson Avenue and Griswold Street,

DREW'S BLOCK,

DETROIT.

DAILY, SEMI-WEEKLY, & WEEKLY

ADVERTISER OFFICE,

Corner Jeff. and Woodward Avenues,

OVER KING'S CLOTHING STORE,

DETROIT.

ALPHEUS S. WILLIAMS, Proprietor.

A. S. WILLIAMS, } Editors.
F. A. HARDING, }

BOOK & JOB PRINTING

DONE WITH NEATNESS, CHEAPNESS AND DESPATCH.

15

Business ad of FREDERICK E. COHEN *in the Detroit Directory of 1846*

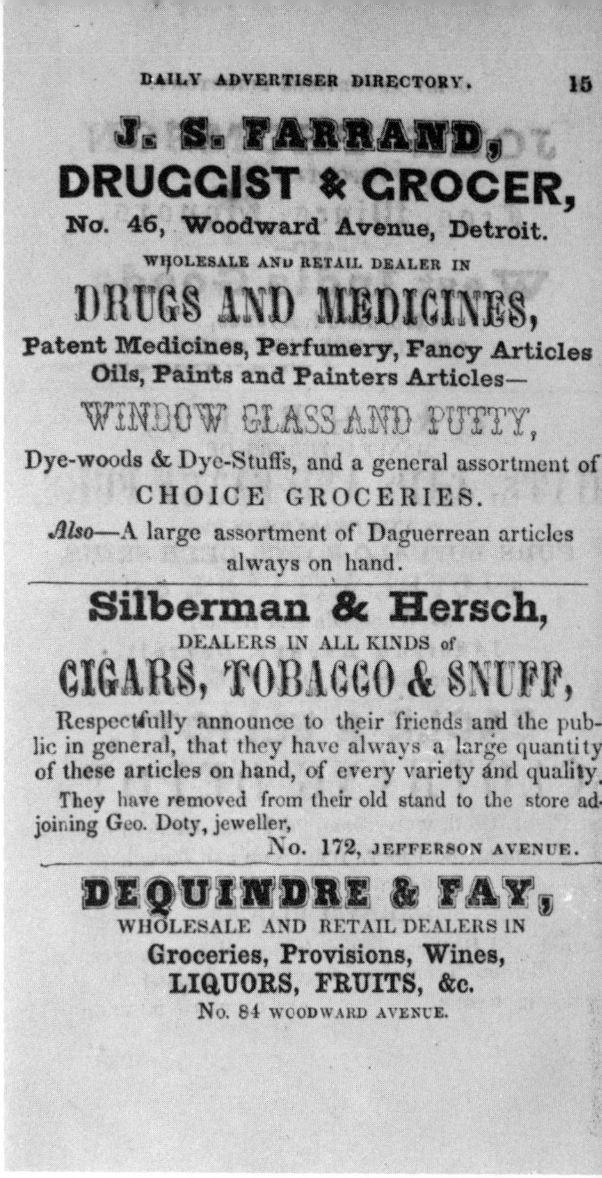

DAILY ADVERTISER DIRECTORY. 15

J. S. FARRAND,

DRUGGIST & GROCER,

No. 46, Woodward Avenue, Detroit.

WHOLESALE AND RETAIL DEALER IN

DRUGS AND MEDICINES,

Patent Medicines, Perfumery, Fancy Articles
Oils, Paints and Painters Articles—

WINDOW GLASS AND PUTTY,

Dye-woods & Dye-Stuffs, and a general assortment of
CHOICE GROCERIES.

Also—A large assortment of Daguerrean articles always on hand.

Silberman & Hersch,

DEALERS IN ALL KINDS OF

CIGARS, TOBACCO & SNUFF,

Respectfully announce to their friends and the public in general, that they have always a large quantity of these articles on hand, of every variety and quality.

They have removed from their old stand to the store adjoining Geo. Doty, jeweller,

No. 172, JEFFERSON AVENUE.

DEQUINDRE & FAY,

WHOLESALE AND RETAIL DEALERS IN

Groceries, Provisions, Wines,
LIQUORS, FRUITS, &c.

No. 84 WOODWARD AVENUE.

Business ad of SILBERMAN *and* HERSCH *in the Detroit Directory of 1850*

he moved to Detroit. Kanter became the first Jewish banker in the city by founding the German-American Bank. He was a very colorful personality and the first Detroit Jew to be active in politics, having been elected among other offices a member of the state legislature in 1857. He was also a great friend of the Indians and because of his bustling activity was named by them "Bosh-Bish'gay-bish-gon-sen," meaning "Fire Cracker." The Indians always had a great liking for Kanter; they never missed an opportunity to call on him in Detroit or to send greetings to him. The merchants of Detroit in the early 1860's were at a loss one day to account for a circle of Indians gravely squatted in front of Kanter's store on the main business street, Kanter making one of the circle, the whole company smoking and maintaining a strong silence, until they (the merchants) were informed that the Indians were a delegation of chiefs on their way to see the Great White Father at Washington, who would not pass through Detroit without smoking a pipe of peace with "Fire Cracker."

Charles E. Bresler, born in Cannstadt, Germany, was a resident of Ypsilanti in the early 1840's (possibly the 1830's), and moved later to Detroit.

Charles, Henry, and Emanuel Lederer, natives of Bohemia who came to Ann Arbor in 1847, moved to Lansing about 1849 where they established a tannery, soap factory and general store. Henry Lederer died in Lansing in 1885. His wife, Frances, whom he married in Ann Arbor in 1850, was a resident of Lansing for over 46 years. She died in 1897.

Jacob Hirsch, born in Germany, was the pioneer Jewish settler in Jackson, arriving there in 1842. Within a few months he was joined by Jacob Levy. Bernard Wolf came in 1846 and Joseph Hanaw in 1847. Henry Lang probably settled there also before 1850.

Mannes Israel of Waldeck, Germany, came to Kalamazoo in 1844, starting a general store. He was reputed to be a very learned man, especially in the physical sciences. In 1855, he took in Simon Rosenbaum,

LOUIS FREIDENBERG

SOLOMON MEYERFELD

SOLOMON BENDIT

JULIUS HOUSEMAN

also a native of Waldeck, as his business partner, who continued the business after Israel's death in 1868. Israel's son, Edward, born in Kalamazoo in 1859, was the astronomer of General A. W. Greely's Arctic expedition of 1881. Young Israel, who joined the United States Signal Corps upon his graduation from the University of Michigan, was a volunteer with the Polar explorers. Though the youngest member of the expedition, he led investigating parties by dogsled and helped discover an overland route to Hazenland in Greenland. Physically frail, Israel died before the expedition returned to the United States, having refused to accept more than his share of rations.

Emil Friedman, H. Stern, and M. Cohn were the other early Jewish settlers in Kalamazoo prior to 1850.

Samuel and Marx Hart, natives of south Germany, came to Marshall about 1848.

Solomon and Andrew Freedman, afterwards members of the Detroit community, were at Adrian before 1850. Louis Freidenberg and Solomon Meyerfeld were the only German-Jewish settlers in Monroe (originally Frenchtown) before 1850.

Julius Houseman was the first Jewish settler in Grand Rapids. He came in 1852 and became a distinguished member of the community and state. He served as mayor of Grand Rapids and as a member of Congress, the first Michigan Jew to hold the office of mayor and the only Michigan Jew to this day to have been elected to the House of Representatives.

A study of the city directories of Detroit published before 1850 disclosed the following:

The 1837 *Directory,* the first to be published, contains 1,330 names but not one that can be safely claimed as Jewish.

In the second *Directory,* issued in 1845 and containing 2,800 names, we find Solomon Bendit and Company, dry goods; Goodkind and Freedman, fancy and dry goods; and Moses Rendskopf (later Rindskof).

In the third City *Directory,* published in 1846 and containing 3,238 names, the following known Jews are listed: S. Bendit and Company, dry goods; Frederick Cohen, portrait painter; Solomon Freedman, fancy and staple dry goods; Adam Hersch, cigar maker; Moses Rendskopf; Jacob Silberman. The *Directory* also contains an advertisement by Frederick E. Cohen, a reproduction of which appears on page 55.

In the 1850 *Directory,* the fourth, in spite of the large increase in the population, which then numbered 21,019, only the following Jewish firms and individuals are listed: A. Amberg and Company, merchant tailors; S. & H. Bendit and Company, dry goods; F. E. Cohen, portrait painter; Solomon Cohen, peddler; S. Freedman and Brothers, dry goods dealers; Alexander Grunwald, clothing store; Joseph Grunwald; Adam Hersch, firm of Silberman and Hersch; Leopold Pappenkeimer (later Pappenheimer), fancy store; Silberman and Hersch, cigar manufacturers; Jacob Silberman, firm of Silberman and Hersch. The *Directory* also contains an advertisement by the firm of Silberman and Hersch, which is reproduced on page 55.

The list of Jews in the 1850 *Directory* is not complete, however, for we know that several other Jews resided in the city. By the fall of 1850, there were, in Detroit, more than the traditionally required *minyan* (ten males over the age of thirteen), to start a congregation, and on September 22, 1850, the little band of Jews in Detroit organized the Bet[1] El Society (now Temple Beth El), Michigan's first Jewish congregation, thus founding the first Jewish community in the state of Michigan.

[1] Original name, phonetically spelled.

A SELECTED BIBLIOGRAPHY

Manuscripts

"John Askin Ledgers and Account Books, 1780–1796," Burton Historical Collection, Detroit Public Library.

"Canadian Archives, 1769–1790," Burton Historical Collection.

Marion Morse Davis, "Michilimackinac Notes," Burton Historical Collection.

"Detroit Notarial Records, 1737–1785," Burton Historical Collection.

"Lieutenant John Hay's Diary, 1763–1765," Clements Library, Ann Arbor.

"Lieutenant James MacDonald Letters, 1763," Clements Library.

Daniel Morison, "Mackinac Journal, 1769–1772," Burton Historical Collection.

"John Porteous Journals," Burton Historical Collection.

"Public Archives of Canada, Lower Canada," S. 13, Ottawa, Canada.

"Public Archives of Canada," B Series, Vol. 217, Ottawa, Canada.

"James Sterling Letter Book, 1761–1765," Burton Historical Collection.

"Wayne County, Michigan, Land Records, 1703–1796," Burton Historical Collection.

"Herschel Whitaker Papers," Burton Historical Collection.

"Thomas Williams Papers," Burton Historical Collection.

Published Manuscripts

American State Papers, Washington, 1832.

The John Askin Papers, ed. Milo M. Quaife, 2 volumes, Detroit, 1928 and 1931.

"The Bouquet Papers" in *Michigan Pioneer and Historical Collections,* Vol. 19, Lansing, 1891.

"Commerce of Rhode Island," in *Massachusetts Historical Society Collections,* Vol. 69, Boston, 1914.

Diary of the Siege of Detroit. . . . ed. Franklin B. Hough, Albany, 1860.

"The Gladwin Manuscripts" in *Michigan Pioneer and Historical Collections,* Vol. 27, Lansing, 1897.

"The Haldimand Papers" in *Michigan Pioneer and Historical Collections,* Vol. 19, Lansing, 1891.

"The Mackinac Register," in *Wisconsin Historical Collections,* Vols. 18 and 19, Madison, 1908 and 1909.

Robert Navarre's Journal of the Conspiracy of Pontiac, 1763, translated by R. Clyde Ford, Detroit, 1910.

Report on Canadian Archives, 1885, Ottawa, 1886.

Territorial Papers of the United States, Michigan Territory, Vols. 10–12, Washington, 1942–1945.

SECONDARY SOURCES

Burton, Clarence M., *The City of Detroit, Michigan, 1701–1922,* Vols. 1 and 2, Chicago, 1922.

Byars, W. V., *B. and M. Gratz, Merchants in Philadelphia, 1754–1798,* Jefferson City, Missouri, 1916.

DeSola, Clarence I., *History of the Corporation of Spanish and Portuguese Jews: Shearith Israel of Montreal,* Montreal, 1918.

Dublin, Frances, "Jewish Colonial Enterprise in the Light of the Amherst Papers (1758–1763)" in *Publications of the American Jewish Historical Society,* Vol. 35, New York, 1939.

Farmer, Silas, *History of Detroit and Michigan,* Detroit, 1884.

Gay, Margaret Cooper, *Hatchet in the Sky,* New York, 1954.

Harvard Guide to American History, Cambridge, Mass., 1954.

Heckewelder, John, "History, Manners and Customs of the Indian Nations" in *Memoirs of the Historical Society of Pennsylvania,* Philadelphia, 1876.

Heineman, David E., "Jewish Beginnings in Michigan Before 1850" in *Publications of the American Jewish Historical Society,* Vol. 13, New York, 1905.

__________ "The Startling Experience of a Jewish Trader During Pontiac's Siege of Detroit in 1763" in *Publications of the American Jewish Historical Society,* Vol. 23, New York, 1915.

Henry, Alexander, *Travels and Adventures in Canada. . . ,* New York, 1809.

Jewish Encyclopedia, 12 volumes, New York and London, 1901–1905.

Jewish Community Blue Book of Milwaukee and Wisconsin, Milwaukee, 1925.

Jewish Quarterly Review, New Series, Vol. 10, 1920.

Katz, Irving I., "Ezekiel Solomon, The First Jew in Michigan" in *Michigan History Magazine,* Vol. 32, September, 1948.

__________ "Chapman Abraham: An Early Jewish Settler in Detroit" in *Publications of the American Jewish Historical Society,* Vol. 60 (Part 1), September, 1950.

Lebeson, Anita Libman, *Jewish Pioneers in America,* New York, 1931.

Marcus, Jacob R., *Early American Jewry,* Vols. 1 and 2, Philadelphia, 1951 and 1953.

Osborn, A. C., "The Migration of Voyageurs from Drummond Island to Penetanguishene in 1828" in *Ontario Historical Society, Papers and Records,* Toronto, 1901.

Palmer, Friend, *Early Days in Detroit,* Detroit, 1906.

Parkman, Francis, *History of the Conspiracy of Pontiac,* Boston, 1851.

Peckham, Howard H., *Pontiac and the Indian Uprising,* Princeton, 1947.

Russell, John Andrew, *The Germanic Influence in the Making of Michigan,* Detroit, 1927.

Sack, Benjamin G., *History of the Jews in Canada,* Montreal, 1945.

Universal Jewish Encyclopedia, 10 volumes, New York, 1939–43.

Wood, Edwin S., *Historic Mackinac,* Vols. 1 and 2, New York, 1918.

A Chronology of the History of

TEMPLE BETH EL

IRVING I. KATZ

The home of MR. & MRS. ISAAC COZENS *on Congress and St. Antoine streets where the first Detroit* Minyan *Services were held*

ISAAC COZENS

A CHRONOLOGY

of the History of

TEMPLE BETH EL

Organization and First Activities
1850–1861

1850

Sarah Cozens and her husband, Isaac, arrived in Detroit the early part of the year and took up their residence in a house near the corner of Congress and St. Antoine streets, where a few months later Marcus Cohen conducted the first *Minyan* in Detroit.

MRS. ISAAC COZENS

JOSEPH NEWMAN, *President, 1855*

JACOB SILBERMAN, *President, 1850–1855, 1855–1857*

MARCUS COHEN

Mrs. Cozens, a pious woman accustomed to worshipping in a synagogue in her native Germany and in New York, urged the small band of her co-religionists to establish a congregation in Detroit.

SEPTEMBER 22 Founding of the "Bet El Society" by twelve German Jews at Cozens' home, first Jewish congregation in the state of Michigan. Joseph Newman was elected temporary chairman. First officers elected were Jacob Silberman, president; Solomon Bendit, vice-president and treasurer; Joseph Freedman, secretary. Rabbi Samuel Marcus of New York was engaged as the first spiritual leader at the recommendation of his friend, Marcus Cohen, who officiated at services up to that time. Congregation was orthodox in its ritual and observances. Rabbi Marcus' duties included that of cantor, teacher, *shochet* (ritual slaughterer) and *mohel* (circumcizer). His annual salary was $200.00. A Hebrew-German-English Day School was opened where children received their secular as well as religious education. Detroit's population of 21,019 included 60 Jews. Estimated Jewish population in the United States was 50,000.

1851

JANUARY 1 Purchase of half an acre of land on Champlain (now Lafayette) Street for cemetery purposes. The purchase price was $150.00, of which half was paid in cash and the other half secured by interest bearing notes, payable in six and twelve months respectively, and for their payment a mortgage was given on the cemetery.

APRIL 21 Legal incorporation of the congregation by Jacob Silberman, Solomon Bendit, Joseph Freedman, Max Cohn, Adam Hersch, Alexander Hein, Jacob Lang, Aron Joel Friedlander, Louis Bresler, Charles E. Bresler, and Leo Bresler. (Articles of incorporation recorded in Wayne County Clerk's office on December 21, 1852). Hebrah Bikur Cholim, a society for attendance on the sick and the dying, was organized, with Charles E. Bresler as president.

Tombstone of RABBI SAMUEL MARCUS, *first Rabbi of Beth Èl, in Champlain (now Lafayette) Street Cemetery*

Champlain (now Lafayette) Street Cemetery of Temple Beth El, Detroit's oldest Jewish Cemetery

CLOTHING EMPORIUM.

Sykes & Guiterman,

South side of Jefferson Avenue, between Bates and Randolph Streets.

IMPORTERS OF

French & Belgian Broad-Cloths, Cassimeres

AND VESTINGS.

MERCHANT TAILORS,

Wholesale and Retail Dealers in READY MADE CLOTHING, keep constantly on hand a general assortment of Gentlemen's Furnishing Goods.

SAMUEL SYKES. SIMON GUITERMAN.

I. KAUFFMANN,

Wholesale and Retail

CLOTHING EMPORIUM,

KEARSLEY BLOCK, JEFFERSON AVENUE,

DETROIT.

CLOTHING MADE TO ORDER. GOOD FIT WARRANTED.

FREEDMAN & BROTHERS,

Dealers in Fancy, Staple, and Millinery Goods,

Wholesale and Retail,

No. 133, Jefferson Avenue, Detroit, Michigan.

Silks, Dress Goods and Shawls, of every description, Cloaks, Visetes, Bonnets, Ribbons, Flowers, Fringes, Gimps, Trimmings, Silk and Thread Laces, Needlework, &c., &c. The Trade and Milliners supplied on the most liberal terms.

JOSEPH FREEDMAN, Detroit Mich. SOLOMON FREEDMAN New York.
WILLIAM FREEDMAN, Cleveland, Ohio.

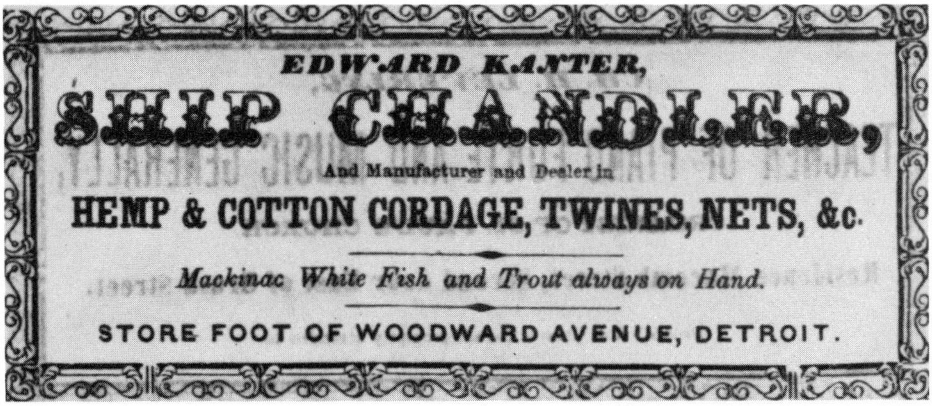

Business ads of Beth El members in the 1853–1854 Detroit Directory

1852

APRIL An account of the founding of Beth El, based on a letter from Joseph Freedman, appeared in *The Occident,* a monthly magazine edited by Rabbi Isaac Leeser of Philadelphia, the leader of Orthodox Judaism in the United States. Rental of room above the store of Silberman and Hersch at 172 Jefferson Avenue to be used as a place of worship. The room was transformed into a synagogue at the cost of $300.00, rent included.

SEPTEMBER 22 Adoption of first Constitution and By-Laws (first German version).

1853

The Detroit *Directory* of 1853–54 stated that Detroit numbered 113 Jews during the summer of 1853.

DR. LIEBMAN ADLER

Title page of Jewish calendar for 50 years, and a page-listing of Beth El

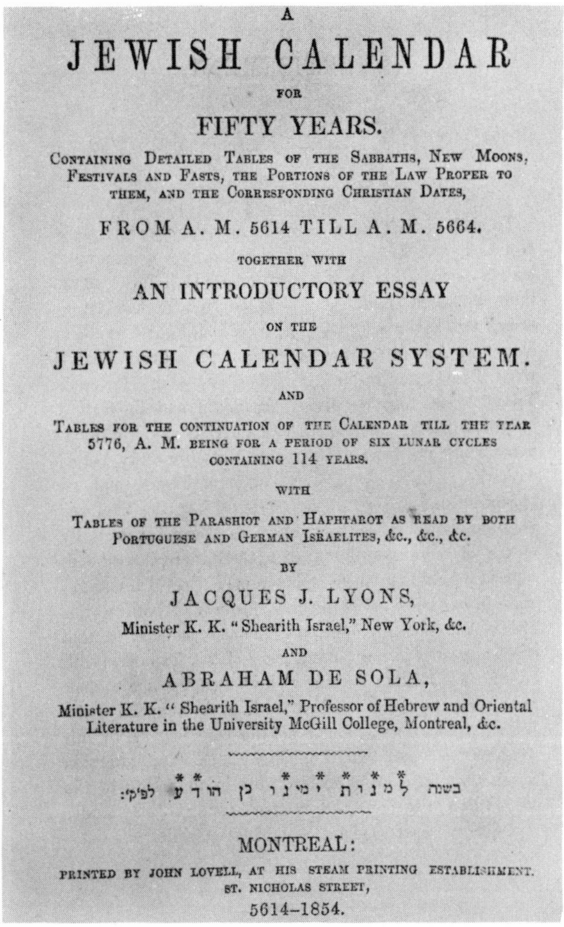

A

JEWISH CALENDAR

FOR

FIFTY YEARS.

CONTAINING DETAILED TABLES OF THE SABBATHS, NEW MOONS, FESTIVALS AND FASTS, THE PORTIONS OF THE LAW PROPER TO THEM, AND THE CORRESPONDING CHRISTIAN DATES,

FROM A. M. 5614 TILL A. M. 5664.

TOGETHER WITH

AN INTRODUCTORY ESSAY

ON THE

JEWISH CALENDAR SYSTEM.

AND

TABLES FOR THE CONTINUATION OF THE CALENDAR TILL THE YEAR 5776, A. M. BEING FOR A PERIOD OF SIX LUNAR CYCLES CONTAINING 114 YEARS.

WITH

TABLES OF THE PARASHIOT AND HAPHTAROT AS READ BY BOTH PORTUGUESE AND GERMAN ISRAELITES, &c., &c., &c.

BY

JACQUES J. LYONS,

Minister K. K. "Shearith Israel," New York, &c.

AND

ABRAHAM DE SOLA,

Minister K. K. " Shearith Israel," Professor of Hebrew and Oriental Literature in the University McGill College, Montreal, &c.

בשנת למנות ימינו כן הודע לפ'ק:

MONTREAL:

PRINTED BY JOHN LOVELL, AT HIS STEAM PRINTING ESTABLISHMENT. ST. NICHOLAS STREET,

5614–1854.

1854

SUMMER Rabbi Marcus died during the cholera epidemic and was laid to rest in the Champlain Street Cemetery. Dr. Liebman Adler, recently arrived from Germany and recommended to Beth El by Dr. Isaac M. Wise of Cincinnati, the founder of American Reform Judaism, was chosen as the second spiritual leader. His annual salary was $360.00 and his duties included that of preacher (in German), cantor, teacher, *shochet* and *mohel*. Rabbi Jacques J. Lyons of New York and Rabbi Abraham De Sola of Montreal, who published a Jewish calendar for fifty years, the first in the United States, listed Beth El of Detroit in this calendar. This listing appeared with about one hundred Jewish synagogues, philanthropic organizations and societies which then served less than 100,000 Jews in the United States and Canada.

1855

OCTOBER Rabbi Adler attended the Cleveland Rabbinical Conference, first in America. Members raised $1,000.00 for the purchase of a site for a synagogue. The congregation numbered 25 members. Joseph Newman was elected the second president. He remained in office for a short period and was followed by Jacob Silberman.

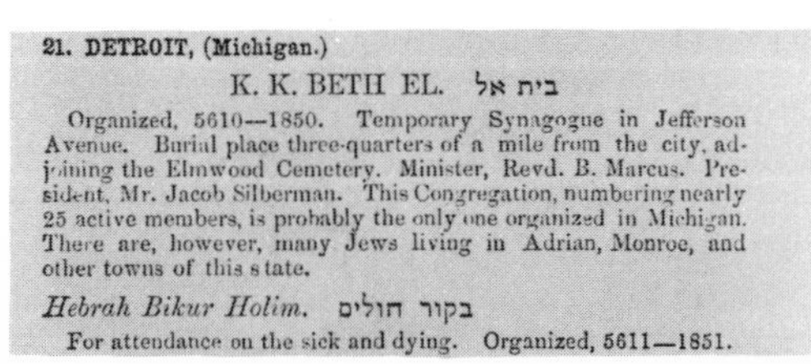

21. DETROIT, (Michigan.)

K. K. BETH EL. בית אל

Organized, 5610—1850. Temporary Synagogue in Jefferson Avenue. Burial place three-quarters of a mile from the city, adjoining the Elmwood Cemetery. Minister, Revd. B. Marcus. President, Mr. Jacob Silberman. This Congregation, numbering nearly 25 active members, is probably the only one organized in Michigan. There are, however, many Jews living in Adrian, Monroe, and other towns of this state.

Hebrah Bikur Holim. בקור חולים

For attendance on the sick and dying. Organized, 5611—1851.

INDEPENDENT ORDER B'NAI B'RITH

BENEVOLENCE, BROTHERLY LOVE, HARMONY.

To all whom it may concern,

Know ye that the District Grand Lodge No. 2 located in the city of Cincinnati State of Ohio at a regular meeting held on the 14th day of May 1857 5618 upon the application of Brothers J. Silberman, M. Cohen, L. Bomfy, H. Friedman, S. Sykes, S. Heavenrich, E. Schloss, S. Schloss, L. Bressler, S. Schwab, A. Hart, M. Hirschman, M. C. Fechheimer has granted a charter for a lodge, to be known by the name, style and title of PISGAH Lodge No. 34 to hold its sessions in the city of DETROIT Mich. on Sunday evening of each week.

Accordingly we the undersigned officers of the District Grand Lodge No. 2 do hereby authorise & empower the above named trusty and well beloved brethren, their successors duly and legally elected, to constitute said Lodge under the name above stated and confer upon them all the rights and privileges guaranteed to a subordinate Lodge by the Constitution of the Order. Provided always, that the said above named brethren and their successors pay due respect to the Constitution Grand Lodge and this District Grand Lodge. PISGAH Lodge No. 34 is in duty bound to conform to the regulations as contained in the Constitution of the Order, and to pay due obedience to the mandates of the District Grand Lodge No. 2 under pain of forfeiting this Charter.

Given under our hand and the seal of the District Grand Lodge No. 2 the 24th day of November 1857 5618

Isaac M. Wise

Lewis Abraham

Countersigned in the name of the ... Constitution Grand Lodge of New York the ...

Julius Bien

B. Rothschild

Charter of Pisgah Lodge, B'nai B'rith, founded by Beth El in 1857

ISIDOR FRANKEL, *President, 1857–1858*

MORRIS HIRSCHMAN, *President, 1858–1859*

1856

New Constitution and By-Laws were adopted containing ideas of Reform Judaism. Dr. Isaac M. Wise of Cincinnati visited Detroit for the first time and gave a brief account of Beth El in *Die Deborah,* the German supplement of *The Israelite,* a weekly edited by Dr. Wise.

1857

MAY Beth El members organized Pisgah Lodge No. 34 of the Independent Order of B'nai B'rith, Michigan's oldest Jewish lodge. The lodge received its charter on November 24, and Jacob Silberman was elected first president.

JULY 14 Rabbi Isaac Leeser of Philadelphia visited Detroit for the first time and gave an account of Beth El in *The Occident.* Isidor Frankel was elected third president of the congregation.

1858

Morris Hirschman was elected the fourth president of the congregation.

1859

JANUARY Dr. Adler was discouraged because of the lack of a synagogue building and submitted his resignation, but was prevailed upon to remain.

The Detroit Jewish Community, in common with Jews throughout the world, held a meeting on January 16 to protest against the Mortara case in Italy. (In 1858, papal gendarmes carried away by force Edgar Mortara, the six year old son of a Jewish family. The child had been christened during illness by his Catholic nurse. The church insisted that the baptism once administered made the boy a Catholic and that he must be brought up as such against the will of his parents.) A spirited controversy on the Mortara case appeared in the *Detroit Free Press* between Dr. Adler and an anonymous writer.

APRIL 25 Dr. Adler urged the members, at the quarterly congregational meeting, to build a synagogue in Detroit. A Synagogue Building Association was formed, with Edward Kanter as president.

MAY 1 A hall over John C. Sherer's drug store, at 39 Michigan Grand Avenue (now Cadillac Square), between Bates and Randolph Streets, was leased at an annual rental of $140.00. The terms of the lease provided that the hall was "to be used as a meeting house and school room."

AUGUST Dr. Isaac M. Wise of Cincinnati visited Detroit and preached at Beth El. An account of his visit appeared in *The Israelite*.

OCTOBER Emanuel Schloss was elected fifth president of the congregation.

EMANUEL SCHLOSS, *President, 1859–1860*

SIMON FREEDMAN, *President, 1860–1865*

1860

The legality of the 1856 Constitution and By-Laws was questioned by the more orthodox members of the congregation. At a congregational meeting on March 4, the matter was debated and the majority re-affirmed the ideas of Reform Judaism contained in the 1856 Constitution and By-Laws and adopted new Articles of Incorporation, which were filed with the County Clerk on March 5. Simon Freedman was elected sixth president of the congregation which now had a membership of forty.

The Rivard Street Synagogue, 1861–1867

1861

MARCH 1 The French Methodist Episcopal Church and adjoining parsonage on Rivard Street, between Croghan (now Monroe) and Champlain (now Lafayette) streets, was purchased for $3,500.00.

SPRING Rabbi Adler accepted a call to K.A.M. Temple in Chicago and was succeeded by Rabbi Abraham Laser, who became the third spiritual leader.

FRIDAY, AUGUST 30 The Rivard Street Synagogue was dedicated by Dr. Isaac M. Wise of Cincinnati and Rabbi Laser. Accounts of the dedication appeared in the *Detroit Free Press,* the *Detroit Tribune and Advertiser,* and *The Israelite* of Cincinnati. The ded-

The Rivard Street Synagogue, 1861–1867

ication exercises, held in the afternoon, and the Friday evening services which followed the exercises as well as the Saturday morning services were supported by a melodeon and mixed choir. This choir was led by Abraham J. Franklin, a liberal-minded member of the congregation, who succeeded in introducing and passing a resolution by the members to permit the participation of music and a choir at these services. Mr. Franklin became the first choir director of the congregation, a post to which he contributed his services for twenty-eight years.

SEPTEMBER 27 The use of music and a mixed choir at worship, an innovation which was contrary to Orthodox Judaism, split the congregation. Seventeen members withdrew and organized the Schaarey Zedeck Society, now Congregation Shaarey Zedek.

NOVEMBER 7 Mesdames Isaac Altman, Isidor Frankel, and Simon Freedman represented Beth El at the organization meeting of the Soldiers' Aid Society, the first such organization in the United States organized during the Civil War. During the Civil War, 210 Jewish soldiers from Michigan served in the Union Army, an excellent military record considering the small Jewish population in Michigan at that time. Many of these were from Detroit, including Joseph Newman, a Temple member.

RABBI ABRAHAM LASER

ABRAHAM J. FRANKLIN

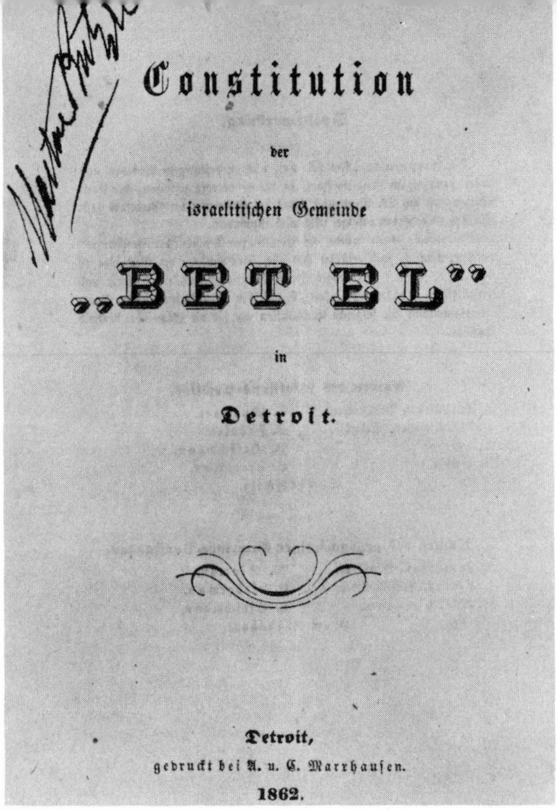

Constitution

der

israelitischen Gemeinde

„BET EL"

in

Detroit.

Detroit,
gedruckt bei A. u. E. Marxhausen.
1862.

Title page of 1862 Constitution and By-Laws of Beth El

Title page of Minhag America *Prayer Book which Beth El began using in 1862*

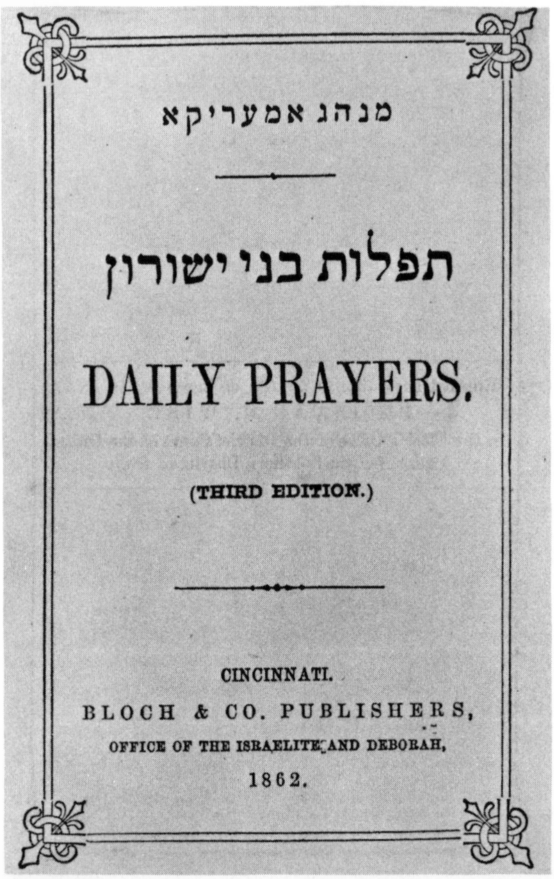

מנהג אמעריקא

תפלות בני ישורון

DAILY PRAYERS.

(THIRD EDITION.)

CINCINNATI.
BLOCH & CO. PUBLISHERS,
OFFICE OF THE ISRAELITE AND DEBORAH,
1862.

DECEMBER *The Israelite* reported that the Hebrew-German-English Day School had an enrollment of seventy-four pupils.

1862

JANUARY 5 A new Constitution and By-Laws (revised German version) were adopted which paved the way for the introduction of greater reforms in ritual.

APRIL Members voted at the quarterly congregational meeting:

1. To replace the *Minhag Askenaz* prayer book (liturgy used in Orthodox congregations) by the *Minhag America* prayer book (American Reform ritual of Dr. Isaac M. Wise).
2. To retain the choir and instrumental music as an integral part of religious services.
3. To introduce the three year cycle of reading from the *Torah* instead of the Orthodox one-year cycle.
4. To abolish *aliyos* (calling up to the *Torah)* at services.
5. To abolish the wearing of the *talis* (prayer shawl) at services and the use of *tachrichim* (shrouds) for the deceased, except the former for the Rabbi.

First page of the minutes of Ladies' Society for the Support of Hebrew Widows and Orphans in the State of Michigan, 1863

Detroit July 12th 1863.

In Folge einer von Herrn A. Laser an die hiesigen israelitischen Damen schriftlich ergangenen Aufforderung versammelten sich dieselben heute in der Odd Fellows Hall.

Herr Laser machte hierauf die Damen mit dem Zweck der Versammlung bekannt: „einen Wittwen und Waisen Verein zu gründen". Folgende Damen erklärten sich zum Beitritt als Mitglieder des Vereins bereit:

Mrs. L. Rice	Mrs. H. Kaichen
" Bendit	" Butzel
" L. Hirshman	" A. Kaichen
" Em. Schloss	" I. Joseph
" S. Schloss	" A. Hersch
" M. Labold	" I. Brenzlor
" A. Lehman	" A. Oppenheimer
" L. Lambert	" M. Mendelson
" I. Frankel	" H. Solomon
" S. Muslimer	" I. Sternberger
" M. Cohen	" R. Blum
" A. Laser	" M. Rosenberger
" E. S. Heineman	" M. Erman
" M. Trounstine	" M. Rindskoff
" I. Kauffman	" S. Wolfson
" H. Freedman	" M. Marks
" S. Freedman	" H. Frenzdorf
" H. Sykes	" Ph. Lichtenberg
" Bernstein	" A. Bresslaur
" R. Ehrman	" S. Sloman
" Knoll	" M. Sloman
" A. I. Franklin	" B. Prell
" Malsh	" Marks
" Brand	" I. Robinson
" Sittig	" D. Amberg
" F. Rothschild Mrs. Loewenstein	" S. Rothschild.

Hierauf wurde beschlossen die Versammlung auf Sonntag den 26. Juli zu vertagen und daß bei dieser nächsten Versammlung die Beamtenwahl stattfinden und die ersten vierteljährigen regelmäßigen Beiträge entrichtet werden sollen.

A. Laser Secty.

DR. ISIDOR KALISCH

SIGMUND ROTHSCHILD, *President, 1865–1866*

6. To permit men and women to sit together at services, instead of women in the gallery and men on the main floor, as is the custom in Orthodox congregations.
7. To introduce on *Shovuos* the ceremony of confirmation for boys and girls, retaining the ceremony of *bar mitzvah* for boys.

FEAST OF SHOVUOS First confirmation of ten boys and girls occurred.

1863

JULY Rabbi Laser organized the Ladies' Society for the Support of Hebrew Widows and Orphans in the State of Michigan, later popularly known as the "Frauen Verein." Louis Hirschman (a man!) was elected first president for a short time and was followed by Mrs. Emil S. Heineman. (The society existed until 1927. It was known then as "Jewish Widows Aid Society.")

1864

AUGUST Dr. Isidor Kalisch succeeded Rabbi Laser as the fourth spiritual leader of Temple Beth El.

SEPTEMBER 10 Dr. Kalisch preached his inaugural sermon.

FRIDAY, SEPTEMBER 22 Dr. Kalisch dedicated Shaarey Zedek's first synagogue on Congress and St. Antoine streets.

1865

APRIL 19 Dr. Kalisch conducted a

Detroit Free Press.

DETROIT, MICHIGAN. THURSDAY MORNING, APRIL 20, 1865.

memorial service for President Abraham Lincoln in the Rivard Street Synagogue. Dr. Kalisch published a volume of his German poems, under the title *Toene des Morgen-Landes* (Sounds of the Orient).

Sigmund Rothschild elected seventh president of the congregation.

1866

Rabbi Elias Eppstein succeeded Dr. Kalisch as the fifth spiritual leader at the annual salary of $1500.00. The members were exceedingly pleased with Rabbi Eppstein and in token of their appreciation they renovated and refurnished his parsonage. David J. Workum was elected eighth president of the congregation.

BETH EL SYNAGOGUE.—REV. DR. KALISCH.

My friends a great national calamity has called us together to meet in this place of worship at an unusual hour. Our bleeding hearts cry to God, and our eyes shed bitter tears at the unexpected death of our late President.

In the fifty-fifth year of his age, in full manly vigor, after four years of heroic labor, trouble and struggle to preserve our sacred constitution, and to restore Union and peace, and shortly after the wicked rebellion received a decisive blow, he, the true champion of national rights, the powerful and successful advocate of universal freedom, the upright and true patriot, was suddenly snatched from our midst.

It is true that he shared the same fate of Moses, the deliverer of Israel from the Egyptian bondage, who was not permitted to lead the freedmen to the promised land, and could only see it from the top of the Mount of Nebo, so could he perceive only from the gigantic mountain of glorious victories over the enemy the revived power and the renewed glory of our blessed Union.

But it is not only his early demise which fills our breasts with sadness, but also the manner in which he found his death especially grieves us to the core of our hearts. It is this that makes millions of men inconsolable.

The faithful and righteous, sitting at the side of his amiable lady, was killed by a base villain.

Why, they moan with heart-breaking anguish, should such a horrible end be the reward of innumerable noble deeds?

But as a servant of our holy religion, I must remind you of the principle of our sages, that the reward of the good is not always given in this life. The real reward begins when the man ceases to be a member of this world. And the memory that he leaves in the hearts of men, the affliction and deep emotions which follow him are the reflected splendor of the heavenly reward that flashes upon earth.

So will the name of our late President be perpetuated in the hearts of the great glorious nation of the Union, and will shine forever among the most distinguished names in the records of all civilized nations. All this, however, is only a shadow of his great reward in the realms of eternity.

Let us, therefore, submit to the divine Providence, whose ways, although a great mystery to us, yet are just, and let us pray that the soul of our late President shall be bound up in the bundle of life in the blissful regions of light for ever and ever. Amen.

Memorial Address for President Lincoln delivered by DR. ISIDOR KALISCH *at the Rivard Street Synagogue on April 19, 1865 (from the* Detroit Free Press)

RABBI ELIAS EPPSTEIN

DAVID J. WORKUM, *President, 1866–1868*

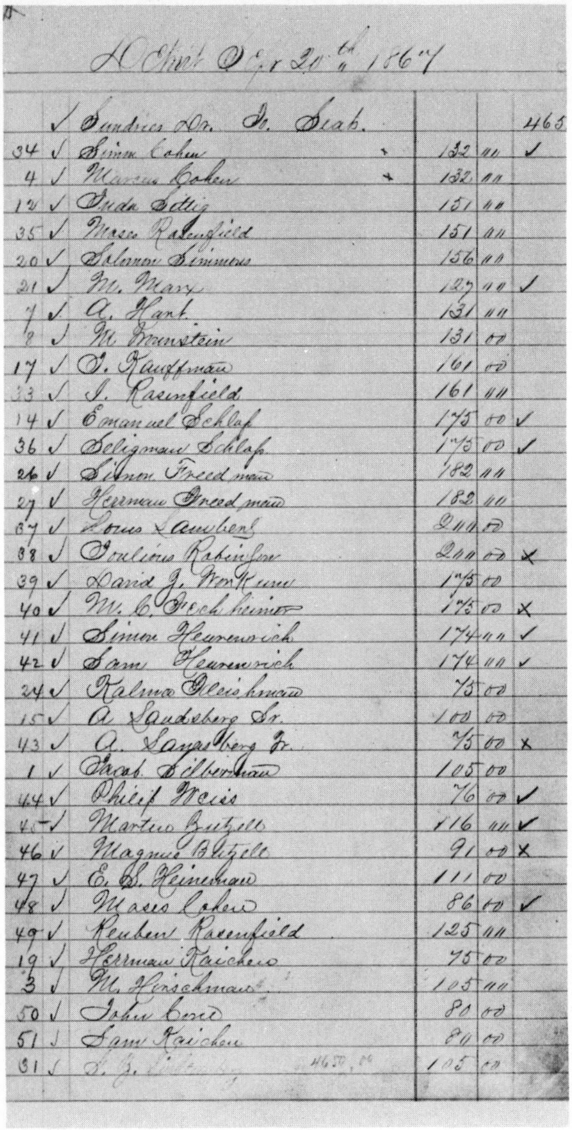

Detroit Dec 20th 1867

	✓	Sundries Dr. to Seat.			465
34	✓	Simon Cohen	132	00	✓
4	✓	Marcus Cohen	132	00	
12	✓	Juda Sittig	151	00	
35	✓	Moses Rosenfield	151	00	
20	✓	Solomon Simmons	156	00	
21	✓	M. Marx	127	00	✓
7	✓	A. Hart	131	00	
8	✓	M. Bornstein	131	00	
17	✓	S. Kauffman	161	00	
33	✓	I. Rosenfield	161	00	
14	✓	Emanuel Schlaf	175	00	✓
36	✓	Seligman Schlaf	175	00	✓
26	✓	Simon Freedman	182	00	
27	✓	Herman Freedman	182	00	
37	✓	Louis Lambert	200	00	
38	✓	Julius Robinson	200	00	✗
39	✓	David J. Workum	175	00	
40	✓	M. C. Bechheimer	175	00	✗
41	✓	Simon Heavenrich	174	00	✓
42	✓	Sam Heavenrich	174	00	✓
24	✓	Kalman Gleishman	75	00	
15	✓	A. Landsberg Sr.	100	00	
43	✓	A. Landsberg Jr.	75	00	✗
1	✓	Jacob Silberman	105	00	
44	✓	Philip Weiss	76	00	✓
45	✓	Martin Butzell	116	00	✓
46	✓	Magnus Butzell	91	00	✗
47	✓	E. S. Heineman	111	00	
48	✓	Moses Cohen	86	00	✓
49	✓	Reuben Rosenfield	125	00	
19	✓	Herman Kaichen	75	00	
3	✓	M. Hirschman	105	00	
50	✓	John Cone	80	00	
51	✓	Sam Kaichen	80	00	
31	✓	[illegible] 4650, 00	105	00	

A page from the Book of Accounts of Beth El (earliest extant), 1867

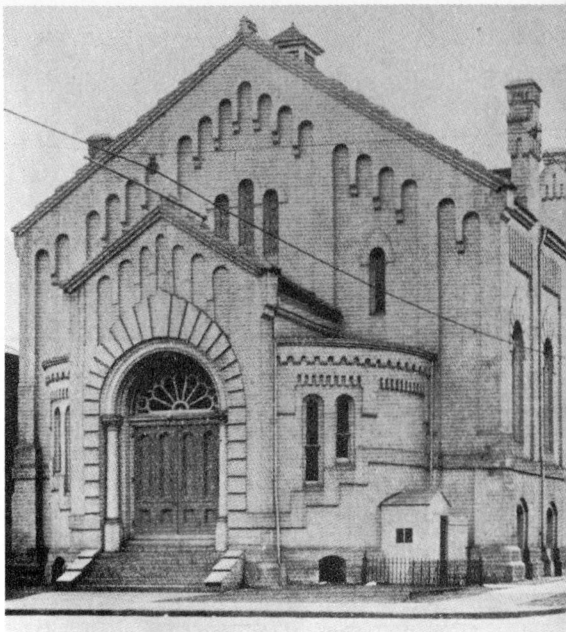

The Temple on Washington and Clifford, 1867-1903

The Washington Boulevard Temple, 1867–1903

1867

MARCH 19 The Tabernacle Baptist Church on Washington Avenue (now Boulevard) and Clifford Street was purchased for $17,000.

FRIDAY, AUGUST 30 The dedication of Washington Avenue Temple took place and was conducted by Dr. Isaac M. Wise of Cincinnati and Rabbi Eppstein. Accounts of the dedication appeared in the *Detroit Free Press,* the *Detroit Tribune and Advertiser,* and *The Israelite.*

1867 Confirmation class

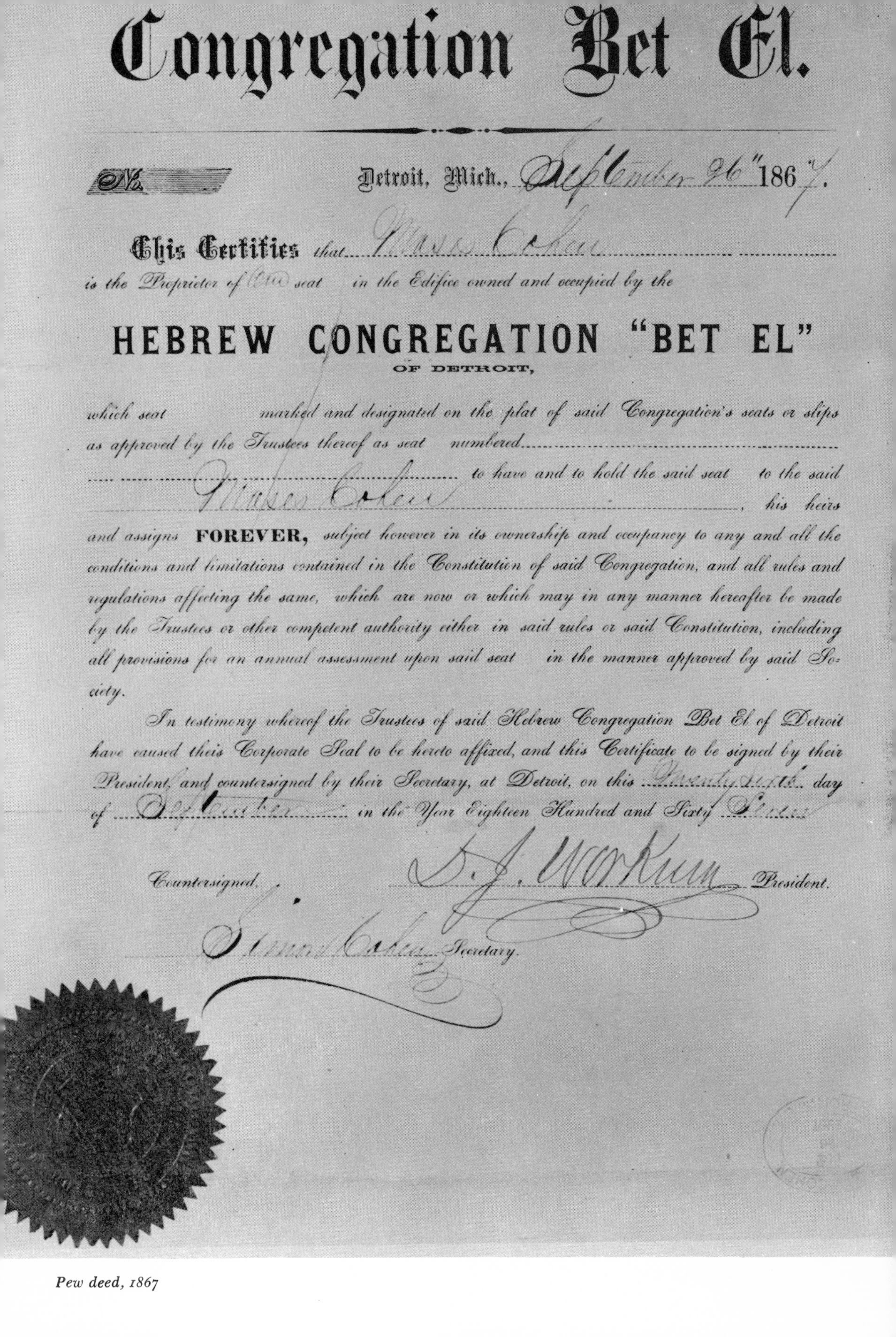

Congregation Bet El.

№ Detroit, Mich., September 26" 1867.

This Certifies *that* Moses Cohen *is the Proprietor of* One *seat in the Edifice owned and occupied by the*

HEBREW CONGREGATION "BET EL"

OF DETROIT,

which seat marked and designated on the plat of said Congregation's seats or slips as approved by the Trustees thereof as seat numbered .... *to have and to hold the said seat to the said* Moses Cohen, *his heirs and assigns* **FOREVER,** *subject however in its ownership and occupancy to any and all the conditions and limitations contained in the Constitution of said Congregation, and all rules and regulations affecting the same, which are now or which may in any manner hereafter be made by the Trustees or other competent authority either in said rules or said Constitution, including all provisions for an annual assessment upon said seat in the manner approved by said Society.*

In testimony whereof the Trustees of said Hebrew Congregation Bet El of Detroit have caused their Corporate Seal to be hereto affixed, and this Certificate to be signed by their President, and countersigned by their Secretary, at Detroit, on this Twenty Sixth *day of* September *in the Year Eighteen Hundred and Sixty* Seven

Countersigned, D. J. Workum *President.*

Simon Cohen *Secretary.*

Pew deed, 1867

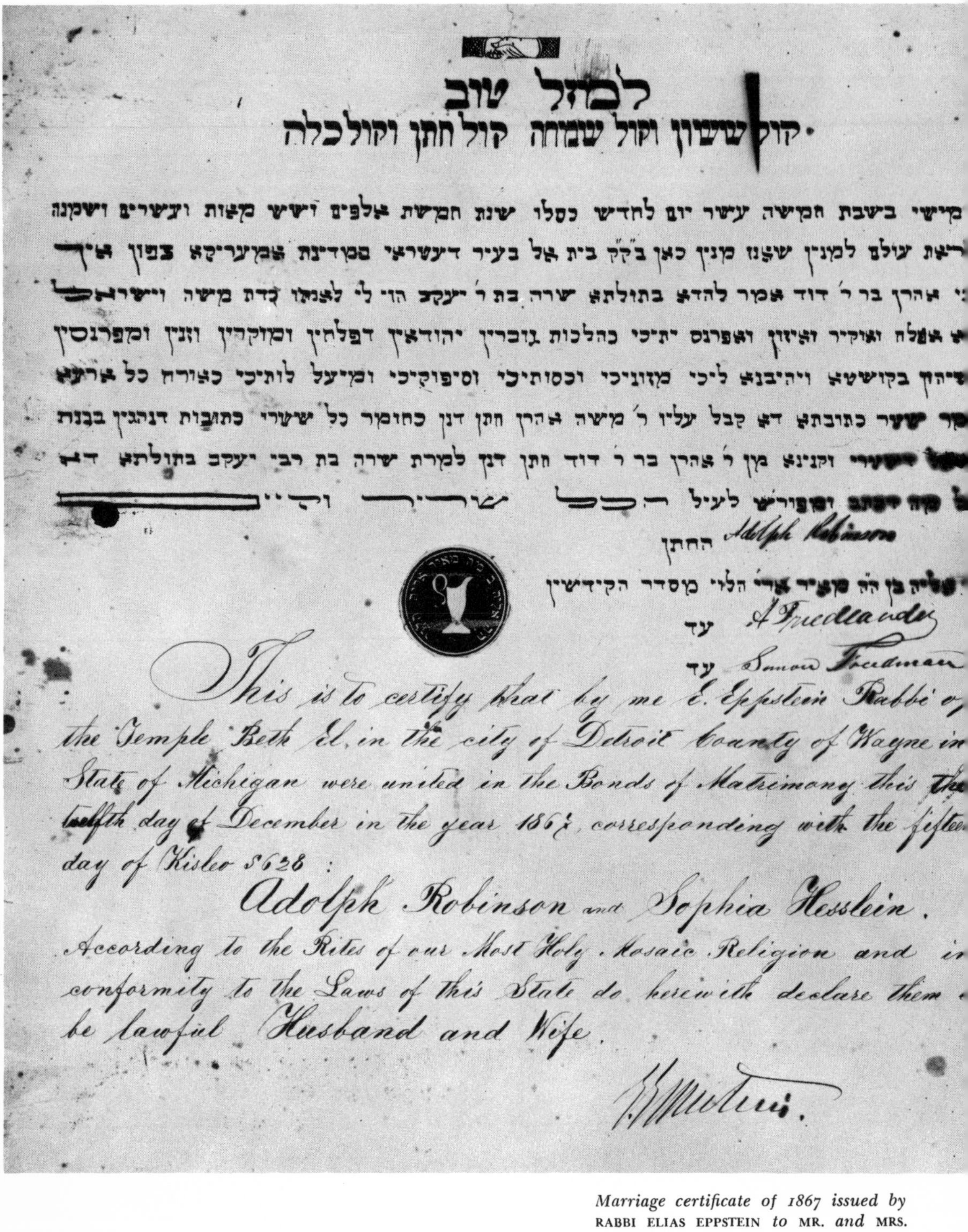

למזל טוב

קול ששון וקול שמחה קול חתן וקול כלה

מישי בשבת חמישה עשר יום לחדש כסלו שנת חמשת אלפים ושש מאות ועשרים ושמנה
ריאת עולם למנין שאנו מנין כאן בק״ק בית אל בעיר דעטראיט במדינת אמעריקא צפון
י אהרן בר ר׳ דוד אמר להדא בתולתא שרה בת ר׳ יעקב הוי לי לאנתו כדת משה וישראל
א אפלח ואוקיר ואיזון ואפרנס יתיכי כהלכות גוברין יהודאין דפלחין ומוקרין וזנין ומפרנסין
יהון בקושטא ויהיבנא ליכי מזוניכי וכסותיכי וסיפוקיכי ומיעל לותיכי כאורח כל ארעא
ר שער כתובתא דא קבל עליו ר׳ משה אהרן חתן דנן כחומר כל שטרי כתובות דנהגין בבנות
ישראל וקנינא מן ר׳ אהרן בר ר׳ דוד חתן דנן למרת שרה בת רבי יעקב בתולתא דא
מה דכתוב ומפורש לעיל הכל שריר וקיים

החתן Adolph Robinson

אליה בן הה׳ מאיר הלוי מסדר הקידשין

עד A Friedlander

עד Samuel Friedman

This is to certify that by me E. Eppstein Rabbi of the Temple Beth El in the city of Detroit County of Wayne in State of Michigan were united in the Bonds of Matrimony this the twelfth day of December in the year 1867, corresponding with the fifteen day of Kisleo 5628:

Adolph Robinson and Sophia Hesslein.

According to the Rites of our Most Holy Mosaic Religion and in conformity to the Laws of this State do herewith declare them to be lawful Husband and Wife.

E. Eppstein.

Marriage certificate of 1867 issued by RABBI ELIAS EPPSTEIN *to* MR. *and* MRS. ADOLPH ROBINSON, *the parents of* SETTA ROBINSON, *a benefactor of Temple Beth El*

CHRONOLOGY

SEPTEMBER Late Friday Evening services were introduced.

1868

Rabbi Eppstein published *Confirmant's Guide to the Mosaic Religion,* first book of Jewish interest published in Michigan. Rabbi Eppstein urged the members to support the establishment of a Jewish Orphan Home in Cleveland, Ohio.

Simon Heavenrich was elected ninth president of the congregation.

1869

JANUARY The Hebrew-German-English Day School was discontinued and a religious school, meeting after public school hours, was opened.

AUGUST Dr. Kaufmann Kohler was brought by Beth El from Germany as the sixth rabbi, to succeed Rabbi Eppstein.

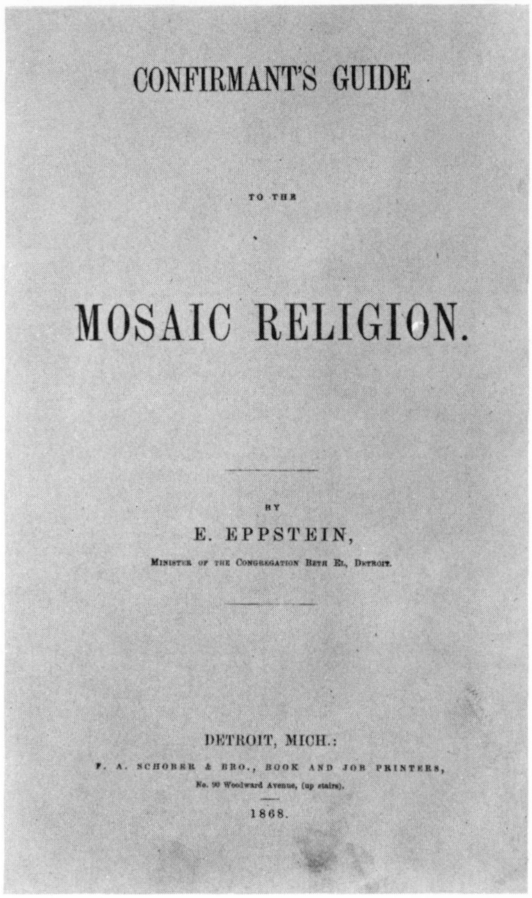
CONFIRMANT'S GUIDE

TO THE

MOSAIC RELIGION.

BY

E. EPPSTEIN,

Minister of the Congregation Beth El, Detroit.

DETROIT, MICH.:

F. A. SCHOBER & BRO., BOOK AND JOB PRINTERS,

No. 90 Woodward Avenue, (up stairs).

1868.

Title page of Confirmant's Guide to the Mosaic Religion *by* RABBI ELIAS EPPSTEIN, *published in Detroit, 1868*

DR. KAUFMANN KOHLER

SIMON HEAVENRICH, *President, 1868–1874*

CONSTITUTION AND BY-LAWS

OF THE

Beth El Hebrew Relief Society,

OF

DETROIT, MICH.

Organized December, 1869.

DETROIT:
PRINTED BY THE DETROIT PRINTING COMPANY, 86 WOODWARD AVE.
1878.

Title page of Constitution and By-Laws of Beth El Hebrew Relief Society

SEPTEMBER 4 Dr. Kohler preached in German his inaugural sermon "The Qualities of a God-called Leader of Israel."

NOVEMBER Dr. Kohler attended the Philadelphia Rabbinical Conference, the first conclave of the leaders of Reform Judaism in the United States.

DECEMBER Beth El and Shaarey Zedek organized The Gentlemen's Hebrew Relief Society, later The Beth El Hebrew Relief Society, Detroit's first centralized Jewish philanthropic agency. David J. Workum was elected as its first president.

1870

Dr. Kohler was married to Johanna Einhorn, daughter of Rabbi David Einhorn, and as a wedding present the congregation furnished his home.

Dr. Kohler abolished the observance of the second day of festivals and the wearing of the *talis* by the rabbi. Reverend M. Greenblatt was engaged as reader, cantor and teacher to assist Dr. Kohler.

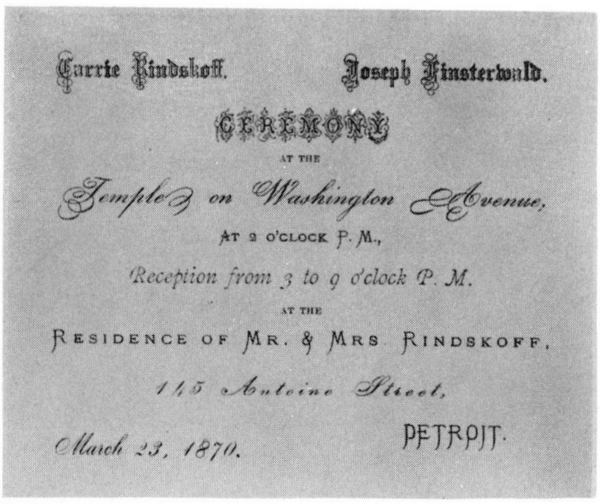
Carrie Rindskoff. Joseph Finsterwald.

CEREMONY

AT THE

Temple on Washington Avenue,

AT 2 O'CLOCK P. M.,

Reception from 3 to 9 o'clock P. M.

AT THE

RESIDENCE OF MR. & MRS RINDSKOFF,

145 Antoine Street,

March 23, 1870. DETROIT.

Invitation to a wedding ceremony at the Washington Blvd. Temple, 1870

1871

OCTOBER Dr. Kohler accepted the pulpit of Sinai Congregation in Chicago.

NOVEMBER Rabbi Emanuel Gerechter, our seventh rabbi, succeeded Dr. Kohler.

English replaced German as the language of instruction in the Religious School.

RABBI EMANUEL GERECHTER

CHRONOLOGY

1873

APRIL Arrangements were made with Woodmere Cemetery for the exclusive use of Section North F by Beth El members and their families.

MAY Dr. Leopold Wintner assumed the religious leadership of the Temple as its eighth rabbi, with Rabbi Gerechter continuing as cantor, reader and teacher.

DR. LEOPOLD WINTNER

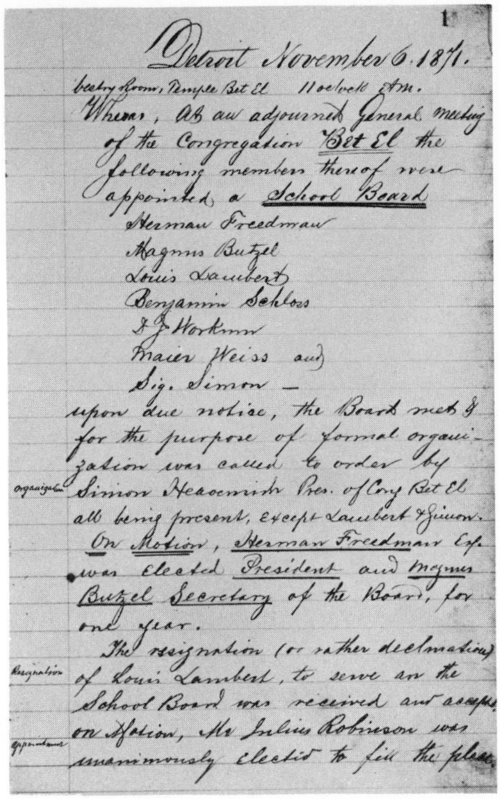

1

Detroit November 6. 1871.

Vestry Room, Temple Bet El 11 o'clock A.M.

Whereas, at an adjourned General meeting of the Congregation "Bet El" the following members thereof were appointed a School Board

Herman Freedman
Magnus Butzel
Louis Lambert
Benjamin Schloss
D. J. Workum
Maier Weiss and
Sig. Simon —

upon due notice, the Board met & for the purpose of formal organization was called to order by Simon Heavenrich Pres. of Cong Bet El all being present, except Lambert & Simon.

Organization — On Motion, Herman Freedman Esq. was elected President and Magnus Butzel Secretary of the Board, for one year.

Resignation — The resignation (or rather declination) of Louis Lambert, to serve on the School Board was received and accepted.

Appointment — on Motion, Mr Julius Robinson was unanimously elected to fill the place.

A page of the first Extant minutes of the School Board of Beth El, 1871

An invitation to a ball, 1872

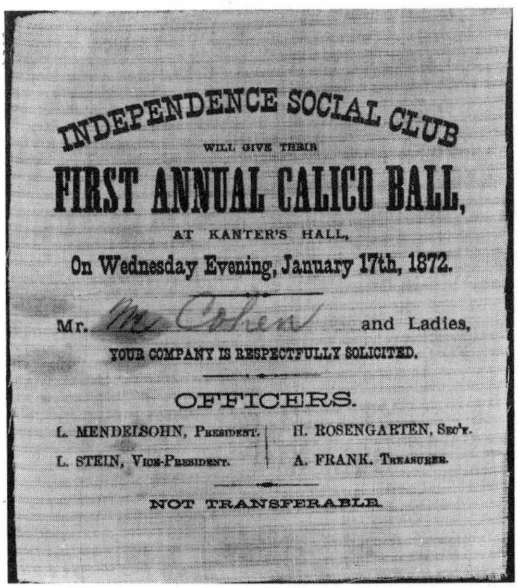

INDEPENDENCE SOCIAL CLUB
WILL GIVE THEIR
FIRST ANNUAL CALICO BALL,
AT KANTER'S HALL,
On Wednesday Evening, January 17th, 1872.

Mr. M. Cohen and Ladies,
YOUR COMPANY IS RESPECTFULLY SOLICITED.

OFFICERS.

L. MENDELSOHN, President. | H. ROSENGARTEN, Sec'y.
L. STEIN, Vice-President. | A. FRANK, Treasurer.

NOT TRANSFERABLE.

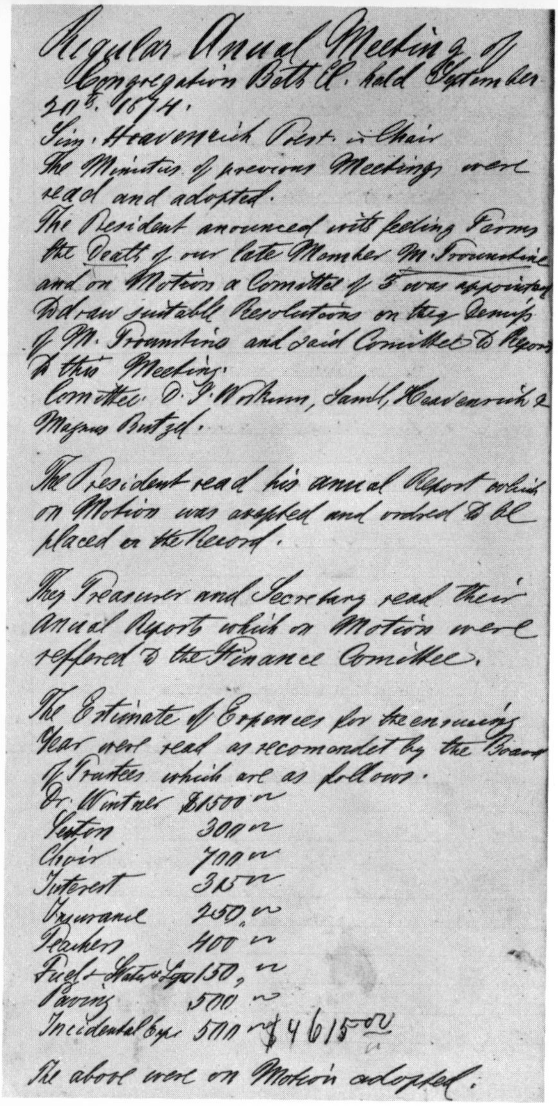
Regular Annual Meeting of Congregation Beth El held September 20th 1874.
Sim. Heavenrich Prest. in Chair
The Minutes of previous Meetings were read and adopted.
The President announced with feeling Terms the Death of our late Member M. Frowntine and on Motion a Comittee of 3 was appointed to draw suitable Resolutions on the Demise of M. Frowntine and said Comittee to Report to this Meeting.
Comittee: D. J. Workum, Saml. Heavenrich & Magnus Butzel.

The President read his annual Report which on Motion was accepted and ordered to be placed on the Record.

The Treasurer and Secretary read their Annual Reports which on Motion were reffered to the Finance Comittee.

The Estimate of Expences for the ensuing Year were read as recomended by the Board of Trustees which are as follows.

Dr. Wintner	$1500.00
Sexton	300.00
Choir	700.00
Interest	315.00
Insurance	250.00
Teachers	400.00
Fuel & Water & Gas	150.00
Paving	500.00
Incidental Exp.	500.00 $4615.00

The above were on Motion adopted.

First page of 1874 Minute Book of Beth El (first extant minute book of meetings of congregation and Board of Trustees).

JULY 8 Magnus Butzel, Simon Heavenrich and David J. Workum attended a meeting of thirty-four congregations in Cincinnati which founded the Union of American Hebrew Congregations.

SEPTEMBER 28 Beth El became officially affiliated with the Union of American Hebrew Congregations.

NOVEMBER 16 Dr. Wintner dedicated Section North F of Woodmere Cemetery.

1874

JULY A Beth El delegation attended the Cleveland Convention of the Union of American Hebrew Congregations where they supported the establishment of the Hebrew Union College, which opened in Cincinnati in 1875.

SEPTEMBER A committee was appointed to solicit funds for the erection of a monument by the Jews of America at the Centennial Celebration of the United States in Philadelphia in 1876.

MAGNUS BUTZEL

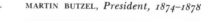

MARTIN BUTZEL, *President, 1874–1878*

CHRONOLOGY

NOVEMBER Rabbi Gerechter accepted the pulpit of Temple Emanuel in Grand Rapids, Michigan.

Martin Butzel elected tenth president of the congregation.

1875

FEBRUARY 2 The Hon. Simon Wolf of Washington lectured at the Temple.

HOLY DAYS President Martin Butzel ordered Dr. Wintner to preach in German only and the members upheld his decision at the subsequent annual congregational meeting.

1876

JANUARY A new Constitution and By-Laws adopted (first English version).

MAY Dr. Wintner was invited to preach at the Church of Our Father (Universalist), the first Detroit rabbi to preach in a Christian Church.

SEPTEMBER Dr. Heinrich (Henry) Zirndorf was brought to Detroit from

DR. HENRY ZIRNDORF

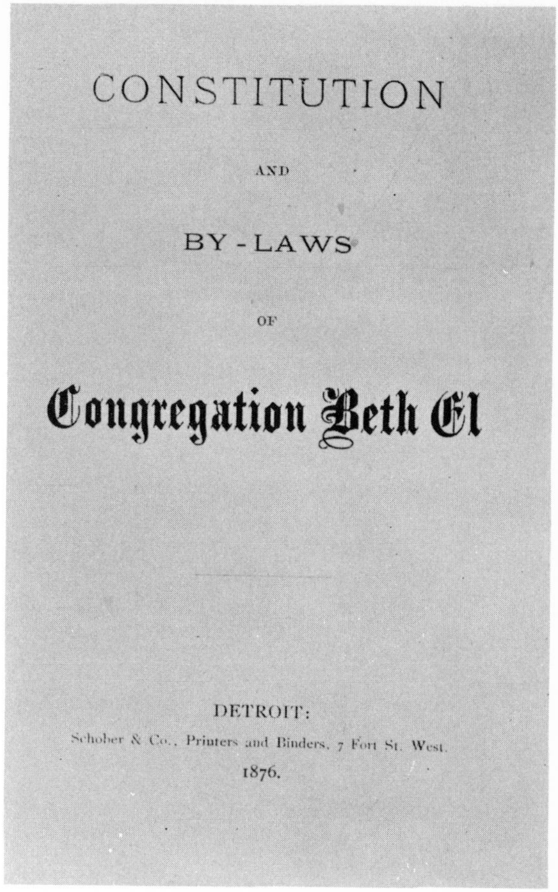

CONSTITUTION

AND

BY-LAWS

OF

Congregation Beth El

DETROIT:

Schober & Co., Printers and Binders, 7 Fort St. West.

1876.

Title page of 1876 Constitution and By-Laws

Notice of the 1876 meeting for the election of a Rabbi

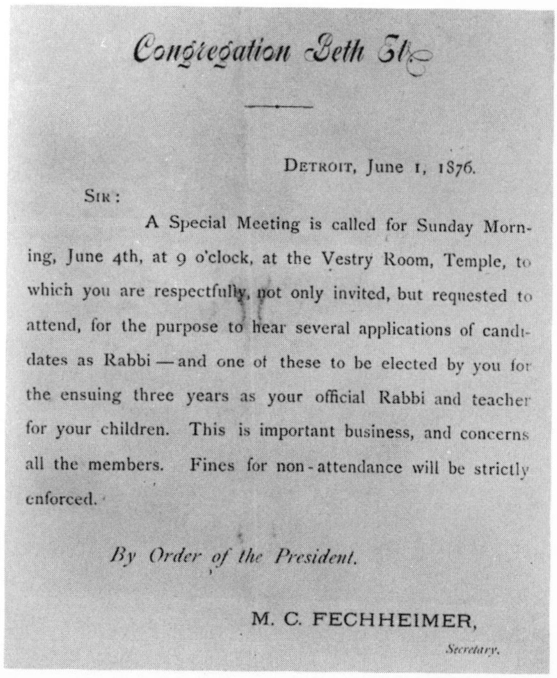

Congregation Beth El

DETROIT, June 1, 1876.

SIR:

A Special Meeting is called for Sunday Morning, June 4th, at 9 o'clock, at the Vestry Room, Temple, to which you are respectfully, not only invited, but requested to attend, for the purpose to hear several applications of candidates as Rabbi — and one of these to be elected by you for the ensuing three years as your official Rabbi and teacher for your children. This is important business, and concerns all the members. Fines for non-attendance will be strictly enforced.

By Order of the President.

M. C. FECHHEIMER,

Secretary.

SELIGMAN SCHLOSS, *President, 1878–1881*

An invitation to a ball, 1876

Admission card to excursion arranged in honor of the Rabbinical Literary Association, 1880

Germany to become the Temple's ninth rabbi.

DECEMBER The congregation purchased its first organ for $1,150.00 to replace the melodeon previously used. First Chanukah Festival held in the Religious School.

1877

JULY 4 The officers, trustees and members of Beth El attended the cornerstone laying ceremonies of Congregation Shaarev Zedek on Congress and St. Antoine streets. Dr. Max Lilienthal of Cincinnati and Dr. Zirndorf officiated at the ceremonies.

A Junior Choir was formed to sing at the Friday evening services and a normal class was opened by Dr. Zirndorf for post confirmands of the Religious School who served as assistant teachers.

1878

Dr. Zirndorf established the Temple Library. Seligman Schloss elected eleventh president of the congregation.

1880

JULY 14–15 Beth El was host to the Rabbinical Literary Association, an association of rabbis organized in 1879 by Dr. Max Lillienthal of Cincinnati.

1881

FEBRUARY A resolution was passed by the Temple Board that no child who observed his *bar mitzvah* at the Temple be permitted to recite anything except the *brochos* (blessings) before and after the reading from the *Torah*.

SEPTEMBER Israel Aaron, a student of the first ordination class of the Hebrew Union College (1883), assisted Dr. Zirndorf at the Holy Day Services.

OCTOBER The preaching of sermons on the eve of festival services, except the High Holy Days, was abolished. Julius Robinson was elected twelfth president of the congregation.

JULIUS ROBINSON, *President, 1881–1891*

1882

FEBRUARY Dr. Zirndorf dedicated the new synagogue of Congregation Shaarey Zedek on Congress and St. Antoine streets. Dr. Zirndorf and Simon Heavenrich organized The Hebrew Ladies' Auxiliary Relief Society (later known as The Hebrew Ladies' Sewing Society) to assist Russian-Jewish immigrants of Detroit. Mrs. Seligman Schloss was elected first president.

1883

Memorial prayers at worship for deceased persons were abolished, except for the Memorial Service on *Yom Kippur*.

1884

JULY A motion made at a congregational meeting that Hebrew not be

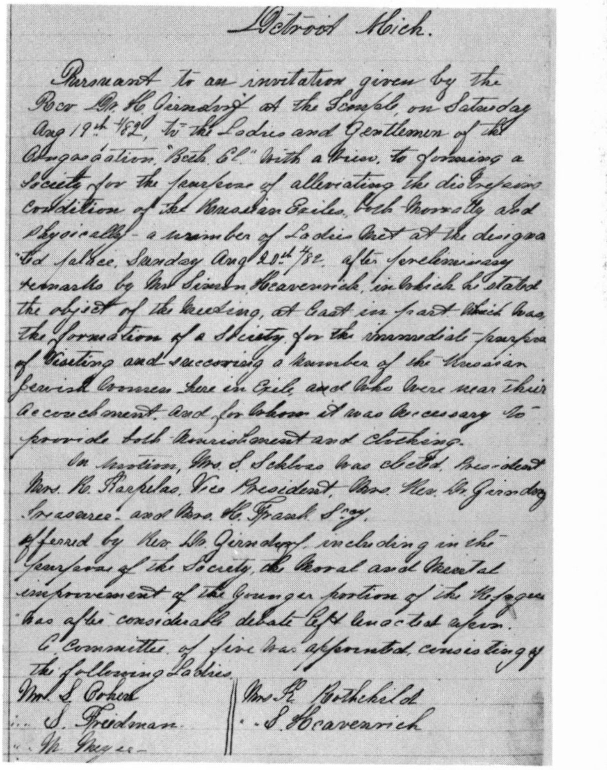

Detroit Mich.

Pursuant to an invitation given by the Rev Dr. H. Zirndorf at the Temple, on Saturday Aug 19th /82, to the Ladies and Gentlemen of the Congregation "Beth El" with a view, to forming a Society for the purpose of alleviating the distressing condition of the Russian Exiles, both Morally and Physically - a number of Ladies met at the designated place, Sunday Aug 20th /82. after preliminary remarks by Mr Simon Heavenrich, in which he stated the object of the meeting, at least in part which was the formation of a Society for the immediate purpose of Visiting and succoring a number of the Russian Jewish women here in Exile, and who were near their accouchment, and for whom it was necessary to provide both nourishment and clothing.

On motion, Mrs. S. Schloss was elected President Mrs. H. [illegible] Vice President, Mrs. Rev. Dr. Zirndorf Treasurer and Mrs. H. Frank Secy.

offered by Rev. Dr. Zirndorf, including in the purposes of the Society, the Moral and Mental improvement of the Younger portion of the [illegible] was after considerable debate left [illegible] [illegible].

A Committee of five was appointed, consisting of the following Ladies.

Mrs. S. Cohen	Mrs. R. Rothchild
" S. Freidman	" S. Heavenrich
" M. Meyer	

First page of minutes of the Hebrew Ladies' Sewing Society, 1882

DR. LOUIS GROSSMANN

taught in the Religious School was lost by a rousing majority.

OCTOBER Service held in honor of the one hundredth birthday of Sir Moses Montefiore, distinguished English philanthropist and statesman.

Dr. Zirndorf accepted the invitation of the Hebrew Union College to occupy the post of Professor of History and Hebrew Literature.

NOVEMBER 27 Rabbi Louis Grossmann, a graduate of the 1884 class of the Hebrew Union College, succeeded Dr. Zirndorf as the tenth rabbi.

DECEMBER 6 Rabbi Grossmann preached his inaugural sermon.

1885

JULY A resolution was passed by the members that Beth El delegates to the forthcoming convention of the Union of American Hebrew Congregations present a resolution on the convention floor urging the adoption of a uniform prayer book by all the Reform congregations in the country.

AUGUST 8 Memorial service was held for former United States President Ulysses S. Grant.

AUGUST 9 Memorial service was held for Sir Moses Montefiore. Congregation adopted the use of the *Minhag America* prayer book on the High Holy Days, to replace the Orthodox *Machzor* (holiday prayer book).

Rabbi Grossmann organized a society for the promotion of culture, named The Emerson Circle.

Beth El Picnic, 1889

1886

MAY Dr. Grossmann organized the Beth El Alumnal Association (now The Young People's Society). Dr. Grossmann, Miss Rose Barlow (now Mrs. Sidney Weinman), Assistant Superintendent, and a number of teachers of the Religious School attended the first convention of the Hebrew Sabbath School Union in Cincinnati.

1889

APRIL A celebration was held in honor of Dr. Isaac M. Wise's seventieth

SAMUEL HEAVENRICH, *President, 1891–1893, 1905–1908*

birthday and a testimonial was forwarded to him.

SPRING Beth El members organized the Self-Help Circle to assist Jewish refugees from Russia. Mrs. Sarah Berger was elected first president.

JULY 9–11 Beth El was host to the Eleventh Council of the Union of American Hebrew Congregations. At this convention, the Central Conference of American Rabbis was founded.

OCTOBER Dr. Grossmann instituted Sunday morning lectures. Dr. Grossmann's book, *Judaism and the Science of Religion,* was published.

1890

APRIL A committee was appointed to locate a new Temple site. A Committee for the Relief of Russian Refugees was organized and an appeal was issued to the Jews of Michigan to support the Palestine Agricultural Colony in Bad Axe, Michigan.

Dr. Grossmann's "Maimonides," a paper read before the Philosophical Society of the University of Michigan, was published.

1891

MARCH Dr. Grossmann organized The Woman's Club of Temple Beth El (which later became The Jewish Woman's Club of Detroit, and in 1925, The Detroit Section of the National Council of Jewish Women). Samuel Heavenrich was elected thirteenth president of the congregation.

1892

SEPTEMBER 4 New Constitution and By-Laws were adopted.

FESTIVAL OF SUKOS Martin Butzel arranged an exhibit at Temple Beth El of the farm products of the Palestine colony in Bad Axe, Michigan. This was the first display of farm products raised by Jews ever shown in the United States.

OCTOBER 14 Four hundredth anniversary of the Discovery of America and twenty-fifth anniversary of the occupancy of the Washington Boulevard Temple were celebrated.

1893

JANUARY $3,100 was raised for a new Temple site.

The use of the facilities of Temple Beth El were made available to the Detroit High School, whose building was destroyed by fire.

Congregation opened a Mission Sunday School, a free afternoon school intended for poor children and for children of parents who belonged to congregations where there was no school.

Julius Freud was elected fourteenth president of the congregation.

1894

DECEMBER A celebration was held in honor of Dr. Grossmann's tenth anniversary in Detroit.

Beth El assumed the responsibility

Program cover of the celebration of the 400th anniversary of the discovery of America and the 25th anniversary of the occupancy of the Temple on Washington and Clifford.

JULIUS FREUD, *President, 1893–1897*

זמירות ישראל

RESPONSES, PSALMS AND HYMNS

FOR WORSHIP

IN

JEWISH CONGREGATIONS

AND SCHOOLS.

EDITED BY

LOUIS GROSSMANN AND F. L. YORK.

שירו לנו משיר ציון:

Psalm, CXXXVII, 3.

DETROIT:

JOHN F. EBY & CO., PRINTERS.

1894.

Title page of a Hymnal, by DR. LOUIS GROSSMANN *and* FRANCIS L. YORK, *published in Detroit in 1894.*

for the maintenance of several beds at the Children's Free Hospital, a project which continued for many years. *Hymns, Prayers and Responses* by Dr. Grossmann and Francis L. York, Temple organist, was published.

Women were appointed as members of the School Board for the first time.

1895

SEPTEMBER Reintroduction of late Friday evening services took place and the *Union Prayer Book No. 1,* published by the Central Conference of American Rabbis, was adopted. Dr. Grossmann's sermons were published in pamphlet form under the title *The Jewish Pulpit.*

1896

MAY Memorial service was held for Baron Maurice De Hirsch, noted philanthropist.

SEPTEMBER A congregational rule was passed prohibiting the covering of the head of male members at services, a practice which had been optional until this year. Dr. Grossmann took a leading part in the fight to eliminate the use of *Readings From The Bible* from the Detroit public schools.

1897

Dr. Grossmann opened a normal school for the training of Religious School teachers.

Louis Blitz elected fifteenth president of the congregation.

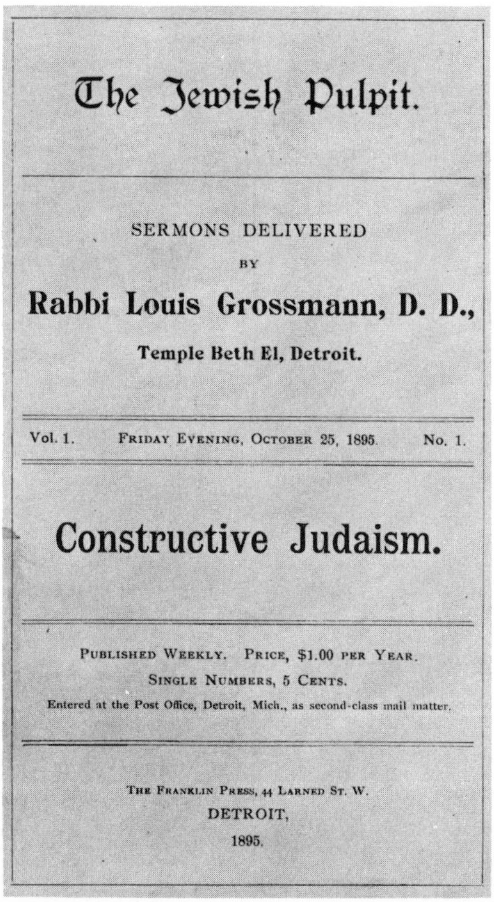

The Jewish Pulpit.

SERMONS DELIVERED

BY

Rabbi Louis Grossmann, D. D.,

Temple Beth El, Detroit.

Vol. 1. FRIDAY EVENING, OCTOBER 25, 1895. No. 1.

Constructive Judaism.

PUBLISHED WEEKLY. PRICE, $1.00 PER YEAR.

SINGLE NUMBERS, 5 CENTS.

Entered at the Post Office, Detroit, Mich., as second-class mail matter.

THE FRANKLIN PRESS, 44 LARNED ST. W.

DETROIT,

1895.

Title page of the first printed sermons by DR. LOUIS GROSSMANN, *1895*

CHRONOLOGY

1898

OCTOBER Dr. Grossmann accepted the call of Congregation B'nai Yeshurun in Cincinnati to serve as Associate Rabbi with Dr. Isaac M. Wise. Testimonials by Beth El and a public farewell reception by the citizens of Detroit were tendered to Dr. Grossmann.

NOVEMBER 30 Rabbi Leo M. Franklin of Temple Israel, Omaha, Nebraska, a graduate of the 1892 class of the Hebrew Union College, was elected eleventh rabbi of Beth El.

1899

JANUARY Rabbi Franklin arrived in Detroit on January 24 and preached his inaugural sermon on January 27. Congregation numbered 136 members.

A Memorial service was held on January 29 for the soldiers and sailors who made the supreme sacrifice in the Spanish-American War.

A subscription was made for a national monument to the fallen heroes.

APRIL Beth El joined in the nationwide celebration of Dr. Wise's eightieth birthday and tendered him a testimonial.

OCTOBER 5 The congregation was reincorporated and a new Constitution and By-Laws were adopted.

NOVEMBER Rabbi Franklin organized the United Jewish Charities, an amalgamation of the Beth El Hebrew Relief Society, Jewish Relief Society,

LOUIS BLITZ, *President, 1897–1905*

Scroll presented by Beth El to DR. ISAAC M. WISE *on his 80th birthday, 1899*

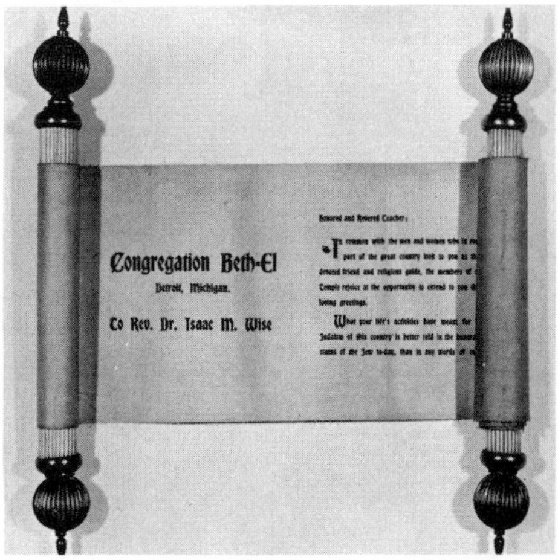

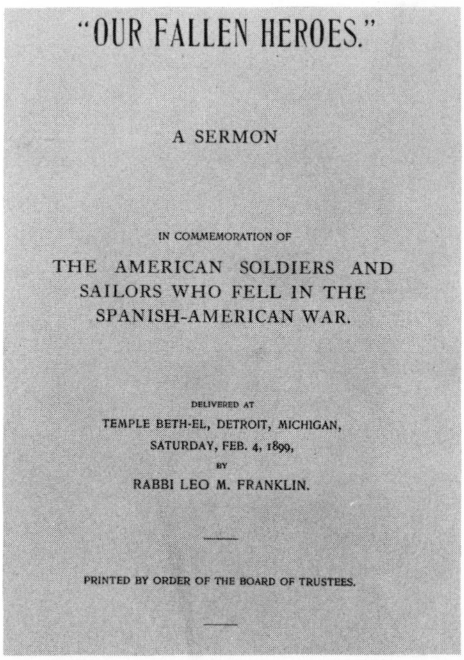

"OUR FALLEN HEROES."

A SERMON

IN COMMEMORATION OF

THE AMERICAN SOLDIERS AND SAILORS WHO FELL IN THE SPANISH-AMERICAN WAR.

DELIVERED AT

TEMPLE BETH-EL, DETROIT, MICHIGAN,

SATURDAY, FEB. 4, 1899,

BY

RABBI LEO M. FRANKLIN.

PRINTED BY ORDER OF THE BOARD OF TRUSTEES.

Title page of Memorial Sermon by DR. FRANKLIN *for soldiers who died in the Spanish-American War, 1899*

DR. FRANKLIN'S *first Confirmation Class, 1899*

ISAAC MAIER WISE.

A MEMORIAL SERMON

DELIVERED AT

TEMPLE BETH-EL, DETROIT, MICH.

Friday evening, April 6, 1900.

BY

RABBI LEO M. FRANKLIN.

PUBLISHED BY THE CONGREGATION.

DETROIT, MICH.:
THE RALSTON-STROUP PTG. CO.
1900

Title page of ISAAC M. WISE *Memorial Sermon delivered by* DR. FRANKLIN

Self-Help Circle and Hebrew Ladies' Sewing Society, out of which sprang the Jewish Welfare Federation in 1926.

1900

APRIL 6 Memorial service was held for Dr. Isaac M. Wise.

OCTOBER 10 A special meeting of the congregation was held at which it was decided to build a new temple.

NOVEMBER 29 The fiftieth anniversary of the congregation was celebrated. A semi-centennial history of the congregation was published, written by Dr. Franklin.

1901

MARCH First Temple bulletin issued.

MRS. ADOLPH SLOMAN, *first President of the Sisterhood*

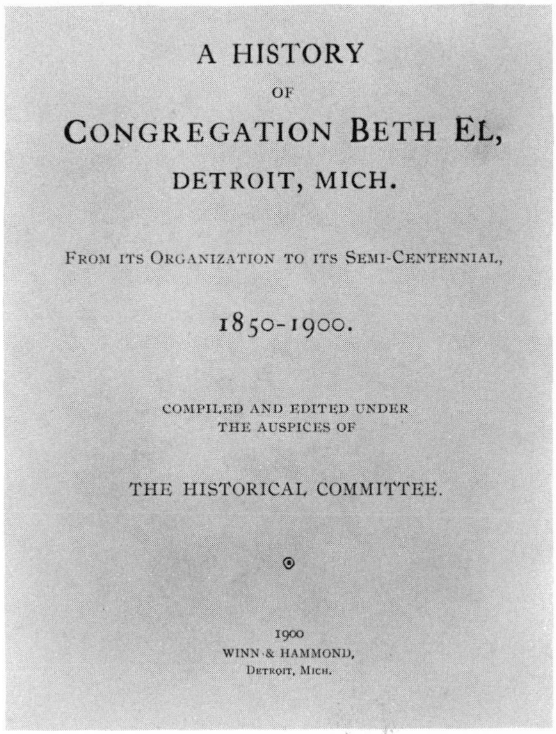

A HISTORY

OF

CONGREGATION BETH EL,

DETROIT, MICH.

FROM ITS ORGANIZATION TO ITS SEMI-CENTENNIAL,

1850-1900.

COMPILED AND EDITED UNDER
THE AUSPICES OF

THE HISTORICAL COMMITTEE.

1900
WINN & HAMMOND,
DETROIT, MICH.

Title page of the Semi-Centennial History of Beth El, written by DR. FRANKLIN *in 1900*

APRIL 3 New Temple site on Woodward near Eliot was purchased.

SEPTEMBER 19 Memorial service was held for President William McKinley.

NOVEMBER 22 Union Thanksgiving service was held with the Unitarian and Universalist churches.

NOVEMBER 25 Ground-breaking ceremonies at the new site took place.

NOVEMBER 26 Dr. Franklin organized the Woman's Auxiliary Association of Temple Beth El. (In 1922 the name was changed to Sisterhood of Temple Beth El.) Mrs. Adolph Sloman was elected first president.

NOVEMBER Dr. Franklin assumed the editorship of *The Jewish American,* Detroit's first English-Jewish weekly, started in 1900, which subsequently became the official organ of Temple Beth El.

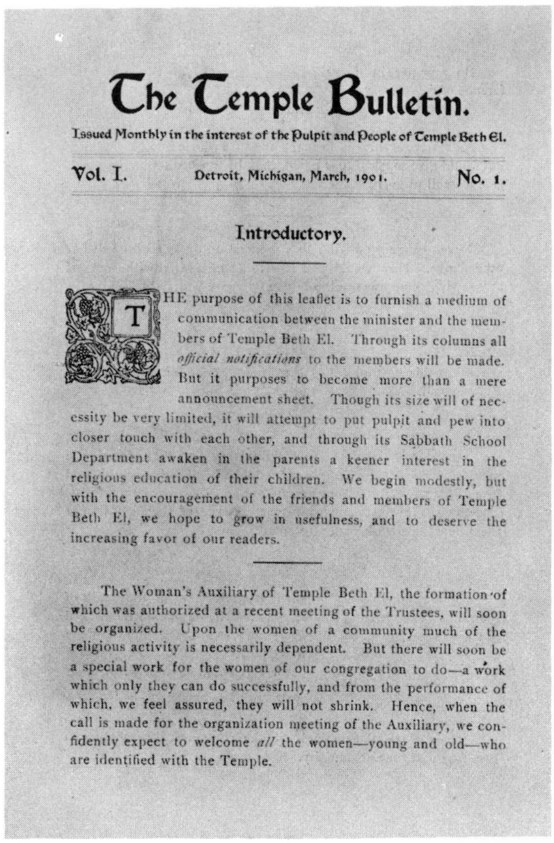

The Temple Bulletin.

Issued Monthly in the interest of the Pulpit and People of Temple Beth El.

Vol. I. Detroit, Michigan, March, 1901. No. 1.

Introductory.

THE purpose of this leaflet is to furnish a medium of communication between the minister and the members of Temple Beth El. Through its columns all *official notifications* to the members will be made. But it purposes to become more than a mere announcement sheet. Though its size will of necessity be very limited, it will attempt to put pulpit and pew into closer touch with each other, and through its Sabbath School Department awaken in the parents a keener interest in the religious education of their children. We begin modestly, but with the encouragement of the friends and members of Temple Beth El, we hope to grow in usefulness, and to deserve the increasing favor of our readers.

The Woman's Auxiliary of Temple Beth El, the formation of which was authorized at a recent meeting of the Trustees, will soon be organized. Upon the women of a community much of the religious activity is necessarily dependent. But there will soon be a special work for the women of our congregation to do—a work which only they can do successfully, and from the performance of which, we feel assured, they will not shrink. Hence, when the call is made for the organization meeting of the Auxiliary, we confidently expect to welcome *all* the women—young and old—who are identified with the Temple.

Front page of the first Temple Bulletin

Temple Beth El on Woodward near Eliot, 1903–1922

1902

APRIL 23 Cornerstone laying ceremony of the new Temple building.

MAY 26–28 National Conference of Jewish Charities in the United States held its Second Biennial Convention at the Temple.

NOVEMBER 27 Dr. Franklin established the Citizen's Interdenominational Community Thanksgiving Service, which is still in existence.

The Temple on Woodward and Eliot, 1903–1922

1903

JANUARY 24 First service held in the chapel of the new Temple.

JANUARY 25 The Religious School

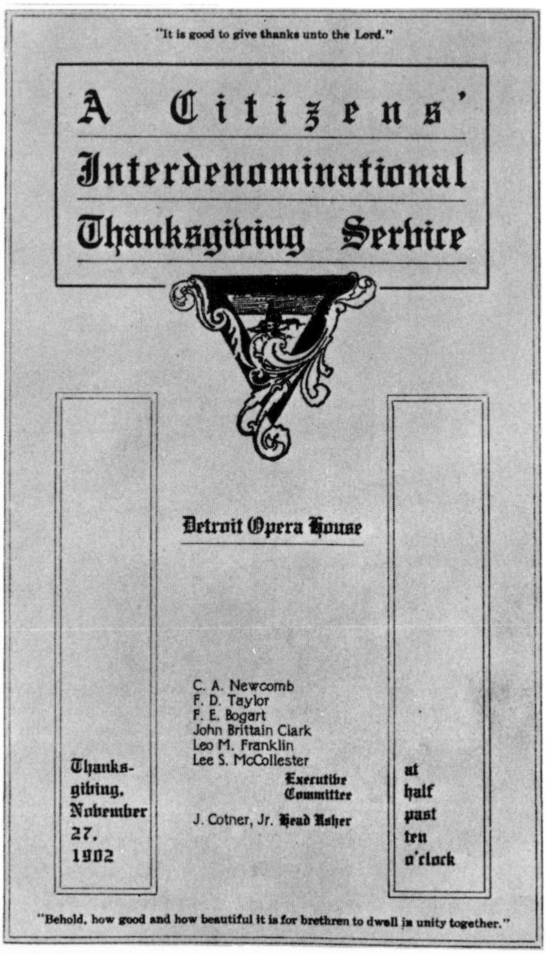

"It is good to give thanks unto the Lord."

A Citizens' Interdenominational Thanksgiving Service

Detroit Opera House

C. A. Newcomb
F. D. Taylor
F. E. Bogart
John Brittain Clark
Leo M. Franklin
Lee S. McCollester
Executive Committee

J. Cotner, Jr. Head Usher

Thanksgiving, November 27, 1902

at half past ten o'clock

"Behold, how good and how beautiful it is for brethren to dwell in unity together."

Program cover of the first Citizen's Interdenominational Community Thanksgiving Service, 1902

ALBERT KAHN

held its first session in the new Temple.

JUNE 29–JULY 4 Beth El was host to the Fourteenth Annual Convention of the Central Conference of American Rabbis.

JULY 8 Sunday morning services, in addition to Saturday morning services, were authorized to begin in January, 1904.

SEPTEMBER 8 Congregation initiated the unassigned seating system, an innovation amongst temples in the United States. Kindergarten and High School Departments were added to the Religious School.

SEPTEMBER 18–19 Dedication of the Temple on Woodward and Eliot. Albert Kahn, internationally famous architect, and a member of the Temple, was the builder.

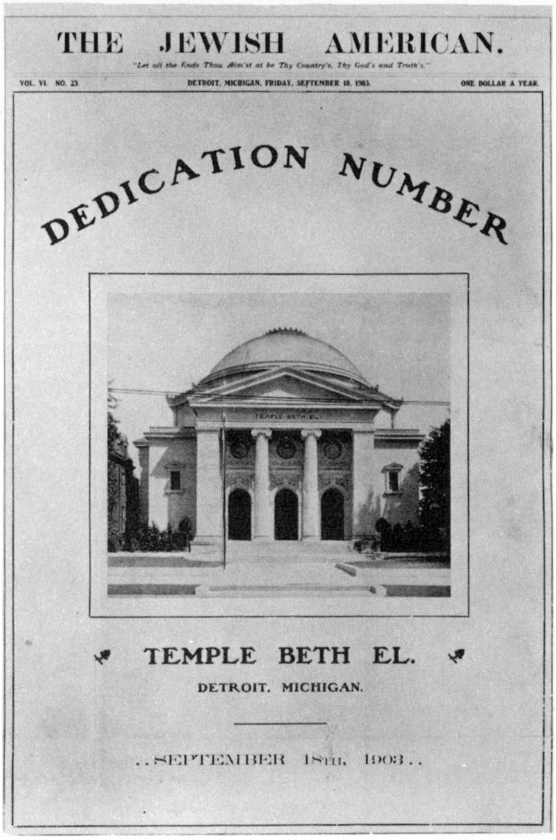

THE JEWISH AMERICAN.

"Let all the Ends Thou Aim'st at be Thy Country's, Thy God's and Truth's."

VOL. VI. NO. 23. DETROIT, MICHIGAN, FRIDAY, SEPTEMBER 18, 1903. ONE DOLLAR A YEAR.

DEDICATION NUMBER

TEMPLE BETH EL.

DETROIT, MICHIGAN.

..SEPTEMBER 18TH, 1903..

The Jewish American *of September 18, 1903, dedicated to Beth El*

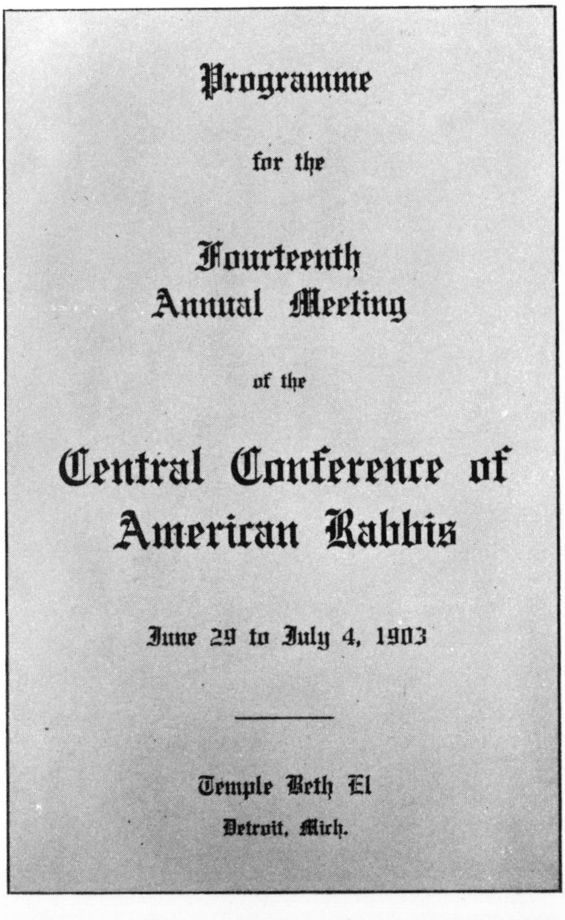

Programme

for the

Fourteenth Annual Meeting

of the

Central Conference of American Rabbis

June 29 to July 4, 1903

Temple Beth El

Detroit, Mich.

Program cover of the 14th annual meeting of the Central Conference of American Rabbis

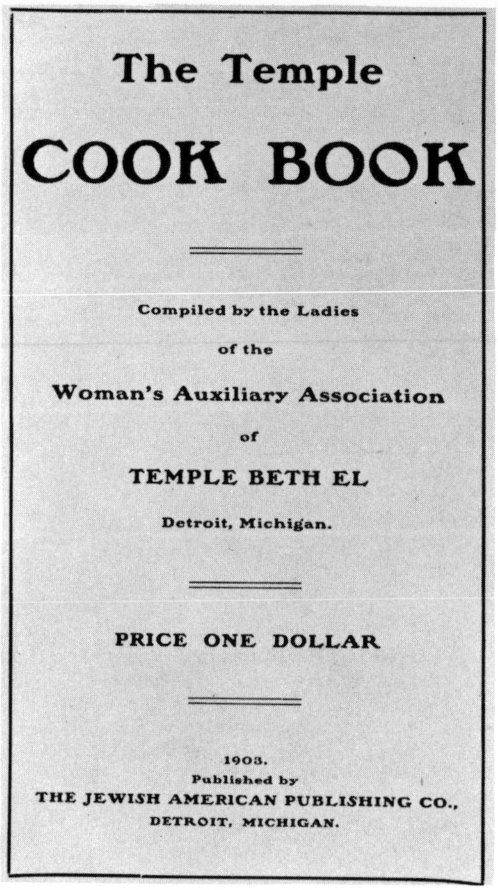

The Temple

COOK BOOK

Compiled by the Ladies

of the

Woman's Auxiliary Association

of

TEMPLE BETH EL

Detroit, Michigan.

PRICE ONE DOLLAR

1903.

Published by

THE JEWISH AMERICAN PUBLISHING CO.,

DETROIT, MICHIGAN.

Title page of Cook Book published by the Woman's Auxiliary Association of Temple Beth El, 1903

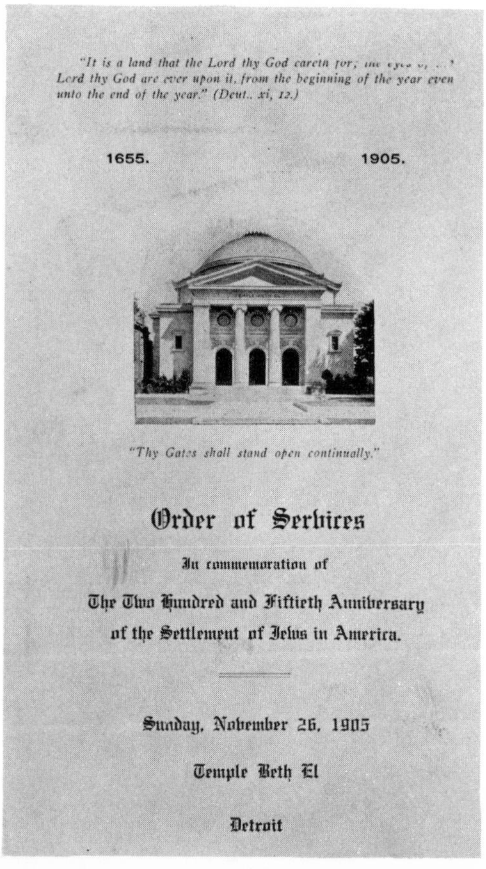

"It is a land that the Lord thy God careth for; [illegible] Lord thy God are ever upon it, from the beginning of the year even unto the end of the year." (Deut., xi, 12.)

1655. 1905.

"Thy Gates shall stand open continually."

Order of Services

In commemoration of

The Two Hundred and Fiftieth Anniversary of the Settlement of Jews in America.

Sunday, November 26, 1905

Temple Beth El

Detroit

1904

APRIL 27 Congregation voted officially to adopt the unassigned seating system.

SEPTEMBER 15 Dr. Franklin inaugurated a temple course, bringing to Detroit outstanding rabbis and lecturers.

1905

JANUARY 1 Dedication of the Temple gym.

APRIL Dr. Franklin instituted exchange of pulpits with out-of-town rabbis.

NOVEMBER 26 Celebration was held in honor of the 250th anniversary of the settlement of the Jews in the United States. Samuel Heavenrich elected president of the congregation for second time.

1906

APRIL 21 Citizen's mass meeting held in the Temple on behalf of the San Francisco earthquake victims.

Memorial shelves and alcoves were inaugurated in the Temple library.

Philanthropic funds established at the Temple.

1907

JUNE 8 Dr. Franklin preached the baccalaureate sermon at the Hebrew Union College.

JULY 15 Dr. Franklin was elected president of the Hebrew Union College Alumni Association.

Program cover of the celebration of the 250th anniversary of the settlement of Jews in the United States

AUGUST 23 Dr. Franklin participated in the installation of Dr. Abraham Hershman as rabbi of Congregation Shaarey Zedek.

DECEMBER 17 Adoption of revised Constitution and By-Laws, incorporating the unassigned seating system.

1908

MAY 17–18 District Grand Lodge No. 6 of B'nai B'rith held its convention at the Temple.

JUNE 6 Public meeting was held at the Temple on behalf of the tuberculosis crusade.

HOLY DAYS Dr. Julian Morgenstern (later president of the Hebrew Union College) assisted Dr. Franklin at the Holy Day services.

OCTOBER 17 First Temple supper was held in conjunction with annual meeting.

NOVEMBER 7 A ceremonial art collection was started.

Henry M. Butzel (now Chief Justice of the Supreme Court of Michigan) elected sixteenth president of the congregation.

1909

JANUARY 24 Tenth anniversary celebration of Dr. Franklin's ministry in Detroit was held.

OCTOBER Afternoon Bible classes for adults were inaugurated. Bernard B. Selling elected seventeenth president of the congregation.

JUSTICE HENRY M. BUTZEL, *President, 1908–1909*

BERNARD B. SELLING, *President, 1909–1912*

BENJAMIN L. LAMBERT, *President, 1912–1913*

1910

MARCH 1 Temple bulletin resumed publication.

JULY 17–24 Jewish Chautauqua Society held its Fourteenth Annual Convention at the Temple.

OCTOBER 23–24 Sixtieth anniversary celebration of the Temple was held. Congregation numbered 422 members.

1911

Members voted to establish a $250 scholarship a year for ten years at the Jewish Technical School at Haifa, Palestine.

1912

First annual service for the students of the University of Michigan was held (which continued for many years). As a result of the successful functioning of the Jewish Student Day in Detroit, the Central Conference of American Rabbis and the Union of American Hebrew Congregations created a Joint Commission on Religious Work in Universities, with Dr. Franklin as its chairman.

Benjamin L. Lambert elected eighteenth president of the congregation.

1913

Dr. Julian Morgenstern delivered a series of lectures on the Bible (and continued the series for the next five years).

LOUIS WELT, *President, 1913–1918*

Mesdames Leo M. Franklin, Monroe Rosenfield, Bernard Selling and Louis Welt attended the organization meeting of the National Federation of Temple Sisterhoods in Cincinnati and the Sisterhood became a charter affiliate of this national organization.

Louis Welt elected nineteenth president of the congregation.

1914

Dr. Franklin established the Student Congregation at the University of Michigan, which was the forerunner of the B'nai B'rith Hillel Foundations.

Congregation was host to the Silver Jubilee Convention of the Central Conference of American Rabbis.

1915

Acquisition of Section Beth El in Woodmere Cemetery which was dedicated November 19, 1916.

$4,000 was subscribed by the members on *Yom Kippur Eve* for the sufferers of World War I and sent to the American Jewish Relief Committee.

Sisterhood organized a Red Cross Unit which became the largest congregational unit in Detroit during World War I.

1916

APRIL Members subscribed $67,726 for the Jewish war sufferers in Europe.

Program cover of 1915 Union Service of the Jewish Student Congregation at the University of Michigan

DR. SAMUEL S. MAYERBERG, *now Rabbi of Temple B'nai Jehudah, Kansas City, Missouri*

1917

Rabbi Samuel S. Mayerberg, a graduate of the 1917 class of the Hebrew Union College, was engaged as the first full-time assistant rabbi.

Religious School was departmentalized into Primary, Intermediate, Junior High, High School, and Normal School departments.

Holy Day supplementary services for non-members were introduced, a unique innovation (which continues to this day). Beth El was reported by the Union of American Hebrew Congregations as the third largest Reform congregation in the country.

BERNARD GINSBURG, *President, 1918–1919*

1918

Union Prayer Book No. 1, Revised, introduced at services.

Temple facilities were placed at the disposal of any organization desiring it for patriotic purposes.

Beth El Honor Roll contained the names of 207 members who had answered the call of their country and four who made the supreme sacrifice.

Boy Scout Troop No. 76 was organized, first Jewish troop in Detroit.

Bernard Ginsburg elected twentieth president of the congregation.

WALTER S. HEAVENRICH, *First President of The Men's Club*

CHRONOLOGY

1919

SUMMER Dr. Franklin was elected president of the Central Conference of American Rabbis.

DECEMBER 17 Men's Club of Temple Beth El was founded. Walter S. Heavenrich elected first president.

Isaac Gilbert elected twenty-first president of the congregation.

1920

PASSOVER First Congregational Seder was held.

Dr. Franklin took a leading part in the 1920's in the fight against the enactment of a law by the state legislature which would have practically put private and parochial schools out of existence. He spoke, among other places, from the pulpit of a Catholic church, the first and only Detroit rabbi to be thus honored. Bishop Michael J. Gallagher of the Catholic Archdiocese of Detroit, who was also a leader of the successful campaign to defeat the proposed legislation, was later an honored guest at one of the fellowship nights of the Men's Club of Temple Beth El held in the social hall of the Temple.

1921

Rabbi Henry Berkovitz succeeded Rabbi Mayerberg as assistant rabbi.

SEPTEMBER 20 Cornerstone laying ceremonies of the Temple on Woodward and Gladstone were held.

ISAAC GILBERT, *President, 1919–1923*

RABBI HENRY BERKOWITZ

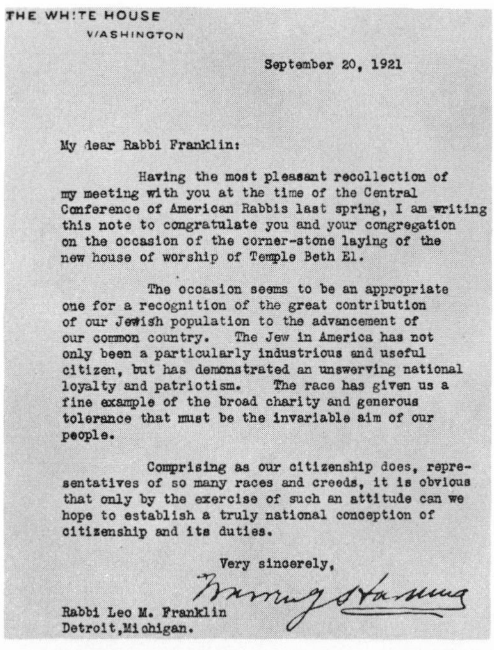

THE WHITE HOUSE
WASHINGTON

September 20, 1921

My dear Rabbi Franklin:

Having the most pleasant recollection of my meeting with you at the time of the Central Conference of American Rabbis last spring, I am writing this note to congratulate you and your congregation on the occasion of the corner-stone laying of the new house of worship of Temple Beth El.

The occasion seems to be an appropriate one for a recognition of the great contribution of our Jewish population to the advancement of our common country. The Jew in America has not only been a particularly industrious and useful citizen, but has demonstrated an unswerving national loyalty and patriotism. The race has given us a fine example of the broad charity and generous tolerance that must be the invariable aim of our people.

Comprising as our citizenship does, representatives of so many races and creeds, it is obvious that only by the exercise of such an attitude can we hope to establish a truly national conception of citizenship and its duties.

Very sincerely,

Warren G Harding

Rabbi Leo M. Franklin
Detroit, Michigan.

Congratulatory letter from PRESIDENT WARREN G. HARDING *on the cornerstone laying ceremony of the Temple on Woodward and Gladstone*

Temple Beth El, Woodward at Gladstone, dedicated in 1922

The Library of Beth El

The Present Temple, 1922—

1922

The congregation worshiped for three months at the First Unitarian Church and at Orchestra Hall.

NOVEMBER 10–12 Dedication of the present Temple on Woodward and Gladstone. Albert Kahn was again the architect.

NOVEMBER 28 Dr. Franklin elected by the congregation for a life tenure. Constitution and By-Laws were revised. Temple Arts Society was founded with Mrs. Frank V. Martin as first president.

The Franklin Memorial Hall of Beth El

THE BETHELITE

The Official Organ of the School of Religion of Temple Beth El

VOL. 1 MARCH 25th, 1923 NO. 1

The Council in Session

(Sitting L. to R.)
Melvin Sands
Janet Welt
Norbert Zuckerkman
Benjamin Cohen
Mildred Jacont
George Ackerman
Julius Pliskow
Gertrude Pearl
Estelle Moskowitz
Herman Lefkowitz
Helen Erlich
Beatrice Erlich
(Standing)
Bernard Segall
Mollie Scholnick
Dr. Franklin
Josephine Magdelin
Ralph Rosen

Greetings From Rabbi Franklin. Council of the City of Justice Very Greetings From Rabbi Berkowitz.

Front page of the first issue of the Bethelite

Brown Memorial Chapel

Sisterhood organized the Michigan State Federation of Temple Sisterhoods. Mrs. Adolph Sloman was elected its first president.

The Cemetery Board was established.

A Book of Memories was inaugurated. A Cradle Roll was started in the Religious School.

1923

Dr. Franklin received an Honorary Doctor of Laws degree from the University of Detroit, a Catholic institution, the first and only Detroit rabbi to be thus honored. Harry R. Solomon and Wallace Rosenheim attended the organization meeting of the National Federation of Temple Brotherhoods in New York City and the Men's Club

ADOLPH FINSTERWALD, *President, 1923–1925*

became a charter affiliate member of this national organization. The first issue of *The Bethelite,* the newspaper of the Religious School, was published.

Adolph Finsterwald elected twenty-second president of the congregation.

Carl C. Adams, building engineer, assumed his post with the Temple, a position which he still holds.

1924

Dr. Franklin's silver anniversary of ministry in Detroit was celebrated.

Girl Scout Troop No. 28 was organized, the first Jewish Girl Scout Troop in Detroit.

CARL C. ADAMS, *Building Engineer since 1923*

1925

Rabbi Leon Fram, of Temple Judea, Chicago, succeeded Rabbi Henry Berkowitz as assistant rabbi.

An amendment to the By-Laws of the congregation was adopted, which provided that the wife of a member of the congregation became a member of the congregation in her own right, with voting and full membership privileges.

Founding of Beth El College of Jewish Studies, one of the first evening schools in this country for adults, by Rabbi Fram. Weekly broadcasts of services over radio station WWJ were instituted.

The seventy-fifth anniversary of the congregation was celebrated on December 13.

DR. LEON FRAM, *now Rabbi of Temple Israel, Detroit*

Beth El murals painted by MYRON BARLOW, *internationally known Detroit Jewish artist, at his studio in Etaples, France. "The Patriarch" depicts the spiritual hospitality of Judaism from the beginning of our history; "Prophet and Priest" represents the spiritual and ceremonial aspects of our religion; "The Student" is a picture of Jewish life in the Middle Ages; "The Immigrant" portrays the hopefulness with which our forefathers looked to America as their land of promise, in his hand a Prayer Book.*

MILFORD STERN, *President, 1925–1928*

MELVILLE S. WELT, *President, 1928–1931*

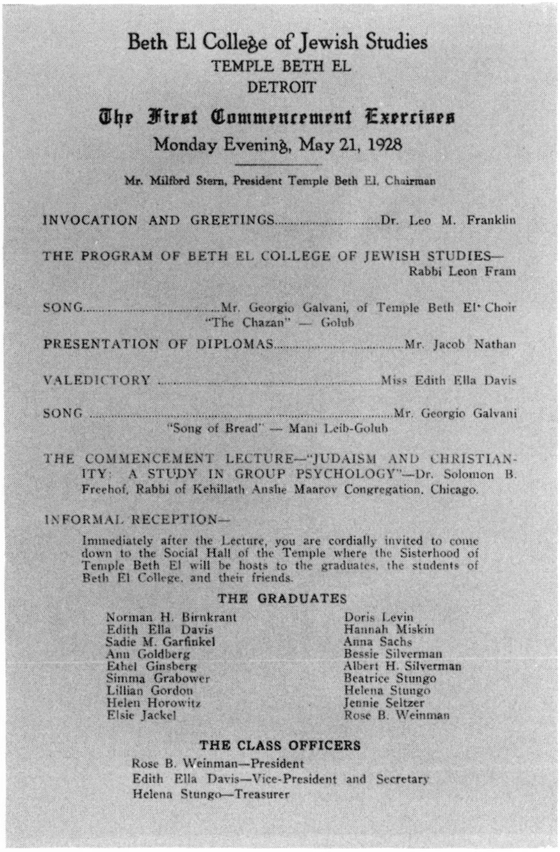

Beth El College of Jewish Studies
TEMPLE BETH EL
DETROIT

The First Commencement Exercises

Monday Evening, May 21, 1928

Mr. Milford Stern, President Temple Beth El, Chairman

INVOCATION AND GREETINGS......Dr. Leo M. Franklin

THE PROGRAM OF BETH EL COLLEGE OF JEWISH STUDIES—Rabbi Leon Fram

SONG......Mr. Georgio Galvani, of Temple Beth El Choir
"The Chazan" — Golub

PRESENTATION OF DIPLOMAS......Mr. Jacob Nathan

VALEDICTORY......Miss Edith Ella Davis

SONG......Mr. Georgio Galvani
"Song of Bread" — Mani Leib-Golub

THE COMMENCEMENT LECTURE—"JUDAISM AND CHRISTIANITY: A STUDY IN GROUP PSYCHOLOGY"—Dr. Solomon B. Freehof, Rabbi of Kehillath Anshe Maarov Congregation, Chicago.

INFORMAL RECEPTION—

Immediately after the Lecture, you are cordially invited to come down to the Social Hall of the Temple where the Sisterhood of Temple Beth El will be hosts to the graduates, the students of Beth El College, and their friends.

THE GRADUATES

Norman H. Birnkrant	Doris Levin
Edith Ella Davis	Hannah Miskin
Sadie M. Garfinkel	Anna Sachs
Ann Goldberg	Bessie Silverman
Ethel Ginsberg	Albert H. Silverman
Simma Grabower	Beatrice Stungo
Lillian Gordon	Helena Stungo
Helen Horowitz	Jennie Seltzer
Elsie Jackel	Rose B. Weinman

THE CLASS OFFICERS

Rose B. Weinman—President
Edith Ella Davis—Vice-President and Secretary
Helena Stungo—Treasurer

Milford Stern elected twenty-third president of the congregation.

1926

Congregation numbered 1,400 members.

1927

Constitution and By-Laws were amended.

The Temple was host to the annual meeting of the Jewish Chautauqua Society.

1928

First graduation from Beth El College of Jewish Studies was held.

Melville S. Welt elected twenty-fourth president of the congregation.

Program of first graduation class of Beth El College of Jewish Studies

First graduation class of Beth El College of Jewish Studies, 1928

1929

Temple was host to the Fortieth Annual Convention of the Central Conference of American Rabbis.

Pre-Kindergarten department was established in the Religious School.

1930

The congregation was reincorporated in perpetuity.

The Temple Activities Committee Plan was inaugurated, whereby the direction of the various activities carried on by the individual societies was entrusted to a central committee.

Eightieth anniversary of the congregation was celebrated with the Hon. Lily Montague of London, England, as the guest speaker.

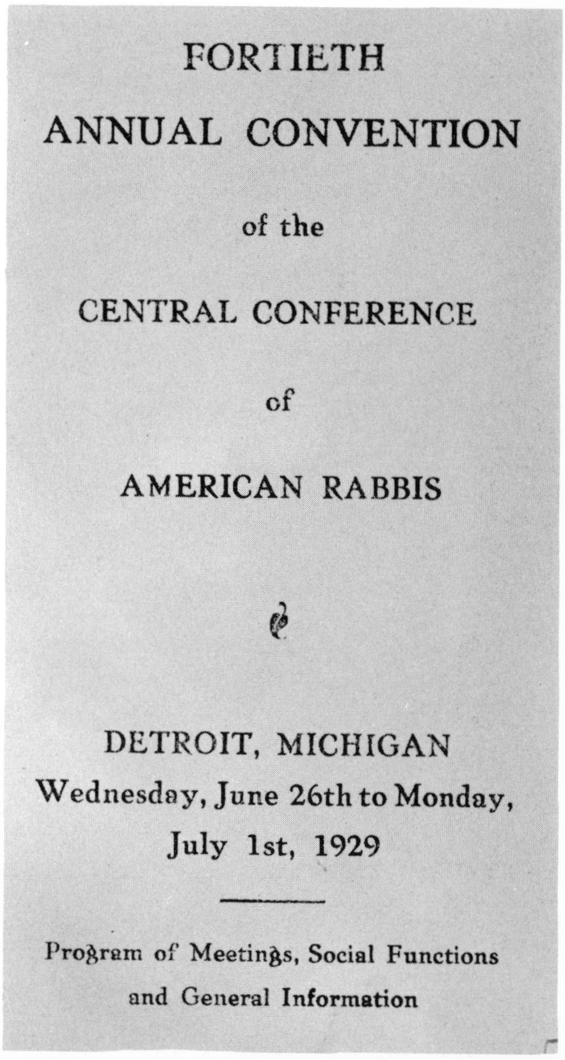

FORTIETH

ANNUAL CONVENTION

of the

CENTRAL CONFERENCE

of

AMERICAN RABBIS

DETROIT, MICHIGAN

Wednesday, June 26th to Monday, July 1st, 1929

Program of Meetings, Social Functions and General Information

Program cover of 40th Annual Convention of Central Conference of American Rabbis, 1929

1931

A school for parents was formed as a part of the College of Jewish Studies.

Israel Himelhoch elected twenty-fifth president of the congregation.

1932

Dr. Franklin was elected president of the Detroit Public Library Commission (a post which he also held in 1938 and 1944).

ISRAEL HIMELHOCH, *President 1931–1936*

A few of DR. FRANKLIN'S *published pamphlets*

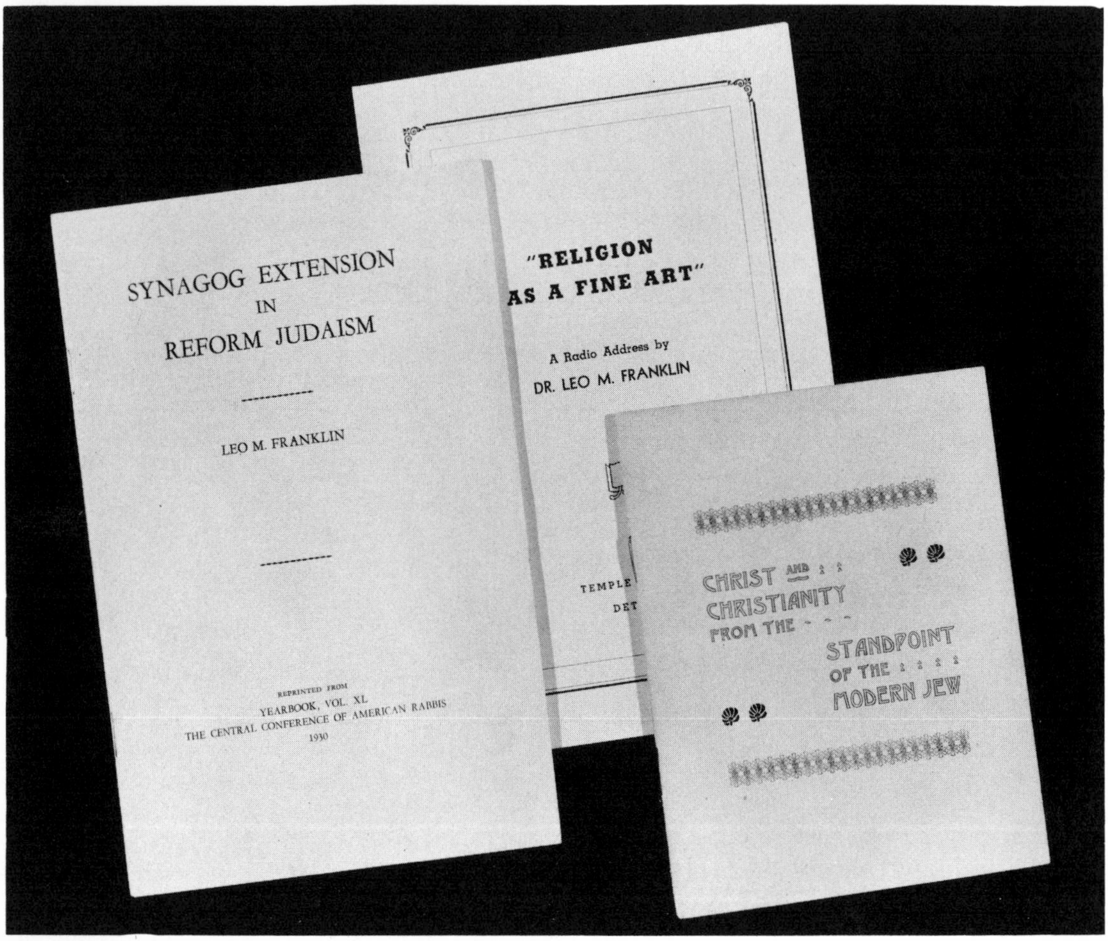

SYNAGOG EXTENSION
IN
REFORM JUDAISM
LEO M. FRANKLIN
REPRINTED FROM
YEARBOOK, VOL. XL
THE CENTRAL CONFERENCE OF AMERICAN RABBIS
1930
"RELIGION
AS A FINE ART"
A Radio Address by
DR. LEO M. FRANKLIN
CHRIST AND
CHRISTIANITY
FROM THE
STANDPOINT
OF THE
MODERN JEW

JASON H. TICKTON, *Music Director*

1933

Jason H. Tickton, present music director and organist of the Temple, assumed his post.

1934

Dr. Franklin's thirty-fifth anniversary with the Temple was celebrated.

The Temple Lecture Forum was instituted.

Inter-congregational Men's Club Dinner was initiated by our Men's Club (which is still in existence).

1935

The Temple Group Plan was inaugurated to stimulate a greater measure of participation by the members in the activities of the congregation and to give members the opportunity to initiate activities and to formulate policies.

The eighty-fifth anniversary of the Temple was observed.

1936

Dr. Franklin broadcast over the "Church of the Air" coast-to-coast radio program, and was invited for another broadcast the following year.

Morris Garvett elected twenty-sixth president of the congregation.

1937

Late Friday evening services were reintroduced at the Temple.

Dr. Franklin delivered the Alumni Lectures and Founder's Day Address

MORRIS GARVETT, *President, 1936–1939*

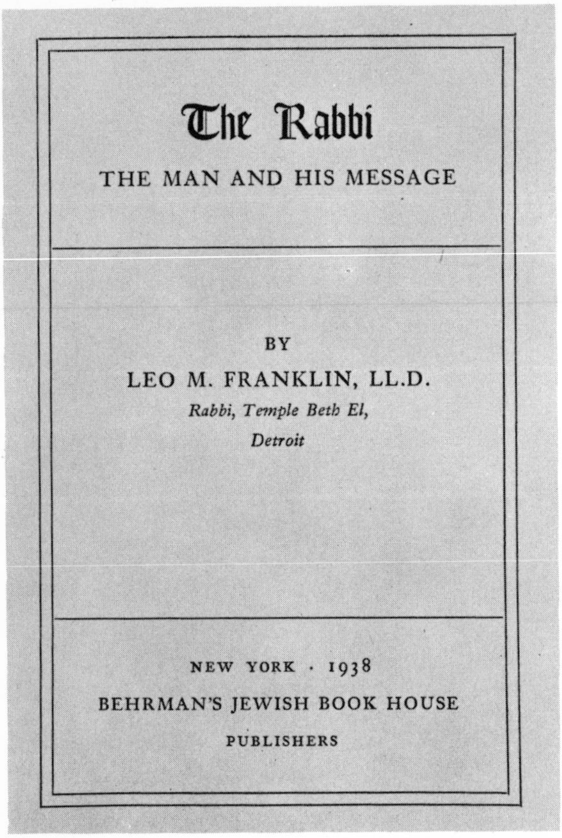

The Rabbi

THE MAN AND HIS MESSAGE

BY

LEO M. FRANKLIN, LL.D.

Rabbi, Temple Beth El,

Detroit

NEW YORK · 1938

BEHRMAN'S JEWISH BOOK HOUSE

PUBLISHERS

Title page of DR. FRANKLIN'S The Rabbi the Man and his Message

at the Hebrew Union College. (These lectures were published in 1938 under the title, *The Rabbi—the Man and His Message*.)

1938

The congregation became a member of the recently formed Jewish Community Council of Detroit.

The bonded debt of the congregation was refinanced.

1939

A testimonial dinner was tendered to Dr. Franklin on his fortieth anniversary in Detroit.

The site of Beth El Memorial Park was purchased on October 3rd.

Irving I. Katz (currently executive secretary) assumed his post with the Temple.

Dr. Franklin was awarded an Honorary Doctor of Divinity degree by the Hebrew Union College and an Honorary Doctor of Laws degree by Wayne University.

Dr. Franklin broadcast over the "Message of Israel" coast-to-coast radio program and was invited to deliver another series of sermons the following year.

Harry C. Grossman elected twenty-seventh president of the congregation.

1940

MAY 28 Sisterhood organized a Red Cross Unit, which became the largest

TESTIMONIAL DINNER
IN HONOR OF
DR. LEO M. FRANKLIN
ON THE OCCASION OF HIS FORTIETH ANNIVERSARY
AS RABBI OF
CONGREGATION BETH EL, DETROIT
1899 - 1939

Program cover of Testimonial Dinner to DR. FRANKLIN *on his 40th anniversary with the Temple*

A view of Beth El Memorial Park

IRVING I. KATZ, *Executive Secretary since 1939*

HARRY C. GROSSMAN, *President, 1939–1941*

In Honor of

DR. and MRS. LEO M. FRANKLIN

on the occasion of Dr. Franklin's retirement from the active ministry

December Seventeenth, Nineteen Hundred Forty-One

Hotel Statler

Detroit

Program cover of Testimonial to DR. FRANKLIN *on his retirement*

congregational unit in Detroit during World War II.

JUNE 4 Ground breaking ceremonies at the site of Beth El Memorial Park were held.

JUNE 22 The Constitution and By-Laws of the Congregation were revised.

NOVEMBER 15–17 The ninetieth anniversary of the congregation was celebrated with Dr. Louis L. Mann of Chicago Sinai Congregation as the guest speaker.

DECEMBER 1 Beth El Memorial Park was dedicated.

DECEMBER 26 First annual *Chanukah* Family Supper was held.

1941

APRIL 14 Dr. Franklin communicated to the Board of Trustees his desire to retire from the active ministry of Beth El after more than forty-two years of continuous service as its rabbi.

APRIL 22 Board of Trustees adopted a resolution creating the status of rabbi emeritus for Dr. Franklin as of October 31, 1941.

APRIL 25–MAY 1 The Temple and its auxiliary organizations were hosts to the Thirty-seventh Council of the Union of American Hebrew Congregations and the concurrent conventions of the National Federation of Temple Sisterhoods, the National Federation of Temple Brotherhoods and the National Federation of Temple Youth.

Resolution creating the status of Rabbi Emeritus for DR. FRANKLIN

SOLUTION ADOPTED BY THE BOARD OF TRUSTEES OF CONGREGATION BETH EL AT A SPECIAL MEETING HELD ON APRIL 22, 1941.

On January 24th, 1899, Leo Morris Franklin entered into the service of Congregation Beth El as its bi. The congregation was relatively a small one, occupying old and inadequate quarters. Since that day, as lived and prospered greatly under his dynamic spirit, increasing six fold in numbers and twice finding it essary to erect magnificent places of worship.

In the four decades that have passed since his coming to Detroit, he has enriched the life of the Congation, the City and the State in a measure far exceeding that given to most men to achieve. A Jew and American, not merely by the accident of birth or nativity, but by the deepest convictions of his soul, he never limited his ministry and works to the people of his own religious faith or of his own native land. iring in his efforts in behalf of Jew and non-Jew alike, he has always had energy to spare for the relief of ering among those living in less fortunate lands across the seas.

No project for the betterment of mankind has ever been foreign to his interest. As a resident of roit, he has given of himself without stint whenever the call to serve came to him. As a consultant in merable matters of public interest during the years, as a member and President of the Library Comsion, as a leader in all cultural activities and in the civic life of the community generally, he has conuted richly to the remarkable progress of the city during his sojourn here. Well earned, indeed, as a zen, were the honorary doctorates conferred upon him by the University of Detroit and Wayne University.

Great as has been his interest in the general life of the community, that which lies closest to his heart ne welfare of Judaism and the Congregation of which he is the spiritual head. As a leader and teacher is people, he has been in the vanguard of the Reform movement in Jewish life and has won the admiration respect of his associates everywhere. Many years ago, his colleagues paid honor to his professional atments by electing him President of the Central Conference of American Rabbis. His alma mater, the rew Union College, has recognized his learning and achievements in advancing the spiritual life of the Jew conferring upon him the degree of Doctor of Divinity. The Union of American Hebrew Congregations has iled itself of his talents by calling him to serve on various Boards and Commissions.

Distinguished as has been his career in so many fields of human endeavor, we, his people, know him as the Rabbi of Temple Beth El; as one who admitted us into the sacred Covenant, who joined us in holy ds with our loved ones, who rejoiced with us in times of gladness and who was ever at our side in times of ow and when the storms of life assailed us. We are proud of his honors and achievements and of the high e he occupies among men of renown, but we shall remember him longest for the love and the spiritual fort he brought to us when a touch of the hand or an understanding word was worth more than all the erial possessions of men. The ultimate record of his attainments will be written by others, but he has self etched the record of his ministry where he would most desire it to be recorded—in the hearts of the and women of his Congregation.

After more than forty-two years of continuous service as Rabbi of Congregation Beth El he has annced to the Board of Trustees his intention to retire from the active ministry.

Be it therefore resolved, by the Board of Trustees of Congregation Beth El, in special meeting asbled, that in accordance with his own expressed desire, Dr. Leo M. Franklin, be retired from the active istry to the Congregation as of October 31st, 1941, and that thereafter his status shall be that of Rabbi eritus.

Be it further resolved, that the good wishes of the Board of Trustees and of the Congregation be exled to Dr. and Mrs. Franklin with the prayer that their days may be long and full of happiness and that blessings of God may be visited upon them in great abundance.

Be it further resolved, that a copy of this resolution, suitably engrossed, be presented to Dr. and Mrs. nklin in behalf of the Congregation.

JUDGE CHARLES C. SIMONS

Judge Charles C. Simons was elected president of the Council. At this conclave, the National Association of Temple Secretaries, an affiliate of the Union of American Hebrew Congregations, was founded by Irving I. Katz, executive secretary of the Temple, who was elected president of the Association.

SUMMER A group of members organized a new Reform congregation, Temple Israel, and called Rabbi Fram to become its spiritual leader.

SEPTEMBER 28 At a special meeting of the congregation, Dr. B. Benedict Glazer, senior associate rabbi of Temple Emanu-El of New York City and a graduate of the 1926 class of Hebrew Union College, was elected rabbi to succeed Dr. Franklin.

NOVEMBER 14 Installation of Dr. Glazer as rabbi of Beth El by Dr. Julian Morgenstern, president of The Hebrew Union College, Dr. Samuel H. Goldenson, rabbi of Temple Emanu-El of New York, and Dr. Franklin.

DECEMBER 17 Community dinner was held at Statler Hotel honoring Dr. and Mrs. Franklin on the occasion of Dr. Franklin's retirement from the active ministry. Dr. Franklin was presented with a citation by the Detroit Round Table of Catholics, Jews and Protestants. Joseph M. Welt elected twenty-eighth president of the congregation.

JOSEPH M. WELT, *President, 1941–1944*

DR. GLAZER'S *first Confirmation Class, 1942*

1942

FEBRUARY Dr. Glazer broadcast over the "Message of Israel" coast-to-coast radio program. These addresses were published under the title *Religion and the World Crisis.*

FEBRUARY 9 Board of Trustees instituted Junior, Intermediate and Senior membership classifications, with full Temple privileges for each classification.

MAY Consecration service for confirmands and their parents at the Sabbath eve services preceding confirmation was instituted.

JUNE 17 By-Laws of the congregation were revised.

A group of Sisterhood women at a Tuesday Red Cross sewing session

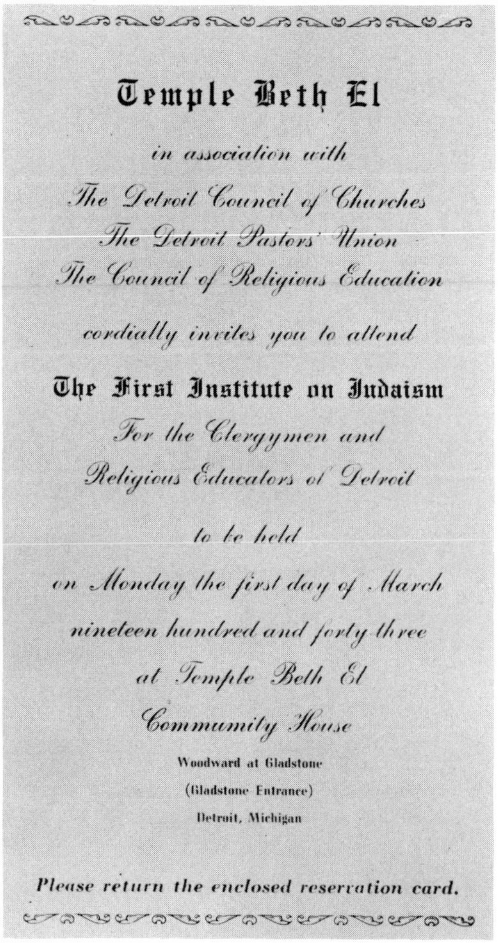

Temple Beth El

in association with

The Detroit Council of Churches

The Detroit Pastors' Union

The Council of Religious Education

cordially invites you to attend

The First Institute on Judaism

For the Clergymen and

Religious Educators of Detroit

to be held

on Monday the first day of March

nineteen hundred and forty three

at Temple Beth El

Community House

Woodward at Gladstone

(Gladstone Entrance)

Detroit, Michigan

Please return the enclosed reservation card.

Program cover of the first Institute on Judaism, 1943

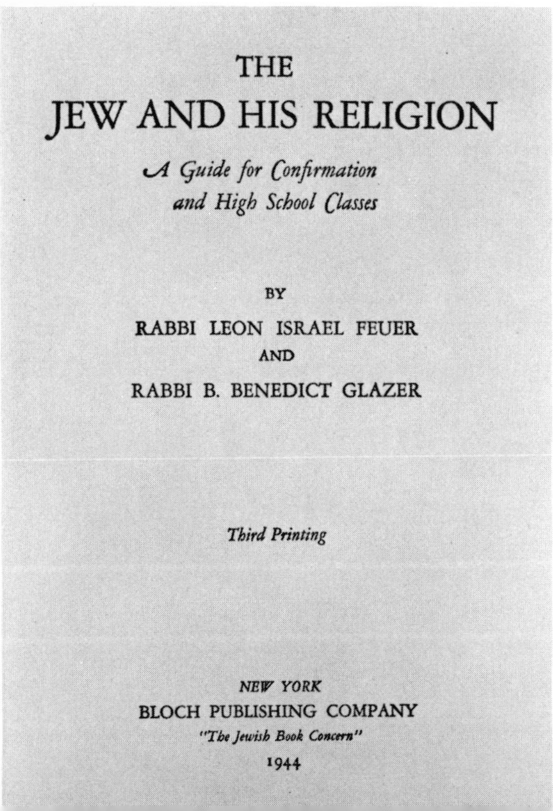

THE

JEW AND HIS RELIGION

A Guide for Confirmation and High School Classes

BY

RABBI LEON ISRAEL FEUER

AND

RABBI B. BENEDICT GLAZER

Third Printing

NEW YORK

BLOCH PUBLISHING COMPANY

"The Jewish Book Concern"

1944

RABBI HERSCHEL LYMON

AUGUST Rabbi Herschel Lymon was appointed minister of religious education.

NOVEMBER Dr. Glazer instituted Annual Book Review Course under the auspices of the Sisterhood.

1943

JANUARY Temple Boy Scouts celebrated the twenty-fifth anniversary of Scouting at Beth El.

FEBRUARY 12 Dedication of Temple Honor Roll of Servicemen and Women of World War II.

MARCH First Annual Institute on Judaism for the Protestant ministers and religious educators of Detroit was founded by Dr. Glazer.

AUGUST Rabbi Lymon entered the chaplaincy of the United States Army and was granted a leave of absence by the Board of Trustees.

Title page of a book by DR. GLAZER *and* RABBI FEUER

SEPTEMBER Mortgage Liquidation and Building Rehabilitation Drive was launched under the leadership of Meyer L. Prentis and Leonard T. Lewis.

YOM KIPPUR EVE Announcement was made at the services that the Temple building was debt free.

1944

JANUARY 23 Burning of the Mortgage Celebration was held.

JANUARY The Michigan Historical Collection at the University of Michigan set aside a section of its library at Ann Arbor to be known as "The Leo M. Franklin Section."

APRIL Dr. Glazer broadcast over the "Message of Israel" radio program.

JUNE 6 D-Day services were attended by a large congregation. Leonard T. Lewis elected twenty-ninth president of the congregation.

1945

JANUARY 19 Ninety-fifth anniversary service was held.

FEBRUARY 26 Board of Trustees and past presidents honored Dr. Franklin at a luncheon on the occasion of his seventy-fifth birthday.

APRIL 14, 15 A memorial service was held by the Religious School for President Franklin D. Roosevelt.

APRIL 20 Dr. Glazer paid tribute to President Roosevelt at a memorial service at the Temple.

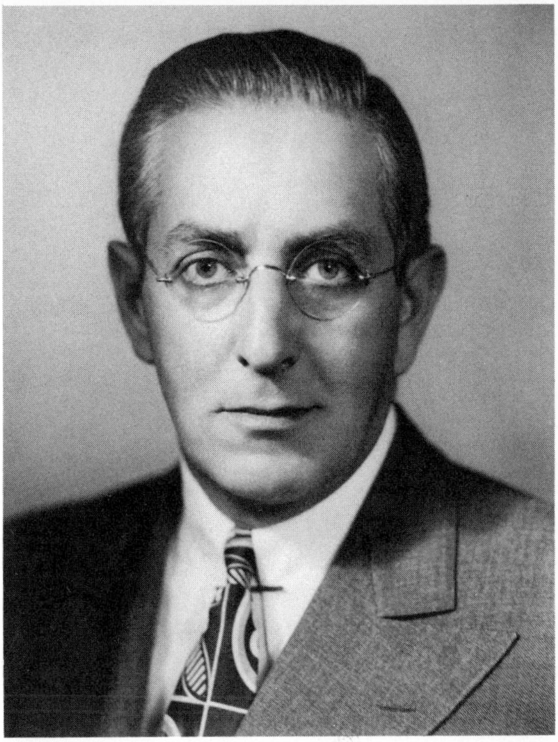

LEONARD T. LEWIS, *President, 1944–1947*

Burning
of the Mortgage
Celebration
TEMPLE BETH EL
DETROIT
JANUARY 23, 1944

Program cover of the burning of the mortgage celebration

MEN'S CLUB OF TEMPLE BETH EL
1919
1945
25TH ANNIVERSARY
CELEBRATION
TEMPLE BETH EL • DETROIT • APRIL 22, 1945

Program cover of Silver Anniversary celebration of the Men's Club, 1945

World War II Memorial Plaque at Temple Beth El

APRIL 22 Silver Jubilee Anniversary Banquet of the Men's Club was held. Rabbi Levi A. Olan of Worcester, Massachusetts, was the guest speaker.

Karl B. Segall, managing director of the cemeteries, assumed his post.

MAY 8 V-E Day services were attended by a large congregation.

AUGUST 15 Victory service was held at the Temple.

SEPTEMBER Consecration ceremony for children entering the Religious School was inaugurated during the week of *Sukkos* by Dr. Glazer.

Men's Club instituted Sunday Morning Breakfast Club and Discussion Group, especially designed for parents whose children attend Religious School, the first in the country.

KARL B. SEGALL, *Managing Director of Cemeteries since 1945*

The Sunday Morning Breakfast Club and Discussion Group, sponsored by the Men's Club

OCTOBER 6 Prayer of intercession on behalf of European Jewry was held.

NOVEMBER *Chanukah* Family Service was inaugurated on Friday evening.

DECEMBER Dr. Glazer won the fight to eliminate discriminatory literature from hotels and resorts in Michigan. Temple Beth El received citation from the government for selling close to $11,000,000.00 in War Bonds, a record for religious institutions in the country, under the leadership of Leonard N. Simons.

1946

JANUARY Nate S. Shapero and Leonard N. Simons were presented with gold medals and special citations by Secretary of the Treasury Fred M. Vinson for their leadership in War

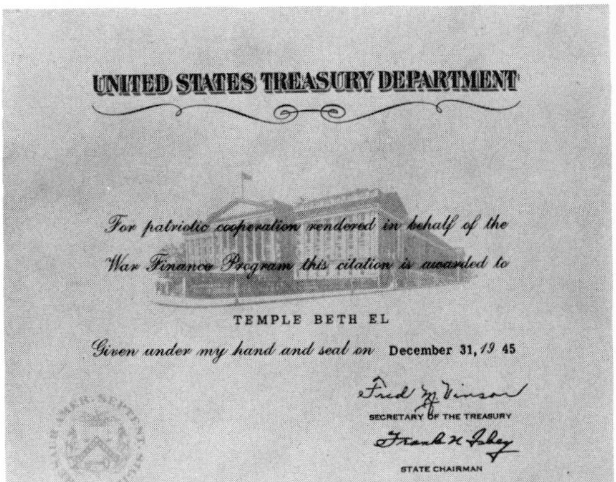
UNITED STATES TREASURY DEPARTMENT

For patriotic cooperation rendered in behalf of the War Finance Program this citation is awarded to

TEMPLE BETH EL

Given under my hand and seal on December 31, 1945

Fred M. Vinson
SECRETARY OF THE TREASURY

Frank H. Foley
STATE CHAIRMAN

Citation awarded to Temple Beth El for the sale of war bonds

Bonds Drives during World War II (only six men in Michigan and fifty in the entire country were thus honored).

MARCH Sisterhood sent 182 boxes of clothing, food, and medical supplies for the Jewish survivors in Europe.

NOVEMBER 5 Fifth anniversary of Dr. Glazer's ministry in Detroit and twentieth anniversary of his ordination as rabbi were observed.

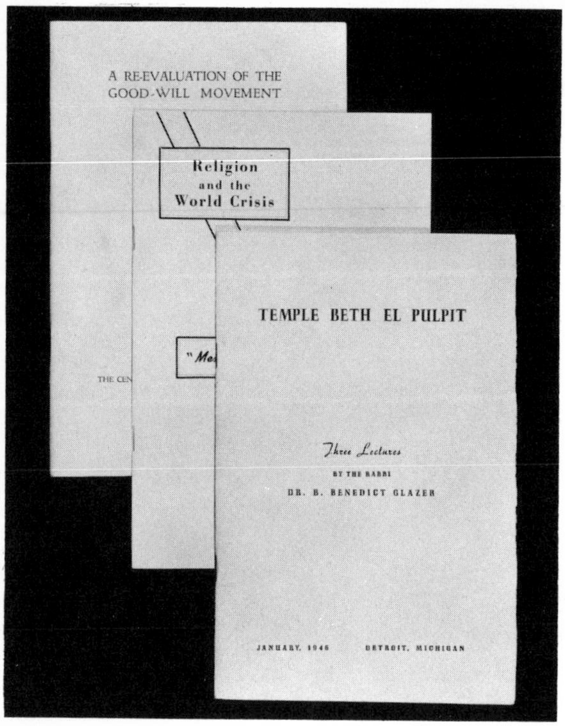

A few of DR. GLAZER'S *published pamphlets*

1947

JANUARY American Jewish Cavalcade Service, sponsored by the Union of American Hebrew Congregations, was held jointly with Temple Israel.

MARCH 1 Mrs. Franklin D. Roosevelt preached at the Saturday morning services under the auspices of the Jewish Welfare Federation.

MAY Temple Endowment Fund was established.

AUGUST 1 Rabbi Sidney Akserad was engaged as assistant rabbi. Dr. Herbert I. Kallet elected thirtieth president of the Congregation.

1948

FEBRUARY 20 American Jewish Cavalcade Service was held jointly with Temple Israel, with Dr. Leo Baeck, formerly chief rabbi of Berlin, Germany, as the guest speaker.

MAY Dr. Glazer was honored by the Negro community of Detroit for his contribution to interracial justice. He

RABBI SIDNEY AKSELRAD

was also honored by the East Side Merchants Association.

JUNE Dr. Glazer presented a paper before the Central Conference of American Rabbis, entitled "A Re-Evaluation of the Good-Will Movement."

AUGUST 8 The Detroit community and the nation mourned the death of Dr. Leo M. Franklin. Funeral was held from the main Temple on August 10. (Interment was in Woodmere Cemetery.)

SEPTEMBER Introduction of double services on the evenings of the Holy Days to accommodate the large membership.

OCTOBER The Leo M. Franklin Memorial Fund was established. Child-naming ceremony at Sabbath morning services was introduced by Dr. Glazer.

1949

APRIL Memorial service on the last day of Passover was inaugurated by Dr. Glazer.

JUNE Nate S. Shapero elected thirty-first president of the congregation.

SEPTEMBER Beth El's centennial anniversary year was proclaimed. Nate S. Shapero proposed to the Board of Trustees that a centennial history of the congregation be published in 1950. An appropriation of $2500 was made. Leonard M. Simons was appointed chairman of the publication committee.

DR. HERBERT I. KALLET, *President, 1947–1949*

NATE S. SHAPERO, *President, 1949–1951*

DR. GLAZER *addressing the congregation at the Centennial Rededication Service of past confirmands. Seated left to right (with class dates), back row,* NATE S. SHAPERO, *President;* JUSTICE HENRY M. BUTZEL *(1885); front row,* A. B. HEAVENRICH, *(1884);* SUSAN KLEIN *(1949);* LEONARD T. LEWIS, *(past president); right back row,* MELVILLE S. WELT *(1895 and a past president);* ALBERT M. COLMAN *(1938);* RABBI SIDNEY AKSELRAD; JOSEPH M. WELT *(1899 and a past president);* ARTHUR L. GOULSON *(1923);* LOIS HOPP, *now* MRS. MORRIS BROWN *(1942);* LAWRENCE J. MICHELSON *(1916);* MRS. IRVING L. HIRSCHMAN *(1903); and* ISRAEL HIMELHOCH *(past president)*

Dr. Glazer was elected president of the newly-formed Wayne County Chapter of the Michigan Society for Mental Hygiene.

SEPTEMBER 29 High Holy Day service was televised over WJBK-TV, an innovation in Detroit.

OCTOBER Board of Trustees established the Leo M. Franklin Memorial Chair in Human Relations at Wayne University.

NOVEMBER 18 Dr. Edgar E. Siskin of North Shore Congregation Israel, Glencoe, Illinois, preached the first in a series of centennial sermons by guest rabbis.

NOVEMBER 25 Dr. Glazer's sermon on the neglect of the mentally ill in Detroit aroused state-wide comment.

DECEMBER 9 Dr. Samuel S. Mayerberg of Congregation B'nai Jehudah,

Kansas City, Missouri, former assistant rabbi of the Temple, preached the second centennial sermon.

DECEMBER 16 Centennial re-dedication service of past confirmands was held.

Temple library received citation of merit from the Jewish Book Council of America.

1950

JANUARY 6 Dr. Julian B. Feibelman of Temple Sinai, New Orleans, preached the third centennial sermon.

JANUARY 24 · Centennial Hebrew music concert was held. Cantor Arthur Wolfson of Temple Emanu-El of New York City was the guest artist.

JANUARY 27 Centennial B'nai B'rith service was held. Dr. Abram L. Sachar, now president of Brandeis University, was the fourth centennial speaker.

DR. JONAH B. WISE *addressing the congregation at the Centennial Anniversary Service. Others seated on the pulpit are left to right (back row)* NATE S. SHAPERO, *President,* DR. JACOB R. MARCUS, *Adolph S. Ochs Professor of Jewish History at HUC-JIR and Director of American Jewish Archives,* DR. B. BENEDICT GLAZER, *(front row)* RABBI ALFRED L. FRIEDMAN *of Lansing,* LAWRENCE J. MICHELSON, *Treasurer,* RABBI SAMUEL UMEN *of Muskegon,* RABBI SANFORD E. SAPERSTEIN *of Pontiac, (right of pulpit, back row)* RABBI SIDNEY AKSELRAD, *Assistant Rabbi,* RABBI FRANK F. ROSENTHAL *of Jackson,* DAVID WILKUS, *Vice President,* RABBI MORTON M. APPLEBAUM *of Flint*

Officers of the Temple on the eve of the Centennial Anniversary Service. Left to right: IRVING I. KATZ, *Executive Secretary;* DAVID WILKUS, *Vice-President;* DR. B. BENEDICT GLAZER; NATE S. SHAPERO, *President;* LAWRENCE J. MICHELSON, *Treasurer*

FEBRUARY 10 Rabbi Leon I. Feuer of the Collingwood Avenue Temple, Toledo, Ohio, preached the fifth centennial sermon.

MARCH Centennial Anniversary Fund was established. $50,000 was raised under the chairmanship of Sidney J. Allen.

MARCH 3 Dedication of the Franklin Memorial Hall in memory of Dr. and Mrs. Leo M. Franklin. Dr. Emil W. Leipziger, rabbi-emeritus of Touro Synagogue, New Orleans, past president of the Central Conference of American Rabbis and a confirmand of Temple Beth El, was the guest speaker.

MARCH 19 Centennial broadcast

Centennial Anniversary Children's Pageant

over radio station WKMH was held.

MARCH 20 A simultaneous television and radio program was presented over WWJ in honor of the Centennial of the congregation. Participants: Dr. B. Benedict Glazer and George W. Stark, City Historiographer.

MARCH 24 Centennial anniversary service was held. Dr. Jacob R. Marcus, president of the Central Conference of American Rabbis, and Dr. Jonah B. Wise of Central Synagogue, New York, son of Dr. Isaac M. Wise, were the guest speakers.

MARCH 25 Centennial anniversary pageant was presented by the children of the Religious School. Centennial

Speakers' Table and a portion of the gathering at the Centennial Anniversary Banquet

anniversary banquet at Book-Cadillac Hotel was held. Guest participants: Dr. Maurice N. Eisendrath, president of the Union of American Hebrew Congregations; Dr. Nelson Glueck, president of the Hebrew Union College; Dr. Solomon B. Freehof of Rodef Shalom Temple, Pittsburgh; the Honorable G. Mennen Williams, Governor of the State of Michigan; The Honorable Albert E. Cobo, Mayor of the City of Detroit; the Right Reverend

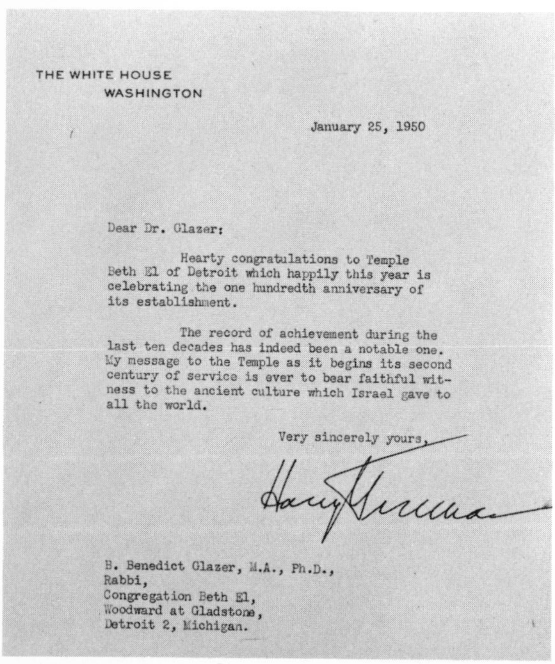

THE WHITE HOUSE
WASHINGTON

January 25, 1950

Dear Dr. Glazer:

Hearty congratulations to Temple Beth El of Detroit which happily this year is celebrating the one hundredth anniversary of its establishment.

The record of achievement during the last ten decades has indeed been a notable one. My message to the Temple as it begins its second century of service is ever to bear faithful witness to the ancient culture which Israel gave to all the world.

Very sincerely yours,

B. Benedict Glazer, M.A., Ph.D.,
Rabbi,
Congregation Beth El,
Woodward at Gladstone,
Detroit 2, Michigan.

PRESIDENT TRUMAN'S *congratulatory letter on Beth El's Centennial*

Richard S. Emrich, Bishop of the Episcopal Diocese of Michigan; the Reverend Chester A. McPheters, president of the Detroit Council of Churches; Dr. David Henry, president of Wayne University. Judge Charles C. Simons was toastmaster.

JULY 2 Dr. Glazer spoke over the "Church of the Air" coast-to-coast program, a Centennial feature of Beth El.

OCTOBER Congregation authorized 10 per cent assessment on dues for the

MISS HATTIE SILBERMAN, *daughter of* JACOB SILBERMAN, *the first President of Beth El, cutting the birthday cake at the Centennial Anniversary Banquet*

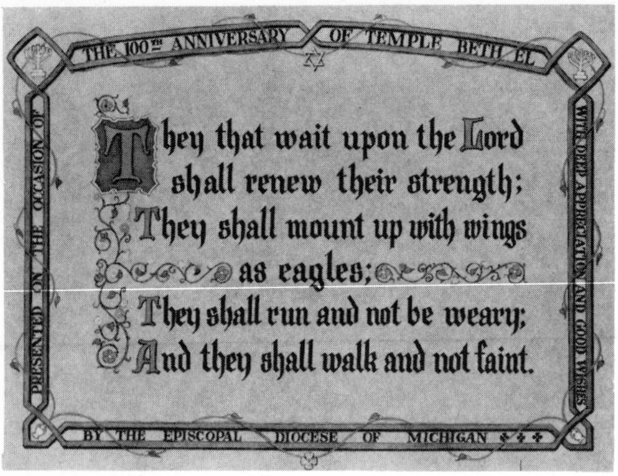

Scroll presented to Beth El on its Centennial by the Episcopal Diocese of Michigan

Certificate presented to Beth El on its Centennial by the Union of American Hebrew Congregations

Toward

BETTER
HUMAN
RELATIONS

LLOYD ALLEN COOK, *Editor*

Holder of the Leo M. Franklin Memorial Chair in Human Relations at Wayne University for the Year 1950-51

1952 · WAYNE UNIVERSITY PRESS · DETROIT

annual maintenance of the Union of American Hebrew Congregations, Hebrew Union College and Jewish Institute of Religion.

DECEMBER *Michigan History,* the quarterly publication of the Michigan Historical Commission, contained a history of Temple Beth El, written by Irving I. Katz.

1951

FEBRUARY 15 Dr. Lloyd Allen Cook, first holder of the Leo M. Franklin Memorial Chair in Human Relations at Wayne University, presented Dr. Louis Wirth of the University of Chicago, who delivered the first Leo M. Franklin Lecture in Human Relations at Wayne University.

APRIL 27 Dr. Glazer's tenth anniversary in Detroit and twenty-fifth in the rabbinate was observed at a special service. Guest participants: Dr. Maurice N. Eisendrath, president of the Union of American Hebrew Congregations; Dr. Samuel H. Goldenson, rabbi-emeritus of Temple Emanu-El of New York City; Rabbi Leon I. Feuer of the Collingwood Avenue Temple, Toledo; Rev. Herbert B. Hudnut, minister of the Woodward Avenue Presbyterian Church and president of the Detroit Pastors' Union; and Ray R. Eppert, vice-president of the Wayne County Chapter of the Michigan Society for Mental Hygiene. The Right Rev. Msgr. Edward J. Hickey, chancellor of

Title page of the first lectures of the LEO M. FRANKLIN *Memorial Chair in Human Relations at Wayne University*

Official Temple family and guests at dinner at the Book-Cadillac Hotel, in honor of DR. GLAZER'S *10th anniversary in Detroit and 25th anniversary in the rabbinate, April 27, 1951*

the Roman Catholic Archdiocese of Detroit, and Father Raymond C. Clancy were present at this service.

JUNE 4 Dr. Glazer was elected by the congregation for life tenure "in recognition of his outstanding ministry in Detroit during the past decade." David Wilkus elected thirty-second president of the congregation.

JULY Dr. Glazer served as a member of the Executive Board arranging

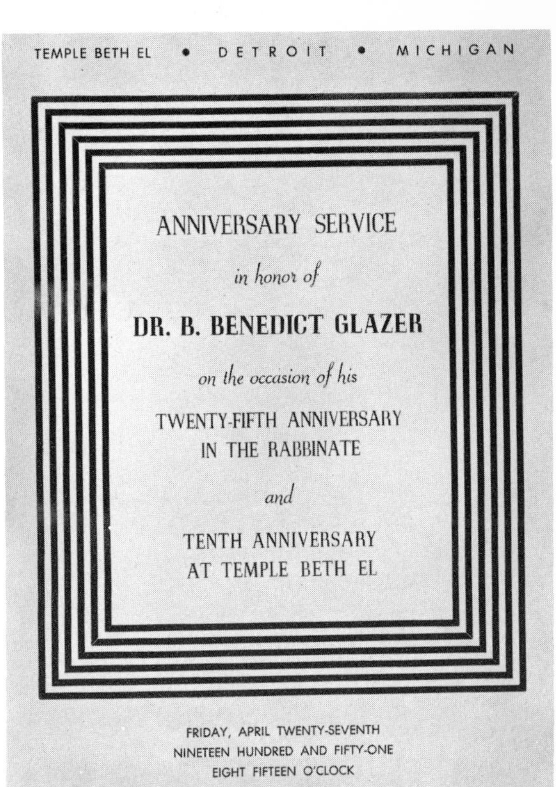

TEMPLE BETH EL • DETROIT • MICHIGAN

ANNIVERSARY SERVICE

in honor of

DR. B. BENEDICT GLAZER

on the occasion of his

TWENTY-FIFTH ANNIVERSARY
IN THE RABBINATE

and

TENTH ANNIVERSARY
AT TEMPLE BETH EL

FRIDAY, APRIL TWENTY-SEVENTH
NINETEEN HUNDRED AND FIFTY-ONE
EIGHT FIFTEEN O'CLOCK

Program cover of DR. GLAZER'S *Anniversary Service, 1951*

DAVID WILKUS, *President, 1951–1953*

To Rabbi B. B. Glazer

In Recognition of Outstanding Services Performed in Connection with Detroit's 250th Birthday Festival, Dedicated to the Causes of International Amity and to the Furtherance of Civic Consciousness Among All Our Citizens.

Albert E. Cobo
Mayor, City of Detroit

Certificate presented to DR. GLAZER *by Detroit's 250th Birthday Festival Committee*

LEON S. WAYBURN, *first President of Temple Players*

Detroit's 250th Birthday Festival. He was honored with a certificate of merit for his participation.

OCTOBER 26–28 Dr. Glazer, Dr. Herbert I. Kallet and Leonard T. Lewis attended the dedication of the House of Living Judaism of the Union of American Hebrew Congregations in New York City.

NOVEMBER 3–4 The congregation was host to the Second Annual Convention of the Great Lakes Region of the Union of American Hebrew Congregations.

NOVEMBER 13 Temple Players, a revival of the Temple Arts Society, was organized by David Wilkus. Leon S. Wayburn was elected the first president.

DR. NORMAN DRACHLER, *Educational Director since 1951*

Rabbi Sidney Akselrad accepted a call to Temple Beth El in Berkeley, California.

DECEMBER Dr. Norman Drachler was engaged as educational director.

1952

MARCH 10 Survey Committee held a meeting at the Temple to discuss the development of additional facilities for the requirements of the Temple membership in the northwest section of the city. Arthur H. Rice and John C. Hopp served as chairman and co-chairman respectively. Raymond K. Rubiner was appointed chairman of the Site Selection Committee.

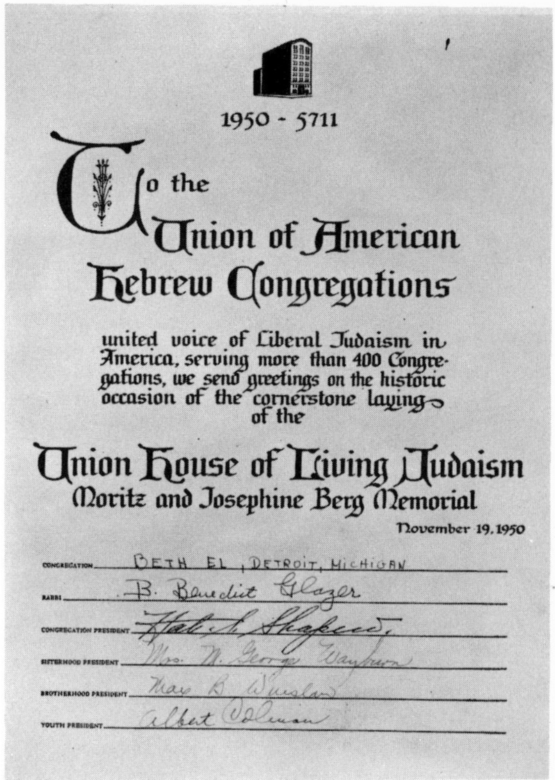

1950 - 5711

To the Union of American Hebrew Congregations

united voice of Liberal Judaism in America, serving more than 400 Congregations, we send greetings on the historic occasion of the cornerstone laying of the

Union House of Living Judaism
Moritz and Josephine Berg Memorial

November 19, 1950

CONGREGATION BETH EL, DETROIT, MICHIGAN
RABBI B. Benedict Glazer
CONGREGATION PRESIDENT
SISTERHOOD PRESIDENT
BROTHERHOOD PRESIDENT
YOUTH PRESIDENT

Cover of a folder deposited in 1950 in the cornerstone of the House of Living Judaism in New York City

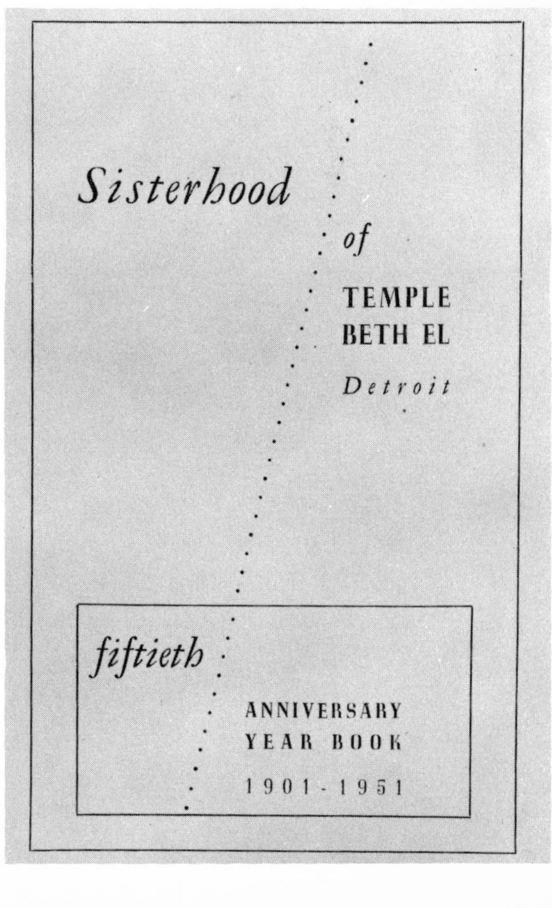

Sisterhood

of

TEMPLE
BETH EL

Detroit

fiftieth

ANNIVERSARY
YEAR BOOK

1901 - 1951

Title page of 50th Anniversary Year-book of Sisterhood

Chanuko Menorah

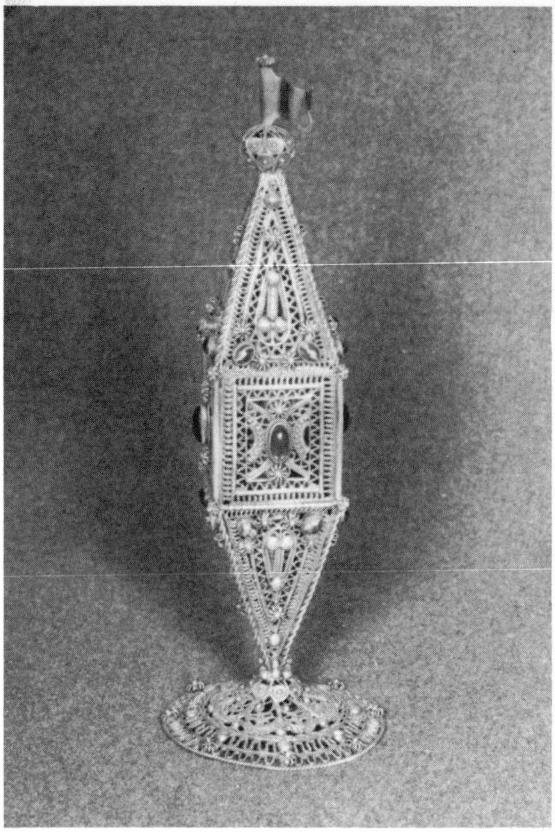

Spice Box

Ceremonial objects from the HARVEY *and* ETHEL GOLDMAN *Ceremonial Collection of Temple Beth El*

MARCH Mr. and Mrs. Harvey H. Goldman presented to the Temple their private collection of 125 rare synagogual and ritualistic art objects, adding considerable prestige to the Temple's ceremonial art collection.

Spice Box

Rimonim (Torah Bells)

Spice Box

The presentation of the Goldman Ceremonial Collection to the Temple. Left to right: MRS. HARVEY H. GOLDMAN, HARVEY H. GOLDMAN, DR. B. BENEDICT GLAZER, DAVID WILKUS.

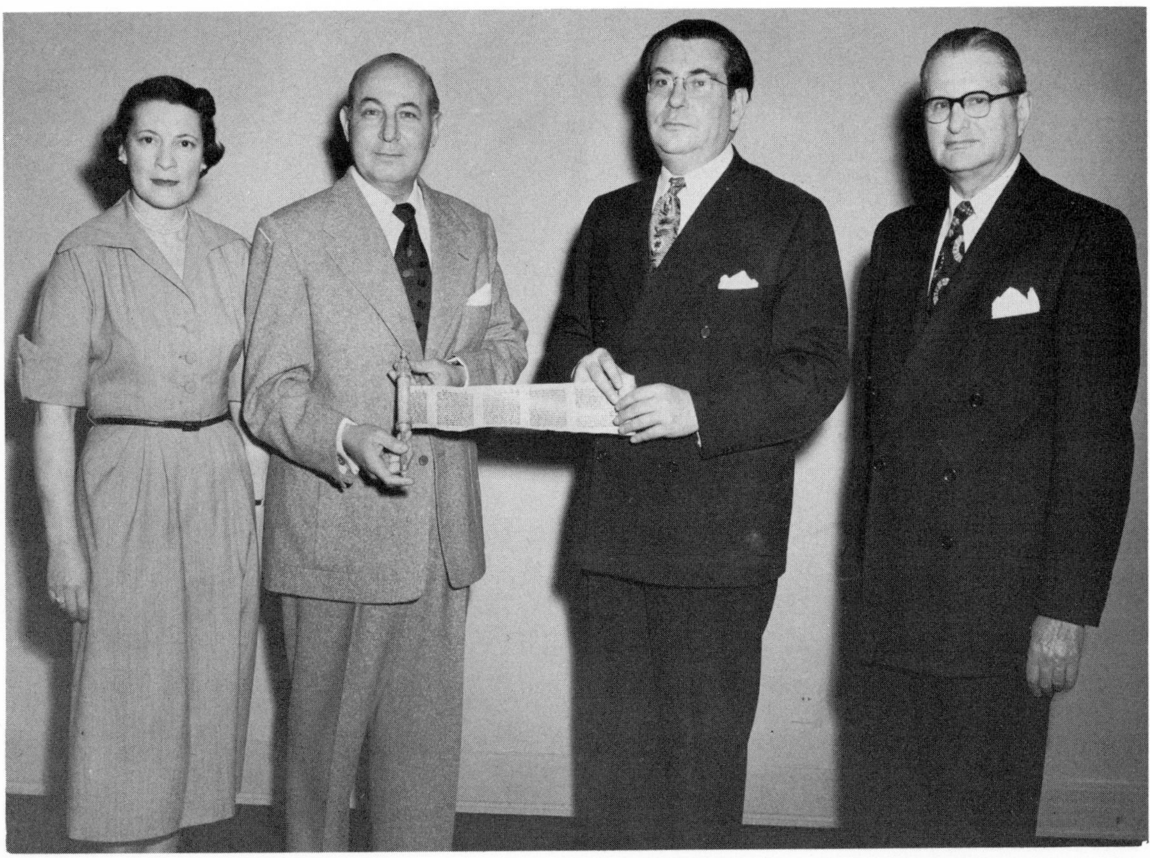

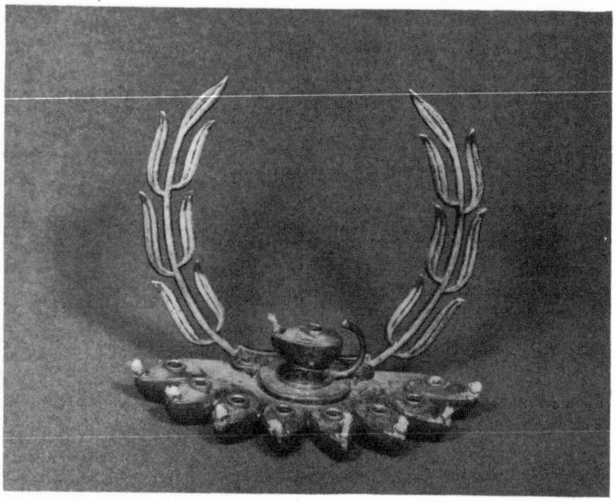

Modern Israeli Chanuko Menorah

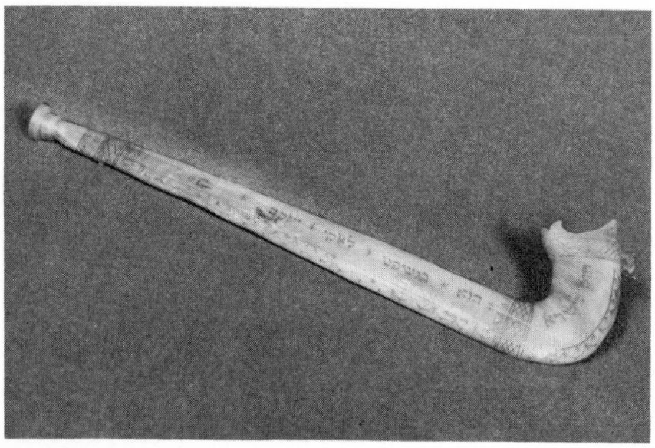

Shofar

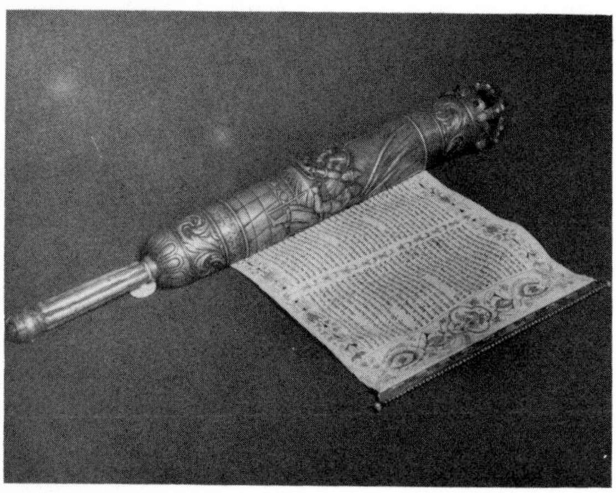

Illuminated Scroll of Esther

Passover Plate

Tass (Breast Plate)

SATURDAY, MAY 3, 1952

The Temple Players

Present The Meller Drammer

PURE

AS THE DRIVEN

SNOW

OR, A WORKING GIRL'S SECRET

Produced and Directed by

LEONARD C. JASLOVE

The 3-Act Meller Drammer
In Which Virtue Triumphs

Featuring the Greatest Galaxy of
Performers in the Art of Histrionics
Ever Assembled on Any Stage

Program cover of first production of Temple Players

WHEREAS, the Protestant and Eastern Orthodox ministers and religious education leaders of the city have been stimulated and inspired by the Annual Institute on Judaism sponsored each year by Temple Beth El, and

WHEREAS, the Institute is to observe its 10th anniversary on May 26, 1952, and

WHEREAS, this project was initiated by DR. B. BENEDICT GLAZER, the distinguished and beloved Rabbi of Temple Beth El,

BE IT HEREBY RESOLVED, that the Detroit Council of Churches, the Detroit Council of Religious Education and the Detroit Pastors' Union express their profound appreciation to Rabbi Glazer, the members of his Staff and the Congregation of Temple Beth El for the fellowship and inspiration provided through this annual occasion, and

BE IT HEREBY RESOLVED, that we voice the hope that Institute on Judaism be continued for many years to come.

BISHOP RICHARD S. EMRICH, President
Detroit Council of Churches

G. MERRILL LENOX, Executive Director
Detroit Council of Churches

VERNER S. MUMBULO, President
Religious Education
Detroit Council of Churches

CARLYLE F. STEWART, President
Detroit Pastors' Union
Detroit Council of Churches

Scroll presented to Beth El by the Detroit Council of Churches, 1953

APRIL 8 A Passover program was presented by the Temple over WJBK-TV.

MAY 3 Temple Players presented "Pure as a Driven Snow," their first production.

MAY 15 The Detroit community and the nation were shocked by the sudden death of Dr. Glazer. The funeral was held from the main Temple on May 18. Interment was at Beth El Memorial Park.

The Board of Trustees proclaimed a thirty-day period of mourning.

The B. Benedict Glazer Memorial Fund was established.

A MEMORIAL PLAQUE

AT THE GRAVE OF

OUR LATE BELOVED

DR. B. BENEDICT GLAZER

WILL BE

DEDICATED

AT THE

ANNUAL MEMORIAL SERVICE

SUNDAY, MAY 31

11:00 A. M.

BETH EL

MEMORIAL PARK

Program cover of the dedication of a Memorial Plaque at the grave of DR. GLAZER

In Memoriam

DR. B. BENEDICT GLAZER

TEMPLE BETH EL

Detroit

Title page of booklet published in memory of DR. GLAZER, *1952*

A memorial booklet was published in tribute to the memory of Dr. Glazer.

JUNE 19 City-wide memorial service for Dr. Glazer was held under the auspices of the Jewish Community Council of Detroit, of which he was vice-president.

JUNE 22 Rabbi Minard Klein assumed the post of assistant rabbi.

HOLY DAYS Services were conducted by Rabbi Minard Klein, Dr. Maurice N. Eisendrath, president of U.A.H.C., and Rabbi Herman E. Schaalman, director of the Chicago Federation of Reform Synagogues.

OCTOBER 11 Young Married Group was formed; Alan E. Schwartz was elected first president.

OCTOBER 17 Installation of Rabbi Minard Klein as assistant rabbi of the Temple by Dr. Samuel S. Mayerberg of Kansas City, Missouri.

Lighting of Sabbath candles at Friday evening services was introduced and the chanting of the *Kiddush* by the cantorial soloist was re-introduced.

OCTOBER 18 The congregation invited a number of out-of-town rabbis to assist Rabbi Klein in the conduct of worship services. Rabbi Sanford E. Saperstein of Temple Beth Jacob, Pontiac, Michigan, preached at the Sabbath morning services.

OCTOBER 25 Rabbi Harry Essrig of Temple Emanuel, Grand Rapids, Michigan, preached at the Sabbath morning services.

RABBI MINARD KLEIN, *Assistant Rabbi since 1952*

OCTOBER 31 Dr. Joseph L. Fink, president of the Central Conference of American Rabbis, preached at the Sabbath eve services.

NOVEMBER 8 Rabbi Alfred L. Friedman of Congregation Shaarey Zedek, Lansing, Michigan, preached at the Sabbath morning services.

NOVEMBER 10 The congregation authorized the purchase of a 22½ acre site on Northwestern Highway between Nine and Ten Mile roads.

NOVEMBER 14 Dr. Julius Mark of Temple Emanu-El of New York City preached at the Friday evening services.

Wayne University Press published *Toward Better Human Relations,* the first series of the Leo M. Franklin Lectures in Human Relations presented in 1951 under the direction of Dr. Lloyd Allen Cook, the first holder of the Leo M. Franklin Memorial Chair in Human Relations.

NOVEMBER 21 Dr. Louis L. Mann of Chicago Sinai Congregation preached at the Friday evening services.

DECEMBER 5 Dr. Louis I. Newman of Temple Rodeph Sholom of New York City preached at the Friday evening services.

DECEMBER 12 Rabbi Klein introduced the *Chanuko* candle lighting ceremony at annual *Chanuko* family service on Friday evening.

DECEMBER 13 Rabbi Harold L.

ALAN E. SCHWARTZ, *first President of Young Married Group*

DR. RICHARD C. HERTZ

Gelfman of Temple Beth Israel, Jackson, Michigan, preached at the Saturday morning services.

DECEMBER 19 Dr. Ferdinand M. Isserman of Temple Israel, St. Louis, Missouri, preached at the Friday evening services.

1953

JANUARY 16 Dr. Solomon B. Freehof of Temple Rodef Shalom, Pittsburgh, preached at the Friday evening services.

JANUARY 20 The Rabbi's Selection Committee, headed by Meyer L. Prentis and Nate S. Shapero, and the Board of Trustees announced the election of Dr. Richard C. Hertz, associate rabbi of the Chicago Sinai Congregation and a graduate of the 1942 Class of the Hebrew Union College, as senior rabbi of the congregation to succeed Dr. Glazer.

JANUARY 30 Mrs. Barnett R. Brickner of Cleveland, Ohio, spoke at the Sisterhood Friday evening service.

FEBRUARY 20 Dr. Tracy M. Pullman of the Church of Our Father of Detroit occupied the pulpit.

The congregation was advised of a $150,000 bequest by Caroline B. Wood of Daytona Beach, Florida.

MARCH 13 Rabbi Eric Friedland of Beth Am People's Synagogue, Chicago, preached at the first Young Married Group Friday evening services.

THE Education of the Jewish Child

A Study of 200 Reform Jewish Religious Schools

BY Rabbi Richard C. Hertz, PH.D.

Union of American Hebrew Congregations

NEW YORK, 1953

Title page of DR. HERTZ'S *book*

Receiving line at DR. HERTZ'S *Installation, 1953. Left to right:* DR. MAURICE N. EISENDRATH, *President, UAHC,* LEONARD N. SIMONS, RABBI MINARD KLEIN, DR. NELSON GLUECK, *President HUC-JIR,* DR. LOUIS MANN, *Rabbi, Chicago Sinai Congregation,* MRS. HERTZ, DR. HERTZ, MRS. A. J. HERTZ *and* MR. A. J. HERTZ, *parents of* DR. HERTZ

MARCH 17 Dr. Hertz's book *Education of the Jewish Child* was published by the Union of American Hebrew Congregations.

MARCH 29 Dr. Hertz and his family arrived in Detroit.

APRIL 3 Installation of Dr. Richard C. Hertz as senior rabbi of the congregation. Guest participants: Dr. Maurice N. Eisendrath, president of the Union of American Hebrew Congregations; Dr. Nelson Glueck, president of the Hebrew Union College and Jewish Institute of Religion; Dr. Louis I. Mann, rabbi of the Chicago Sinai Congregation.

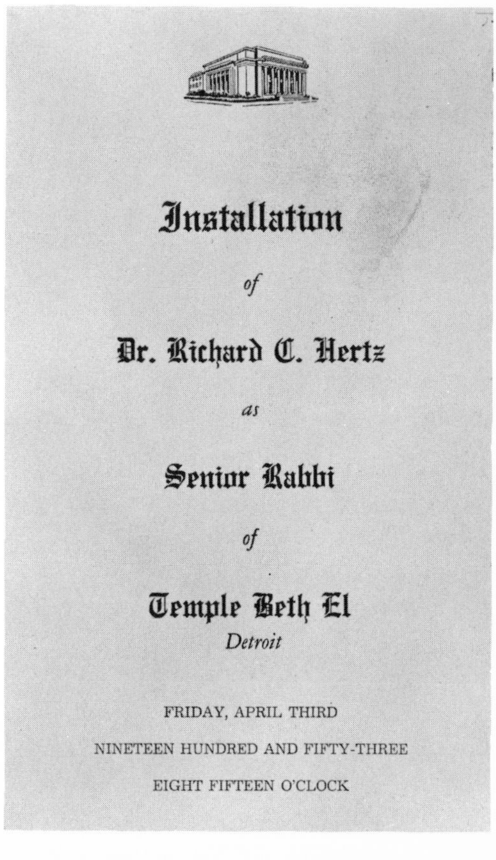

Installation

of

Dr. Richard C. Hertz

as

Senior Rabbi

of

Temple Beth El

Detroit

FRIDAY, APRIL THIRD

NINETEEN HUNDRED AND FIFTY-THREE

EIGHT FIFTEEN O'CLOCK

Program cover of the installation of DR. RICHARD C. HERTZ *as Rabbi of Beth El*

Speakers' Table at Congregational Seder, 1953

MAY 4 Twentieth anniversary of Jason H. Tickton as music director and organist of the Temple was observed at a testimonial dinner.

MAY 11 Leonard N. Simons elected thirty-third president of the congregation.

MAY 15 Memorial service for Dr. B. Benedict Glazer was held. Rabbi Leon I. Feuer of Toledo delivered the memorial address.

JUNE 7 The thirtieth anniversary of Carl C. Adams, building engineer of the Temple, was observed.

SEPTEMBER The congregation was advised of a $50,000 bequest by Setta Robinson, a life-long member of the Temple.

LEONARD N. SIMONS, *President, 1953–*

DR. HERTZ'S *first Confirmation Class, 1953*

JOHN ALEXANDER, *first President of the Young Adult Group*

OCTOBER 14 Young Adult Group was organized; John Alexander was elected its first president.

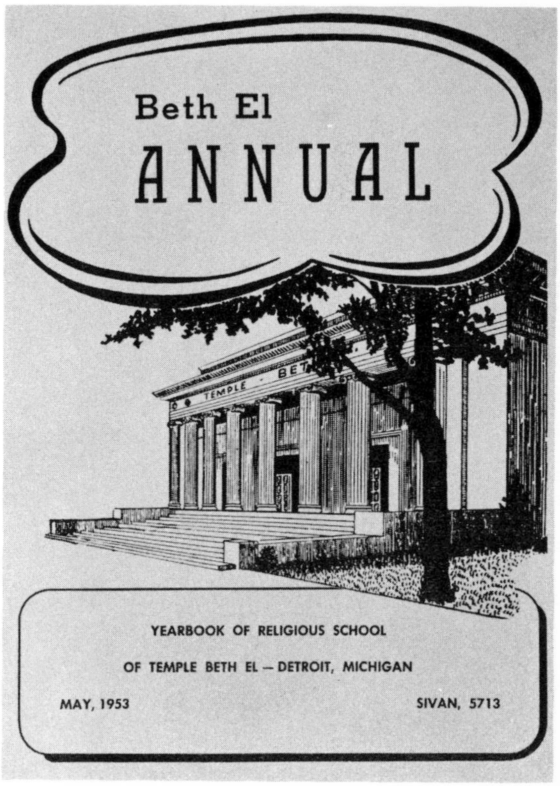

Beth El
ANNUAL
TEMPLE BETH
YEARBOOK OF RELIGIOUS SCHOOL
OF TEMPLE BETH EL — DETROIT, MICHIGAN
MAY, 1953
SIVAN, 5713

Cover of first published Annual of Religious School

IRVING I. KATZ, *Executive Secretary of the Temple, presenting* DR. HERTZ *(seated) on behalf of the Temple staff a Bible published in Israel on the occasion of his first anniversary with the Temple. Left to right:* RABBI MINARD KLEIN, MR. KATZ, JASON H. TICKTON, DR. NORMAN DRACHLER, KARL B. SEGALL

NOVEMBER A parking lot on Gladstone Avenue was opened, made possible through the generosity of the Richard Cohn Foundation, Maurice Aronsson, and David Wilkus.

DECEMBER 15 Dr. Hertz and the Board of Trustees announced the reintroduction of the *bar mitzvah* ceremony and the introduction of the *bas*

A few of DR. HERTZ'S *published pamphlets*

mitzvah ceremony on an optional basis.

1954

JANUARY 15 Dr. Jacob R. Marcus of the Hebrew Union College, author of important works in Jewish history, spoke on "Three Hundred Years in America," in honor of the forthcoming Tercentenary observance of the settlement of the Jews in the United States. A testimonial dinner was tendered to Irving I. Katz, executive secretary, on his fifteenth anniversary with the Temple.

FEBRUARY 7 Mrs. Franklin D. Roosevelt, the late United States President's widow and recently United States representative to the United Nations, lectured under the auspices of the Young Married Group.

FEBRUARY 19 Bishop Richard S. Emrich of the Episcopal Diocese of Michigan occupied the pulpit during Brotherhood Week.

JUNE The Temple contributed $21,768.75 to the 1953–54 combined campaign of the Union of American Hebrew Congregations, Hebrew Union College, and Jewish Institute of Religion, the largest amount in Beth El's history.

Front page of Beth El Happy Day and Memorial Funds pamphlet

Three Hundred Years in AMERICA

DR. JACOB R. MARCUS

To Our Jewish Brethren in the United States of America

PEACE BE WITH YOU AND YOUR NEIGHBORS

BE IT KNOWN UNTO YOU that in Elul 5714 (September 1954) the Jewish community of the United States will commemorate the 300th anniversary of Jewish settlement in this country.

BY THE GRACE OF GOD and under the protection of the Constitution of the United States, we have lived and prospered in this land. We have been an integral part of American life. We have worked with all other Americans in the never-ending search for the democratic way of life and for the light of faith. Our ancient prophetic ideals and the teachings of the sages have been foundation stones of this nation. Our work, our hopes, and above all, our living religion, have been among our proudest offerings to the American community.

IN SOME LANDS ACROSS THE SEAS our brethren have felt the searing flame of prejudice, persecution and death. We in America have had the sad yet inspiring opportunity to save the lives of scores of thousands – to bring comfort to the oppressed, to help in the making of a new and honored nation on the ancient soil of Israel, and to acquire a new recognition of our responsibility for human welfare in keeping with the ancient teachings of our faith. In some lands across the seas our brethren have been pressed to give up their religious beliefs and practices and to disappear in a well of namelessness. BUT WITHIN THE HOME OF AMERICA we have succeeded in preserving the unique identity of the Jewish religion, worshipping in keeping with our historic tradition; and we have preserved our ancient teachings, our ethics, and our religious ideals in the free climate of our nation. Our religion is strong, as our American loyalty is strong.

MINDFUL OF THESE BLESSINGS and with deep gratitude in our hearts to the God of Israel, who, in 1654, led our fathers to the shores of this great new land,

WE HEREBY PROCLAIM the period from Elul 5714 (September 1954) to the end of Sivan 5715 (May 1955) as one of thanksgiving, prayer, study and celebration of the American Jewish Tercentenary.

WE CALL ON ALL OUR BRETHREN throughout the nation to participate in the observance of this anniversary; to offer thanks unto the Lord for the blessings bestowed on us in America; to pray for the continued peace and prosperity of our country and all its inhabitants and to rededicate ourselves to the ideals of our faith within the freedom of American democracy.

Barnett R. Brickner
CENTRAL CONFERENCE OF AMERICAN RABBIS

Simon G. Kramer
AMERICAN JEWISH TERCENTENARY

Theodore L. Adams
RABBINICAL COUNCIL OF AMERICA

Harry Halpern
RABBINICAL ASSEMBLY OF AMERICA

Max J. Etra
UNION OF ORTHODOX JEWISH CONGREGATIONS OF AMERICA

Chas. Rosengarten
UNITED SYNAGOGUE OF AMERICA

Maurice N. Eisendrath
UNION OF AMERICAN HEBREW CONGREGATIONS

Norman Salit
SYNAGOGUE COUNCIL OF AMERICA

American Jewish Tercentenary Proclamation

DR. JACOB R. MARCUS

Three Hundred Years in America

TEMPLE BETH EL is really a pioneer congregation. This is the oldest extant Jewish institution in this great state of Michigan. We Jews are proud of such pioneer institutions—proud of the fact that we are pioneers, in the literal and truest sense of the word, in this great republic which we cherish. We came to this country—our spiritual ancestors—long before there were Baptists and Lutherans. We held religious services in New York City long before even the Roman Catholics gathered together to worship God. We were an organized community three hundred years ago in 1654. Our ancestors came from Brazil. They were refugees from the Portuguese Inquisition, because, in 1654, Brazil had been taken—retaken—by the Portuguese; and the Jews, who had settled there under the Dutch, had been compelled to leave. Most of them returned to the old homeland—to Holland. One particular ship was captured by Spanish pirates. The Spanish pirate ship, in turn, was taken by a French man-o-war. Captain de la Motthe, the captain of this French ship, the *St. Charles,* asked these Jews what their citizenship was, and when he found out they were Dutchmen, Hollanders, he took them to the nearest Dutch port, and he literally dumped them, in September, 1654, on the Battery at New Amsterdam, a town which ten years later became New York. That was the beginning of our communal life in this country.

I know that some of you will ask me if those Jews who came in September, 1654 were the first Jews in the colonies. My friends, you know what the basic principle in all Jewish history is—no Jew is ever the first Jew anywhere. There has always been one who has been there before him—and that was true at this particular time, because one Jew came down to take a look at these "greenhorns." His name was Jacob Barsimson. He was an oldtimer, prepared to teach them the ropes, because, after all, he had been in the country for almost three weeks!

Among those who landed in September, 1654 was a butcher by the name of Asser Levy. A very competent man, he was a *shochet*—a very bold man, a very courageous man. I've often suspected, too, that there was in him something of the old Hebrew Prophets. He could foresee the future. He must have known what was going to happen to the poor Jews of New York in November, 1929, and a few gentiles, too, at the time of the great stock market crash, because when this butcher built his slaughterhouse, he built it on what is today Wall Street. It was called "Wall" Street, because it was the last street in town. It was the street that had the wall to keep off the English and the Swedes on the Delaware and the Indians. Asser Levy found out that, when he was prepared to do his duty with the trainband—with the militia men—and to fight against Indians, he was told by Peter Stuyvesant that because he was a Jew he couldn't fight. They wouldn't let him fight, but they expected him to pay a special tax that was exacted only of Jews. He said that he would not pay the tax but that he was determined to fight with his fellow burghers on the wall. He went to court, fought through his case, and won his case. He laid down a principle that we Jews have attempted to maintain to the present day—*equal rights and equal responsibilities.*

The first congregation, which was established in 1654, was a Sephardic congregation, a Spanish and Portuguese congregation. Among the Jews who followed this Spanish and Portuguese ritual in the next century, was a very well known family of merchants in Philadelphia. This was the firm of B. &. M. Gratz Bros. The Gratzes first were merchant

REBECCA GRATZ. *Courtesy of the American Jewish Archives*

BARNARD GRATZ. *Courtesy of the American Jewish Archives*

shippers. But when the English began to enforce the blockade against smugglers and when they applied British laws with respect to international commerce, most of the Americans found themselves in difficulties. The Gratzes turned their attention to trading with the Indians across the Allegheny Mountains. After trading with the Indians, they acquired large grants of land and attempted to establish great colonies here in this country. Ben Franklin, Washington, the Gratzes and others were engaged in this colonial activity. At one time the land speculators thought of establishing a fourteenth colony, called Vandalia. There were to be 20,000,000 acres in this colony. The Gratzes and their Jewish associates engaged for a time in the attempt to start another colony on the Illinois and Chicago rivers. They, at one time, owned all of the site of the present city of Chicago, in Cook County. Unfortunately, they were not able to hold on to the lands which they owned in those days.

In spite of the fact that they were officers of the Spanish and Portuguese congregation in Philadelphia, which was known as "The Hope of Israel," the Gratzes were, in reality, not Spanish or Portuguese Jews; they were, in truth, Polish Jews, who had come from the German border. What was it that brought German Jews to this country in the seventeen-fifties? They came here for the same reason the German Jews came here in 1939—they were experiencing persecution. Just about the time that we were getting ready to write our Declaration of Independence, the German independent principalities were publishing and promulgating laws such as the following, and I quote one literally: "All jugglers, bear-trainers, tramps, German Jew peddlers and Polish Jews are forbidden access to this country, under penalty of being sent to the penitentiary. All gypsies caught will be hanged or shot." This was the type of legislation that was by no means unusual in Germany in the eighteenth century, and it was the type of legislation that induced Jews, German Jews, to migrate to this country at that time. The Jews, however, as a rule, never leave the land of their nativity, until they are forced to leave.

Many of the German Jews hoped that after the American Revolution conditions would improve in Germany and that Germany would ultimately establish republics along the American line. The Revolution of 1848 convinced many German Jews, however, that there was no possibility of an improvement in the conditions in central Europe. So, by that time, the more cultured and wealthy German Jews, who had held on with the hope of a change in the political life, also thought it advisable to migrate and to come to these shores.

We know the stories of some of those German Jews who migrated during the year 1848 and shortly after. There was one very interesting family in the city of Prague, and they were determined to come here; but before they came they thought they would send a young member of the family to see what the country was like. This young man was sent over in the fall of 1848. His first name was Adolf. He came to the great metropolis of New York. Actually, at that time, in the winter of 1848, it had 400,000 people. He wandered up and down the streets, and he saw something that interested him very much. In front of every brown stone house he saw a jug—a milk jug. In each milk jug were two or three cents for a quart of milk. He was very much interested as he watched for a while—nobody went up and down the streets taking the two or three cents out of the jug; so he wrote back to the family, "Come on over to America. This is an honest country—it is the only place to raise a family." And so the clan came over, in the spring of 1849. But they were "funny" Jews, (you know, there are some Jews who are very strange), and these Jews didn't like New York City. They didn't care to remain there, so they went up the Hudson River to Albany, where they probably ran into a *landsman*

DR. ISAAC M. WISE. *Courtesy of the American Jewish Archives*

from Bohemia by the name of Isaac Mayer Wise, stayed there very briefly, took the canal boats west, and finally landed in the "Queen City of the West" (and, as all of you know, the "Queen City of the West" is none other than Cincinnati, Ohio), stayed there briefly, then moved to Madison, Indiana, on the Ohio, and finally crossed the Ohio to the city at the falls of the Ohio, which we know today as Louisville. There, in 1856, Adolf, already married, had a son, and he called him Louis Dembitz Brandeis.

Now the Brandeis and the Goldmarks, who came over in '48, were really not characteristic of the typical Jew who emigrated in the '30's and

LOUIS D. BRANDEIS. *Courtesy of the American Jewish Archives*

'40's and after that time. The average German Jew who came over in the middle of the nineteenth century was a poor man—some Jewish background (not too much) —a person who had never had the advantages of any real education. We know a great deal about them, because that Bohemian rabbi, Isaac Mayer Wise, in the city of Albany, liked to write, and he has written his memoirs. He told us about his congregation. Most of them were peddlers. He wrote of his experience with these peddlers. If the peddler had any capacity, after a while he graduated from being a peddler. He became what was called, in those days, a "merchant baron." A merchant baron was a man who didn't carry his pack upon his back but actually had a horse and buggy. Then, he would find some likely crossroad spot and settle down. After he settled down, he would open a little retail store. After he was successful, if he was—and frequently they were not; but if he was successful, he would expand. He had two choices:— he could decide to open a larger store and become a jobber for other peddlers, finally a wholesaler and even a manufacturer; or he could decide to stay strictly in the retail business, open a larger store and, finally, become a department store owner. Now of course it is important for men to make a living. That was the first thing that they had to do. But once they had made a living, they thought of other things. They began to open their synagogues and their little meeting places, just as this little community did in Detroit, in 1850, when they established Beth El (which, of course, you know, means "the House of God"). Once they had built their *shuls*, their little synagogues, and their charities, they began to think in larger terms of national religious organizations, and the first national organization of the Jews came in the 1850's, because of an incident that occurred over in Italy.

In Italy, in the little university town—famous for its law school—of Bologna, which belonged to the Papacy, there was a family called the Mortaras. In 1856 the Mortaras had a four year old boy by the name of Edgar, who became very sick and, when it was feared that Edgar might die, the nurse, a very pious Roman Catholic, secretly baptized the child, without the knowledge of the parents. Two years later, the girl left her employer, the Mortara family, and informed the Papal authorities of what she had done. The Pope, at that time, therefore, issued a warrant, sent the Swiss guards with the warrant for the arrest of young Edgar Mortara, and this child of six, in 1858, on a June night, about 10 o'clock, was literally taken out of the arms of his mother and never returned again to the home of the Mortaras.

When this became known all through the world, the American Jews felt that, even in this free land, "eternal vigilance is the price of liberty," and so they organized *the first civic defense organization for Jews,* which was known as the Board of Delegates of American Israelites, and that was in the following year, in 1859. Within two years, they had plenty of work to do, because the great Civil War broke out, and in this war thousands upon thousands of Jews volunteered. There were nine men of Jewish origin in the Northern army, the Union army, who were generals. In spite of the fact there were so many Jewish generals and so many Jews who fought and died to preserve the Union, no rabbi could serve as a chaplain in the United States Army, because of the fact that the law passed by Congress limited that right and privilege only to the Christian clergy. The Board of Delegates went to work and changed that law.

Even as the people in the North fought for what they thought was right, the Jews in the South fought for the Confederacy, and the Jews in the South had a very notable record. The Quartermaster General of the Confederate Army was Colonel Myers of Charleston, the Surgeon General was Dr. Camden De Leon. There was one Jew in the South who was Attorney-General, Secretary of War and, finally, Secretary of State. Many people maintain that he was the brains of the Confederacy, and he was the Jew, Judah P. Benjamin.

JUDAH P. BENJAMIN. *Courtesy of the American Jewish Archives*

After the war was over, all the struggle and effort that had gone into destruction went into building this great country. By 1869 the last spike was driven into a railroad in Utah. That created a transcontinental railroad system. The people of this country were united, and, as the people were united, they believed, that is, the Jews believed,—that we should also be united. In 1873, Isaac Mayer Wise, that young Bohemian, who had gone to Cincinnati, the second largest Jewish community in America, there succeeded in uniting all of the Hebrew Congregations of America into a union. Two years later, he built the Hebrew Union College, the largest and oldest Jewish theological seminary in the Western World.

This man Wise was a rather remarkable person. He was also a great journalist. He had a newspaper called *The American Israelite,* which went into almost every Jewish home in this country. In 1877, he had an interesting bit of news to report to his readers. He reported the fact that the richest Jew in America, and a man who had been one of the outstanding bankers helping the Union during the Civil War, Joseph Seligman, of the firm of Seligman Brothers, had been refused a night's lodging in the Grand Union Hotel in Saratoga, the Spa in New York State. Wise and the Jews of this country were very much disturbed—not because Mr. Seligman would not have a place to sleep, because he could well afford to buy all the hotels in Saratoga and not miss the money (he was reputedly worth $30,000,000)—but they were indignant at the thought that a man should be discriminated against because of his religion. They considered that bigoted and un-American. What did the Jews of this country do when they noted this action? They didn't do what our generation has been accustomed to do. In our generation, we do things differently. When we notice any discrimination of that type, we call a meeting of the most prominent Jews, we very carefully lock the door, we look under the chairs and tables, to be sure nobody is listening to us, and then we do—absolutely nothing! These Jews were conscious of the fact that the firm that owned the Grand Union Hotel was a firm that also owned the largest drygoods wholesale concern in America, known as A. T. Stewart and Company. A great many of the Jews in the 1870's were in the drygoods and in the furnishings businesses. They were determined to boycott that un-American institution. They didn't do it secretly; they came out with notices in the press, and they signed their names. It wasn't long after that, because of this boycott in all probability, that A. T. Stewart went into bankruptcy and was bought by a more enterprising and more liberal business man by the name of John Wanamaker.

The Jews of that generation were able to do what they did because they were a small community of about 250,000. Most of them were central Europeans, most of them were small business people, most of them were members of the Reform synagogues. That whole picture, the picture of 1877, changed radically four years later, when someone threw a bomb in Russia and destroyed one of the rulers of Russia—one of the Czars. That started a wave and a flow of immigration. Today, as a result of that immigration of east European Jews, we are no longer a group of 250,000, but we are a group of 5,000,000. This is the largest group of Jews, in all probability, that has ever existed at any one time in any one country. All of these Jews, no matter what their background or affiliation, are attempting, to the best of their ability, to make their contribution to the American scene. They have their ideals, and they are attempting to lead exemplary lives.

I believe that their ideal can be typified, to a large extent, in the life of one particular American family that I have in mind. This family came here also after 1848 and they settled in the South, in Alabama. One of the most important members of this family was a young Jew whose first name was Mayer. Mayer became a very ardent Southerner. During the period of the Civil War, he heard that a great many of the Alabama soldiers were suffering in the Northern prison stockades for lack of proper care, medicine and nutrition. He knew, as we know, there was no proper agency for them, because this was long before the days of the American Red Cross. He determined to do something about it. He went to see Governor Watts, at Montgomery. He said, "Governor, I've got an idea—let's take half a million dollars worth of good Southern cotton, and ask the North to accept the cotton, turn it into gold, and use the money solely for humanitarian purposes. The North needs the cotton awfully bad." The Governor agreed with him, and decided to see Jefferson Davis, at Richmond. Davis approved of it, and he opened negotiations with Grant, who had just been transferred from the West to the East, and was before Richmond. Grant refused to do anything, and nothing could be done. Young Mayer returned, back to Montgomery, without having accomplished his purpose. After the war was over, Mayer knew that it would be years before the South would rise again. He moved to the city of New York, married, and had a family. His youngest son, who is still living today, has been governor of New York State for four terms, and is now in the United States Senate. The father, Mayer Lehman, did everything he could, in his own humble way, to feed some hungry, starving and sick Alabama soldiers in Northern prison stockades. The father was unsuccessful. The son, Herbert Lehman, as director general of the United Nations Relief and Rehabilitation Administration, successfully fed hundreds of millions of suffering human beings all over the world.

This is the story of one American family. We are proud of the

HERBERT H. LEHMAN. *Courtesy of the American Jewish Archives*

Lehmans—we are proud of all Jews who have, with honesty and integrity, attempted to be and to maintain themselves as good citizens. Sometimes, however, in the quiet and the solitude of our thoughts, we lift up our eyes and we recall what has happened abroad since 1939, particularly in central Europe. We are disturbed by the fact that a Jewry that we thought was secure has been destroyed; that five million Jews have been destroyed. We sometimes ask ourselves, How can we attain security? How can we survive as Jews and as an integral part of this great American Republic? What is the formula for survival for our children? Of course, there are many Jews who have the answer. Some tell us that we ought to go into politics, like Bernard Baruch, and secure the gratitude of our fellow citizens. There are others who maintain that we should engage in scientific activity. There are some who have learned so little from the pages of history that they believe that the only salvation of the Jew lies in the acquisition of the almighty dollar. I am the last person in the world to decry the influence of wealth, of political power, or of scientific achievement, but I maintain that if the Jew is to survive he can survive only through *the integrity of the individual.* If American

Judaism is to rise and not to fall, it will depend upon the individual Jew in his relation to his Jewish community and the larger community into which he is integrated.

This personal integrity of which I speak I believe to be a compound of three elements—*generosity, honor,* and *loyalty.* There is no need today, anywhere in the United States, to speak to American Jews about generosity. Do you realize that, since 1914, these facts, these figures, are literally true—one thousand million—one billion dollars—has been sent abroad by American Jews for the support and sustenance of other Jews, whom they have never known and will never know, purely out of a fine sense of kinship and fellowship? There is nothing like it in all the pages of recorded history!

Certainly I have not come all the way from the "Queen City of the West" to talk to you people about integrity; although I know that you will be the first to say to me that no individual, no Jew, is so righteous and so perfect that he cannot possibly be a little bit better. I know that some of you will say to me that it is hard for us to pull ourselves up by our very own boot straps—that there is a certain amount of social prejudice against us. That is true—and I happen to have a large, unabridged dictionary on my desk that was published in the early part of this century, and it still carries the term "Jew" as a synonym for "scoundrel and usurer," but the fact that such prejudice does exist—that the term "Jew" is for many people a term of reproach—all of that should serve as a challenge to us to take that term of reproach and transmute it into a patent of nobility. If you tell me that it cannot be done, I would like to tell you that there was once a Protestant sect in this country that was hated and despised as the Jew has never been hated and despised. Individuals of this group were actually lynched in the American colonies, but these people persevered in their integrity and today throughout the world, there is no group that is more respected than the Society of Friends, the Quakers. What they have done we can also do. Every Jew should so live and conduct himself as if the future welfare of his people were dependent upon his own personal moral activity. Of course that takes courage, my friends. We have our great spiritual leaders, such as you have in this congregation; we have our great religious institutions; we have our Bible, our Talmud, our Rabbinic traditions, all of which have taught us, for the last 4,000 years, to fight for right and for liberty and for decency and happiness, not only for the Jews, but for every living being; for every man, woman and child that breathes, black and white, Jew and Gentile.

And you may say to me, "If I am generous and honorable, and a decent human being, is this an absolute guarantee that I am going to have a future for myself and my children?" My friends, I wish I could give you that guarantee, but there are no guarantees for individuals, no guarantees for great empires and great states; but, if there is a road which the Jew should tread, I believe it is the path which I have described.

I believe that when every Jew is distinguished among his fellow citizens for his personal integrity—then I believe, I hope, that nothing in God's green earth will ever shake or disturb his position. *Character is the most important thing in life.* If you are good men and women, then all the winds and storms of prejudice may whistle and howl about your ears, but, when the din and the noise and turmoil have passed away, and the dawn of a new day comes shining over the horizon, you will still be standing here erect, unflinching, undaunted—AN ETERNAL PEOPLE.

Dr. Jacob R. Marcus is the foremost living Jewish historian in the United States. He occupies the Adolph S. Ochs Chair of History at the Hebrew Union College, Cincinnati, Ohio, and is Director of the American Jewish Archives in Cincinnati. He is also a past president of the Central Conference of American Rabbis.

He received his A.B. degree at the University of Cincinnati and his degree of Rabbi at the Hebrew Union College. He served with distinction overseas in World War I. He studied at Lane Theological Seminary and the University of Chicago and attended academies in Europe from 1922 to 1926. He received his Ph.D. degree from the University of Berlin and continued his graduate work in Paris and Jerusalem. He has an honorary LL.D. degree from the University of Cincinnati.

He is the author of a series of books important to Jewish life and letters, among which might be included *Israel Jacobson, A Brief Introduction to the Bibliography of Modern Jewish History, Jewish Festschriften, The Rise and Destiny of the German Jew.* He has also written *The Jew in the Medieval World,* first source book in English on medieval Jewish history, and *Communal Sick Care in the German Ghetto,* an absorbing story of the origins of Jewish community sick care and hospitals in medieval Jewry. His latest book is *Early American Jewry,* an informal study, in two volumes, of the life and background of the Jews in the Colonial and early American period. Numerous scholarly articles by him have been contributed to the Hebrew Union College Annual and other scholarly journals.

Dr. Marcus is chairman of the Publication Committee of the Jewish Publication Society. He is also a charter member of the Board of Governors of the Training Bureau for Jewish Communal Service. He is vice-president of the American Jewish Historical Society.—I.I.K.

Appendix

IRVING I. KATZ

in collaboration with

DR. LOUIS L. FRIEDLAND

Appendix

I. Original Articles of Incorporation of Congregation Beth El—1851
II. Transcript of Manuscript Letter from Joseph Freedman to Rabbi Isaac Leeser—1851
III. Congregation Beth El in 1852
IV. 1856 Constitution and By-Laws of Congregation Beth El
V. Rabbi Leeser's Account of Congregation Beth El
VI. Rabbi Liebman Adler Warns Detroit Jews Not to Buy Meat from Unauthorized Detroit *Shochet*
VII. Rabbi Isaac M. Wise Visits Detroit and Congregation Beth El
VIII. Invitations to Social Gatherings by Beth El Members in the 1860's
IX. Account of the Dedication of the Rivard Street Synagogue
X. Advertisement for a Rabbi in *The Israelite* of August 6, 1864
XI. Accounts of the Dedication of the Washington Avenue Temple
XII. Letter of Isaac Hart, a Member of Beth El, to Rabbi Isaac Leeser
XIII. Rabbi's Selection Committee of Congregation Beth El Writes to Dr. Kaufmann Kohler, June 9, 1869
XIV. Letter of Notification to Dr. Henry Zirndorf of his Election as Rabbi of Congregation Beth El, June 9, 1876
XV. Program of the Eleventh Council of Union of American Hebrew Congregations and Delegate's Badge, July 9–11, 1889
XVI. Program of the Semi-Centennial Celebration of Congregation Beth El, November 29, 1900
XVII. Religious School Program of the Semi-Centennial Celebration of Congregation Beth El, December 2, 1900
XVIII. Program of the Dedication of the Temple on Woodward near Eliot
XIX. Services of Dedication of Present Temple at Woodward and Gladstone, November 10–12, 1922
XX. Program of Seventy-Fifth Anniversary Celebration of Congregation Beth El, December 13, 1925
XXI. Perpetual Articles of Incorporation of Congregation Beth El
XXII. Program of the Thirty-Seventh Council of Union of American Hebrew Congregations, April 26–May 1, 1941
XXIII. Excerpts from Addresses at the Centennial Anniversary Banquet of Congregation Beth El, March 25, 1950
XXIV. Presidents of the Sisterhood of Congregation Beth El, 1901–1954
XXV. Presidents of the Men's Club of Congregation Beth El, 1919–1954
XXVI. Membership Statistics of Congregation Beth El, 1850–1954

I ORIGINAL ARTICLES OF INCORPORATION OF CONGREGATION BETH EL—1851

(As recorded December 21, 1852)

Rec'd & Recorded December 21. 1852.

H. Van Rensselaer. Clerk.

The undersigned Israelites of the City of Detroit have this day assembled for the purpose of forming a Society to provide themselves a place of Public Worship, Teacher of their Religeon and Burial Ground and give such Society the name. Congregation Bethel, and adopt the following laws for the administration of the affairs of their Congregation.

Article I.

Name of the Congregation

1 The Name of the Congregation shall be Bethel.

2 The name of the Congregation shall never be changed.

Article II.

Administration.

1 The business of the Congregation shall be administered by a Board of Directors consisting of a President, Vice President, and Three Trustees.

2 None of the above Officers shall receive a Salary of the Congregation.

Article III

Election of Officers

1 The election for Officers shall take place every year in the third week of the Month of Tishri.

2 The President and Vice President shall be elected for one year and Three Trustees for two years.

3. The election for officers shall be by ballot.

4. Every member of good standing who is not more than six months in arrears with his dues, shall be entitled to give a vote, try all transactions of the Congregation and is eligable to any Office

Article IIII.

Duties of Officers

1 The President shall preside at al meetings of the Congregation.

2 By equal number of votes he shall have the casting vote

3 The President shall countersign all certificates of the Congregation and orders for disbursements out of the Treasury

4 On application for charitable purposes the President shall have a right to grant a sum not exceeding five Dollars.

5. The President shall have a right to call extra or special meetings, or shall do so when applied to in writing by seven members.

6 All documents, papers, deeds &c shall be in safe keeping of the President, who shall deliver them on leaving Office in open meeting to his Successor. It shall be his special duty to see that all the rules and regulations of the Congregation are carried out.

Article V.

Duties of the Vice President

The Vice President who has the Office of Treasurer shall take in safe keeping all the Monies of the Congregation and shall disburse them on a written order of the President, countersigned by Secretary.

2. Before entering on his duties as Treasurer he shall have to give satisfactory security to the President & Trustees for the faithfull performance of the duties of his Office.

3 The Vice President as Treasurer of the Congregation shall keep a correct account of all the receipts & disbursements of the Monies of the Congregation and shall deposit all sums in his hands exceeding fifty Dollars according to the direction of the Officers of the Congregation and place the Certificates of Deposit in the hands of the President. He shall make a report of the State of the finances at every quarterly meeting or do so to a Committee appointed by the Congregation for that purpose. By leaving Office he has to deliver books, papers &c of the Congregation in open meeting to his Successor

Duties of the Trustees -

It shall be their duty to be present at all meetings of the Congregation, to see that the rules and regulations of the Congregation are strictly carried out and do their best to promote the welfare of the Congregation -

Article VI.

Duties of the Secretary -

1 A. Secretary shall be elected by the Congregation and if the services of such a one cannot be obtained gratuitously the Congregation shall determine the amount of Salary -

2 The Secretary shall keep a record of all the transactions of the Congregation

3 He shall keep a list of all the members of the Congregation.

4 He shall countersign all the orders and [illegible] of the President

5 Also keep a record of all the interments in the burial ground of the Congregation, By leaving Office deliver papers books to his successor in Office -

VII

Candidates Admission

1 Israelites only can become members of this Congregation

2 Candidates shall be elected by ballot.

3 Candidates for admission will have to make application to the President, deposit $3.25 - admission fee with the Sec. who will give notice at the next meeting of such application which will lay over for actions to a subsequent meeting and if not more than one fourth of the votes are against him he shall be admitted

Candidates for admission will have to sign the Constitution

No member shall have a right to vote on the same meeting of his admission -

VIII

Dues for members shall be according to By laws

526

VIIII

Expulsions

A member who is in arrears with his dues or offerings for twelve months shall be suspended for six month and should on the expiration of that time he not have settled such dues be then expelled

X

Burial

1 Every member secures a place of burial in the burying ground of the Congregation.

2 The Wife of a member or unmarried son under twenty one years of age shall likewise have a free burial place secured.

3 For unmarried daughters of a member shall be the same privileges.

4 Wife or children of a member that have not been raised in the Jewish faith, neither adopted such shall be excluded from the burial ground of this Congregation.

XI.

Burial of Strangers.

The fees for burial place for non members shall be determined by the President and Trustees and shall be no less than five nor more than twenty five Dollars.

The President and Trustees shall have a right to grant at their descretion burial places for indigent persons without charge to their families.

XII

Synagogue

If the Congregation secures a Synagogue or other ~~place~~ building for Divine Service such Service shall be held according to the German

Ritual (Minhag) and not be changed as long as the Congregation exists under the name of Bethel

XIII

The Congregation reserves for itself the right to enact such By Laws as the necessities of this Congregation require.

Detroit April 21, 1851

Signatures

Jacob Silberman Pr
Solomon Bendit. Treas
Joseph Freedman
Max Cohn
Adam Hersch
Alex Hein
Jacob Lang
Aron Joel Friedlander
L Bresler
C E Bresler
L Bresler

II TRANSCRIPT OF MANUSCRIPT LETTER FROM JOSEPH FREEDMAN TO RABBI ISAAC LEESER—1851

(*From the Leeser Collection at Dropsie College, Philadelphia*)

DETROIT November 13, 1851

Rev Isaac Leeser
Phila.

Your favor of the 28th ult and also your valuable Magazine came to hand. We enclose $3 for our subscription & $3 for C & C E. Bressler Detroit to whose address you will also please to send the Occident.

We shall when an opportunity offers gladly speak to our friends of the Occident & your translated bible & solicit subscription.

As regards our congregation here it counts only a very limited number of members, and is of a quite recent organization. Several men having moved here with their families (some time last year) the total want of all opportunities for the religious instruction of their children was severely felt, especially as their business called them away from home most of the time. Subsequently, at a meeting called among those few Yehudim residing here, 12 in number, it was resolved to call a teacher and Shochet and also to buy a piece of burying ground. The incident expenses, though considerable, were contributed with a good deal of liberality, & the above resolution carried out. The number of our members has since then augmented to 18.

The prospects for erection of a Synagogue are rather remote yet being so few in number it will have to be deferred to a later and more auspicious period.

Should on your contemplated western tour you happen to visit Detroit allow us to invite you to call on us. We shall cheerfully attend to any thing that might be of service to your cause.

Wishing you health & happiness

We remain Respectfully
S Freedman & Brothers

by Joseph Freedman

III CONGREGATION BETH EL IN 1852

(The Occident, *Vol. 10, p. 58, April, 1852*)

58 THE OCCIDENT.

DETROIT, MICHIGAN.—A letter before us speaks as follows: "As regards our congregation here, it counts only a very limited number of members, and is of a quite recent organization. Several men having moved here with their families, some time last year, the total want of all opportunities for the religious instruction of their children was severely felt, especially as their business called them away from home most of the time. Subsequently, at a meeting called among those few Jews residing here, twelve in number, it was resolved to engage a teacher and Shochet, and also to buy a piece of ground for a burial-place. The incidental expenses, though considerable, were contributed with a good deal of liberality, and the above resolution was carried out. The number of our members has since then increased to eighteen. The prospects for erecting a Synagogue are rather remote yet; for, being so few in number, it will have to be deferred to a later and more auspicious period." Our readers will see that, at all events, a beginning has been made; and if we view the rapid increase of American cities, it is not too much to predict that the Israelites will not overlook Detroit, as a place well calculated to promote their material prosperity, and that hence the eighteen now there, will not be left so entirely dependent on their own resources, as they now deem themselves.

IV 1856 CONSTITUTION AND BY-LAWS OF CONGREGATION BETH EL

(The Israelite, *Vol. 3, p. 196, December 26, 1856*)

The Constitution and By-Laws of K. K. Beth El, Detroit, Michigan.

We have received a copy of the constitution and by-laws of this young congregation, (established 1850.) and make some extracts from it, for the benefit of our readers. It will be seen, that our friend, the Rev. Mr. Adler is working on a fertile and remunerative soil.

The laws are in German, we can give the translation only. The book begins with the following seven principles.

1. An Israelitish congregation should cultivate concord and peace for all; the members thereof should meet each other in friendship and fraternity; they should assist and support each other with words and actions; they should be one great family.

2. The members of an Israelitish congregation ought to be true Israelites by birth or profession, and their actions should, in every case, testify to this fact.

3. An Israelitish congregation is obliged to establish and support a regular and public divine worship, not only by defraying the necessary expense to this purpose, but by a warm, earnest and cordial participation of the members in public worship.

4. The education of the young in all branches, especially in religion, is a duty involving on the whole congregation. Although the first duty of education devolves on the parents, still the congregation should superintend the school, and always be ready to sacrifices for the elevation and prosperity, of the school.

5. An appropriate, dignified and religious treatment of the dead is likewise a duty of the congregation.

6. The support of poor co-religionists is also a duty of the congregation.

7. The congregation shall, in all its religious institutions, pay due attention to the progress of the age, and maintain the respect due to customs or laws handed down to us by our pious fathers. In cases of innovation, this congregation, shall attempt to remain in unity with the majority, at least, of the American congregations, and shall always attempt to produce uniformity in the American Synagogue.

After these principles, follows the constitution, which is a concise and complete code of rules to govern a body of men, well written and systematically connected. We must, however, object to Art II, in which it says, that all paid officers of the congregation are elected for one year only. This is the cause of continual and unpleasant agitation in the congregation, causes many disturbances and hard feelings, ties paid officers down every year to the whims of every body, and prevents many from accepting office.

In the by-laws the very first point interests us, and we translate it. It says there about the Synagogue;" The *Piutum* of the Sabbaths and feasts, the *Megilos* shall be abolished from divine service, with the expedition of the *Marovis* and the last part of the *Tal* and *Geshem*.

All *Selichos*, except on *Yeme Noraim*, shall be abolished.

The 9th day of Ab the *Krobez* and Kinos, with the exception of three for the evening, and three for the morning, are also abolished.

There shall be omitted in the *Tephilah*, several *Berachoth*, in the morning, *Eschu Mekoman*, *Whehu Raehum*, Bamah *Madlikin*, *Welamalshinim*, *Necom leenenu* and other passages.

The service shall conclude with *Olenu*, and *Kaddish*, followed by *Yigdal* or *Anim semiroth* on the holidays. This is followed by regulations which take care of a proper order and decorum, and give the whole service a rounded and complete appearance.

The other laws are nearly the same as usual, and have only a local interest. We only wish to call attention to the fact, that the spirit of the Cleveland conference moves in this reform, the congregation, having been represented there by their minister, Rev. Mr. Adler, remains faithful to its pledge and fairly opens the way to the *Minhag America*, and to the formation of the Synod, which is clearly expressed in the seventh principle. We for our part, have not the least doubt that at least the western congregation, (and the west grows fast,) will in a few years be a united body in the Synagogue, Synod, Orphan asylum and College. We have plenty of intellect and wealth on this side of the Alleghanies to carry out what we conceive beneficial to the sacred cause of Israel.—Let our brethren remain firm. Step by step, let us proceed; we go safely.

V RABBI LEESER'S ACCOUNT OF CONGREGATION BETH EL

(The Occident, *Vol. 15, pp. 306-307, September, 1857*)

Detroit, Michigan.—On our way from Sandusky we passed through Toledo, Ohio, and Adrian and Monroe, Michigan. There are many Israelites in the first named place, but no attempt has been yet made, at least so far as we have heard, to organize a congregation; and in Adrian, as is just mentioned, they have been left in the lurch after making a commencement, though we trust that they will not become disheartened by the first failure. We could not learn any thing of Monroe, though no doubt there are Jews there also, as they are in almost every town to the west of Pennsylvania. The situation of Monroe seemed to us to be both beautiful and well suited for many kinds of business, and will no doubt attract settlers before long, who may desire to escape from the crowded cities, where the greatest efforts can scarcely procure more than the barest living. As our readers know, Detroit is one of the towns which evidently must attract to it a large commerce from its very favorable position. The Israelites already are numerous there, and appear to be doing well. We could only spend one day, the 14th of July, among them, owing to the fact that our engagements at home compelled us to be absent only about four weeks on a very long journey. We were kindly received by the Rev. Lipman Adler, who officiates as Hazan, Shochet, Teacher and Mohel, having thus ample engagements to fill up all his time. We visited the Synagogue with him; it is situated on a favorable position, only a little *too* high for comfort, though when you are once in it, you will find every thing well and properly arranged. They speak of making an effort soon to erect a suitable Synagogue, and we believe that many donations from Christian residents would be obtained for that purpose. We had no opportunity of visiting the school of the Rev. Mr. Adler, though from what we saw of the youths under his charge at his own house, we should judge that he would train them both well and correctly. We also learned that some *reforms* have been introduced into the worship, such as reading the Haphtorah in a German translation, and having some prayers in the same language in place of the Yekum Purkan; but we also perceived that the whole people were not satisfied with what had been done, and nearly all would resist any radical and farther changes. We trust that for the sake of the public peace, no more alterations will be attempted; for it is one thing to have order, but quite another to force measures on a part of the community which would necessarily provoke resistance. There appears, however, a good spirit to prevail among the few Israelites whom we had an opportunity to see, and we should judge that Mr. Adler has it in his power to effect much good by diffusing knowledge among the people, and we trust that we shall always hear that he has been duly supported in all the good he may undertake.—We promised to be present when the new Synagogue is dedicated; and we shall, with pleasure, keep our word whenever we are called on, which we trust will be before many years.

VI RABBI LIEBMAN ADLER WARNS DETROIT JEWS NOT TO BUY MEAT FROM UNAUTHORIZED DETROIT SHOCHET

(The Occident, *Vol. 17, pp. 491-492, January, 1859*)

DETROIT.—RELIGIOUS NOTICE.

הורעה לעוברים ושבים מבני עמנו הנזהרים לאכול בשר נבלה וטרפה:

יהודי אחד מתושבי עירנו מאיר ווייס שמו עמד ימים כבירים ברחוב העיר בשבת כעוברא דחול בחנותו למכור סחורתו והלך בשוקי העיר לארכה ולרחבה למכור אותה ויהי כאשר ראה שחלול שבת לא הביא ברכה לתוך ביתו התחיל לשחט ולמכר שחיטתו במקולין ושטו העם ולקחו ואכלו משחיטתו והכשר עודנו בין שניהם · והא״ש הזה לא היה לו קבלה משום בר סמכא בארץ הזאת וגם לא הראה לי או לשום אדם אשר לו יד לקרא ולהבין לשון עברית קבלתו אשר לו לפי דבורו כהארץ אשר יצא משם ככר כמו ד׳ או ה׳ שנים ולפי הוראת פיו ועדות אנשי מכירו לא היה מימיו שוחט מוחזק ומורגל רק למד לפני צאתו מארץ מולדתו לצורך שעה ולומד זקן ידוע ששכחה קרובה · ואחרי אשר הותכחיו בדברים ערבים והתריתי בו ולא שמע עבר עליו הכרוז בבה״כ בהסכמת פרנסי קהלתנו ששחיטתו היא נבלה וטרפה · אבל גם בזאת לא חזר מרשעתו · ופיו הכשילו להודות שאיננו מוכשר לקבלה עד עתה ולהשיב על השאלות אשר ישאלו לו אבל אחרי אשר תמצא ידו די זה ילך אל רבני צינציננאטי לכור הבחינה · וכאשר שמעתי זאת כתבתי אל מכירי דר׳ וויס מעשה שהי׳ כאשר היתה · ועתה האיש ההוא שם לדרך פעמיו ואתו כתב יקר שהרותא מהכת אוהבי בשרו אל הרב הניכר לאמר הקבל אותו וקדשתו ומשנה כסף נתנו בידו וצידה לדרכו ואחרי חזירתו שמעתי אומרים שקבלתו אתו לא ידעתי מי שם אותה בשקו והמכשלה הזאת תחת ידו · ומחדש הוא הולך הרוג בקר ושחוט צאן ומריר מביא מארה לבית יהודים אשר עד עתה בכשרות ינהגו · כי אף אם נאמר שעדות פיו לא הכשילו כי אין אדם משים עצמו רשע ונחזיקנו גם עתה אם אמת אתו שעמד בכור הבחינה למפרע בחזקת כשרות · זיל קרי בי׳ רב הוא ששחיטת מחלל שבת בפרהסיא נבלה וטרפה וגם רגלים לדבר שלא עשה תשובה אף אם יכלה עתה רגלו מן השוק כי נראה בעליל שהוא שובת עתה לבצע כסף כאשר חלל לפנים למצוא חפצו:

ועתה אליכם אישים אקרא ואודיע לכל החרדים על דבר התורה בבואם הנה שלא יסערו בבית איש יהודי עד שיבררו מאיזו מקולין הם לוקחים בשר מאכלם:

ק״ק דטראיט לסדר ויבא לבן באהל יעקב תרי״ט לפ״ק

ליעבמאן אדלער הכהן:

VII RABBI ISAAC M. WISE VISITS DETROIT AND CONGREGATION BETH EL

(The Israelite, *Vol. 6, pp. 62-63, August 26, 1859*)

DETROIT.—Last week, for the first time, we visited Detroit, the metropolis of Michigan, a fine and lively city with wide and regular avenues, handsome buildings, romantic vicinity and an active, industrious population. The site of Detroit is so level, that one can view the land for miles up the lake, down the river and into the interior of Michigan. General Cass, one of the wealthiest men of the city, has an old residence here, which, the ground excepted, is worth about $500. This is the general's homestead. A Frenchman of this city, who is worth millions, lives in a frame house that is worth about $200, the ground not included. Several more wealthy men thus retard the progress of the city, still it improves rapidly, notwithstanding the damages done to all the lake cities by the rail roads.

About sixty families of our people live in this city united in a congregation. Few of them are actually rich, none are actually poor. They follow different pursuits and are concerned in almost all branches of city trade. Most all of them are young and active men. Some of them play a prominent part in politics, and are very popular.

The Rev. L. ADLER is the popular minister of this congregation.. He attempted successfully to improve divine service by his lectures, exegetic expositions of the biblical sections read every Sabbath, and by omitting from the liturgy such prayers as belong to by-gone ages. Three times a week Mr. A. gives instruction to the young in the religion of our fathers.—In consequence of Mr. A's being *Schochet* and *Mohel* he can not attend as fully as he desires to the functions of a teacher. Our brethren of Detroit have no Synagogue of their own and no expectation to get one very soon.—There is not that enterprise and energy in congregational affairs among our brethren of Detroit as among the rest of our Western congregations. They need a synagogue, a school, a benevolent society, and they could have all these with but little exertion on the part of the leading members. Several of them told us they would contribute several hundred dollars toward the building of a new synagogue; this is the case especially with Messrs. Breslauer, Sykes and others, if the matter would be agitated.

We preached there Sabbath before last to a large auditory and with the help of God we hope to have cast a blessed seed on a fertile soil. We return our thanks to our brethren of Detroit for the kind treatment we experienced in their midst, and especially to our friendly host Mr. and Mrs. Trounstine.

VIII INVITATIONS TO SOCIAL GATHERINGS BY BETH EL MEMBERS IN THE 1860's

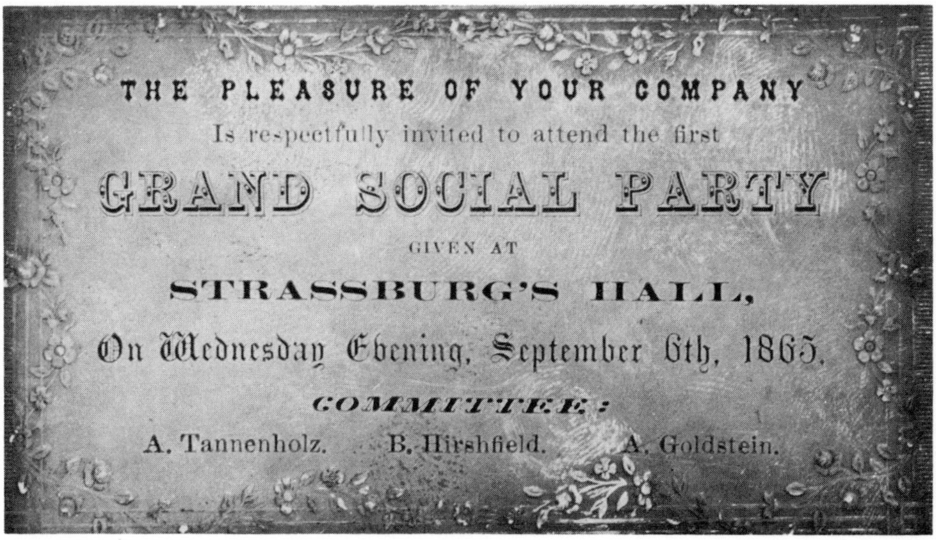
THE PLEASURE OF YOUR COMPANY
Is respectfully invited to attend the first
GRAND SOCIAL PARTY
GIVEN AT
STRASSBURG'S HALL,
On Wednesday Evening, September 6th, 1865.
COMMITTEE:
A. Tannenholz. B. Hirshfield. A. Goldstein.

SOCIAL PARTY.
You are respectfully invited to attend a Social Party, at the
URANIA THEATRE,
Wednesday, Dec. 28, 1864.
E. H. VAN BAALEN. L. M. FRIEDMAN.

IX ACCOUNT OF THE DEDICATION OF THE RIVARD STREET SYNAGOGUE

(The Detroit Tribune and Advertiser, *August, 1861*)

THE CITY.

Religious Intelligence.

DEDICATION OF THE HEBREW SYNAGOGUE. —The Hebrew Synagogue was dedicated yesterday. It is a neat substantial building, the inside arrangement being, with the exception of the holy arch, so near like our churches, that no description of it need be given.

The sermon of Rev. Dr. Wise, who preaches in a classical language, is equalled by no German in this country, with the exception of Judge Sallo and Schurz. Not the least interesting was the entry into the Synagogue of the celebrated J. J. Benjamin, the great oriental traveler, the author of the great work "Eight Years in Asia and Africa." He has just arrived in town from an overland trip from California, having thereby concluded his voyage around the world, and hastened to the synagogue to meet his not less celebrated friend Dr. Wise.

At 3 o'clock P. M. the ceremonies commenced with a Hebrew song by the choir accompanied by a melodeon, during which Rev. Mr. Lasar, Mr. S. Freedman and Mr. Schloss carried the sacred scrolls of the law in procession through the Synagogue, preceded by six girls dressed in white, carrying burning wax tapers. Having reached the altar, the celebrated Rev. Dr. I. M. Wise, LL. D., opened the services with an English prayer. Several psalms were then sung by the choir, and the Rev. Dr. Lasar, after which the sacred scrolls were deposited in the arch of the covenant. The consecration hymn was then sung, and the Rev. Dr. Wise preached the dedication sermon, taking his text from the end of the 4th and 6th chapters of Isiah. He said the congregation deserved particular praise for having erected a monument to the ancient sacred cause of Judaism in the city of Detroit, being few in number, and in these hard times it certainly required heavy sacrifices to accomplish the object. But it might be said there are plenty of churches as there is, so inconsiderately plaid with oaths, sacred pledges and the honor of manhood, as we see it in our days. We might think religion has no influence, but it is not the fault of the churches, it is the fault of misconstruction in the churches. There is too much sectarianism and too little religion, too much dogmatism and too little moral truth. This house, however, shall be dedicated to the purpose of teaching you that the Lord is our righteousness, i. e., the object of our religion is to make men righteous, just, veracious, honest and truthful, generous, humane, and philosophic. The speaker then continued, philosophers say truth has no criterion, but the evidence of history is certainly undeniable, and three thousand years of history speak in our favor. He also reviewed the principal nationality of antiquity. Their religious and philosophic systems show how all the works of fiction fall to the ground, and truth stands triumphant. In every age the system defended by him was opposed by the majorities—by Paganism first, by the Greek and Roman philosophy, then by the church of the middle ages, but we never yielded, but stood our ground firmly, and will stand yet, when all these systems are gone, leaving behind them mere shadows, as Rome is of the Rome of antiquity. We have a principle to defend, a mission to perform, so the milenium of history said, and if the present age tells us we are wrong, as all the systems of past ages pretended, and we answer we may be right after all, for us thirty-five centuries of history speak.

The speaker then went through the peculiarities and doctrines appertaining to his system as the unity of God the perfection of the human race, the dominion of right—salvation by righeousness—universal salvation by the progress of arts, science and liberty—dwelling principally on the point that right should rule and not might—and freedom should be the standard-bearer of humanity and not oppression. This being the land of all truths and all fictions—a chaos from which will rise a new civilization—new arts—new science, new philosophy and a new world. It is for us to deposit our peculiar doctrines in this very chaos, a laven in the huge mass, to this purpose—Judaism—and also this Synagogue.

The speaker then, on behalf of Israel, consecrated the new edifice, and prayed for peace and Union in this great and glorious Republic.

After this the choir sung another hymn, when the Eev. Mr. Lasaer appeared in the pulpit and explained in German the object of the present occasion. He spoke in eloquent terms of the generosity of the congregation, the object of the great work accomplished—and the lessons which in future should be learned in this house of the Lord.

The Rev. Mr. Lasaer and the choir then concluded the solemnities by the usual rites of the Sabbath services. The whole was very impressive, the ceremonies very imposing—and the whole proved that the race of the prophets—the offspring of the Divine bards—is not yet extinct.

X ADVERTISEMENT FOR A RABBI IN THE ISRAELITE *OF AUGUST 6, 1864*

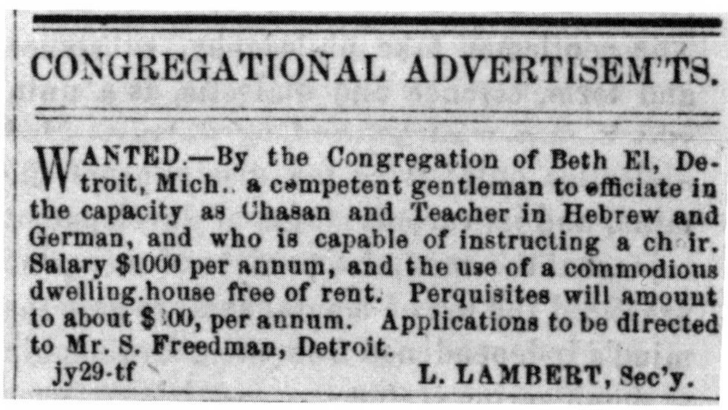

CONGREGATIONAL ADVERTISEM'TS.

WANTED.—By the Congregation of Beth El, Detroit, Mich.. a competent gentleman to officiate in the capacity as Chasan and Teacher in Hebrew and German, and who is capable of instructing a ch ir. Salary $1000 per annum, and the use of a commodious dwelling.house free of rent. Perquisites will amount to about $ 00, per annum. Applications to be directed to Mr. S. Freedman, Detroit.

jy29-tf L. LAMBERT, Sec'y.

XI ACCOUNTS OF THE DEDICATION OF THE WASHINGTON AVENUE (BOULEVARD) TEMPLE

(The Detroit Free Press, *August 31, 1867*)

(The Israelite, *Vol. 14, p. 6, September 6, 1867*)

TEMPLE DEDICATION.

The New Jewish Congregation Beth El.

Interesting Ceremonies of the Occasion.

During yesterday afternoon was witnessed the interesting and, in this city, unusual exercises of the dedication of a Jewish temple. The church edifice, on the corner of Washington avenue and Clifford street, recently purchased by the congregation Beth El, has been renovated and fitted up for the purpose, and was yesterday solemnly dedicated according to the rites of the Jewish faith. The interior arrangements of the altar and chancel, so unlike those of our Christian churches, may make some brief description of interest.

Just within the middle of the altar rail is the desk for the scrolls of the law when in use. From this rise semi-circular steps, upon the fourth of which, in rear of the first desk, is that of the minister, and upon either hand stands a highly ornamented candelabrum, each with the seven candlesticks bearing lighted candles. Upon the summit of the pyramid of steps, which are carpeted with crimson, stands the "Ark of the Covenant," inclosed by double columns on each side and concealed by a crimson veil in front, heavily ornamented with gold. The columns support an arch, beneath which is a circular stained glass window, upon which are represented the two tables of stone bearing the ten commandments in the Hebrew tongue. The veil of the ark also bears an inscription in the same characters. High above the ark depends from the ceiling a lamp, where within a blood-red globe burns the "perpetual light." The five distinctive colors used in the ornamentation, viz.: orange, blue, red, purple and green, are shown in the circular openings above the windows, and also in the highly gilt and embroidered coverings of the five books or scrolls of the Mosaic law.

Tickets had been issued to avoid an over-crowding of the house, which was comfortably filled, and about four o'clock the exercises commenced with the arrival at the door of the temple of

THE PROCESSION.

This consisted of damsels thirteen in number: Misses Barbara Hirschman, Clara Amberg, Fanny Hart, Sarah Van Baalen, Caroline Rosenberg, Rachael Van Baalen, Annie Simmons, Sarah Joseph, Sarah Hirsch, Louisa Van Baalen, Minnie Rindskoff, Cecilia Sloman and Hannah Laboid, all bearing wreaths and bouquets of flowers, and followed by members of the congregation bearing the five scrolls of the law, with the officers of the several committees. The Rabbi knocks at the door and says in Hebrew and English, "open unto us the gates of righteousness, that we may enter to praise the Lord." The procession then entered and marched up the platform, the congregation rising to their feet and the splendid choir singing, "Blessed be he who cometh in the name of the Lord" etc., when, the men having deposited the scrolls upon the desk, all took seats.

After the introductory prayer by Rev. I. M. Wise, of Cincinnati, the procession reformed, and proceeded slowly around the room, the damsels bearing the wreaths, and the men the scrolls, returning again to the desk, the choir singing the 42d psalm, which had been first read by the minister, Rev. Mr. E. Eppstein: "As the host panteth after the water brook, so panteth my soul after Thee, O God." At the close of the singing the President of the congregation, Mr. D. J. Workum, ascended to the step in front of the ark, and prepared to light the holy, perpetual fire, which he lighted, and pronounced a benediction: "Blessed be Thou, O Lord, our God, King of the Universe," etc. The minister then read the "Hallelujah," the 150th psalm, in Hebrew and English, which was then sung as the procession completed a second circuit around the temple, in the same order, preceded by the forerunner. The hymn, "Wir schau'n zu Dir," followed, after which Rev. Mr. Eppstein, minister of the congregation, delivered the following discourse, taking for his subject the proposition: "The House of God to unite all mankind."

Jesaias 66. 18. "For I know their works and their thoughts; the time shall come that I will gather all nations and tongues, and they shall come to see my glory."

Blessed be the Most High who has given us power to erect this house which we have set apart to His service, and blessed be the Most High, who in His kindness has favored me to take an active part therein.

It is a happy gala day to the members of Beth El and when they turn their eyes toward Heaven, they will surely pronounce with me the benediction: "Blessed be Thou, Lord our God, King of the universe, who is good, well doeth good.

Blessed be the Most High, who has been with us and enabled us to succeed in our undertakings; hallowed be He for His kindness and sanctified be His name, for He has protected, guarded and enabled us to dedicate to His name this house.

So, then, be this edifice consecrated to the Most High and His service.

Be it sanctified to the living God; to the everlasting God; to the Omnipotent; may His spirit rest upon it and His countenance hallow it to Israel and mankind.

It is a gratifying thought to us mortals to be able to dedicate to Him "who has planted the earth and expanded the heavens," a place where He might be nigh unto us when we pray, where He might hear the more readily our supplications and thanksgivings. Although we know that "the heavens are His throne and the earth His footstool," still cling to the idea that places like this are hallowed by His spirit, and well be it so.

We mortals know that His spirit cannot be confined to place nor time, but a place like this, where we feel His presence—a place like this, where we devote ourselves unto Him and His service—and a day like the Sabbath, which we have set apart to serve Him both place and time—we call holy, for both bring us in nearer relationship to Him, our Heavenly Father.

But it is not enough to know or feel, that a place like this is sanctified; it is not enough to be convinced, that the father of mankind reveals himself here unto his children. This thought needs vitality, it needs to be carried into life.

It is stated from the Temple of Solomon, that the windows thereof were of uncommon make. They were wide on the outside and narrow on the inside To give evidence that a Temple of God should not receive its light from the world, but should impart it to the world.

Churches, temples, places of worship, should take an active part in the mission which is assigned to mankind, to make the earth an Eden, where all men shall live in peace and harmony together. Therefore I repeat, "*The House of God, to unite mankind.*"

Jesiah in his speech against the vain desire to sanctify a spot to the service of the Most High, says: "Where is a house that ye build unto me, where is a place for my rest? For all those things hath my hand made, and all those things have been! is the declaration of the Eternal. The Heavens are my throne and the earth my footstool." Our sages add thereto a wise word in saying, "He is the soul, the spirit that fills the whole universe;" but all the universe cannot contain Him; every spot in Heaven and on earth, and all created hosts are full of His spirit. His spirit vibrates everywhere, and it would be a vain desire to think that a building like this should be favored more than the rest of the earth, and be in particular a sanctified spot to Him, and invested by His spirit, which is everywhere. The main object of a place of worship is contained in the word of Jesiah: "For I know their works and their thoughts; the time will come that I will gather all nations and all tongues; and they shall come to see my glory."

The house of God to unite mankind. I. In brotherly love. II. In one voice. III. To glorify the Lord. The All Merciful bless my efforts to explain this to His praise.

1. The house of God, to unite mankind in brotherly love.

"For I know their works and thoughts." When Solomon had dedicated his temple in the presence of Israel; when the glory of God was seen therein, he knelt and prayed: "And also unto Him, who is not a son of thy people, the stranger who shall come from afar to pray unto Thee in this house; for the sake of Thy great name; mayest Thou in Heaven, from the place of Thy abode, do according to the supplication of the stranger; that all the nations of the earth may know Thy name, learn to fear Thee and to recognize Thy name, by which this house, which I have built, is called."

The example set by Solomon was followed by all the succeeding ages to this day. The Synagogues of Israel have been schools where brotherly love was taught. Within the sacred walls of a synagogue it was taught: "Love thy neighbor as thyself." This is the great object of the law. Even in the dark ages, when oppression rested heavy upon our fathers; when they were driven from nation to nation and from kingdom to kingdom; when even a grave was denied unto them; even then they could lament in their Synagognes, but in no instance did they forget that their oppressors were their brothers before God, and they prayed that their hearts might be enlightened—in the Lamentations which time has preserved, we find no hate, no revenge—hope is their principle feature, hope for the future.

The temples of Israel taught us to unite in brotherly love with mankind. Israel never did, nor never will seek to make proselytes, and still the law of Israel has made thousands of them; they do not bear the name—but they adhere to the teachings of Israel and have adopted the law of Judah, that there is but one God, that mankind is but one family and that churches, temples or places of worship are to unite them in brotherly love. "For I know "their works and their thoughts" sayeth the eternal.

Any man, Jew or Gentile, who enters his church or temple to praise the Lord in his way or manner and leaves hate to his fellow man does not live up to his law, for enlightened Christianity, as well as Judaism teach the doctrine: Man is the image of God, and there is but one God, that has created us alike.

The time has come that the various forms of

religions, which in the vital essence, are but one, do not any more shut the portals of their temples to the members of other sects; the time has come, which has trodden down the prejudice, as though a Jew pollutes a church; the time is passed when the two great sects of Christianity called each other infidels and closed doors and portals of places of worship to each other.

We are happy to live in a time and in a country where the word of our text has become true, for I know their works and their thoughts. It is known now that the church does not sanctify men, but the works and thoughts of man hallow the church, and there is no better work than to unite man to man; there is no better thought than the one "I am a link in the great family of mankind; we are brothers."

It is a sign of the dawn of happy days, that religion, progressing religion, commenced the move and opened wide the portals of its churches and temples and receives every one in love and affection; no more will we be asked after our creeds—as though these words make the man—but the works will be investigated, and if worthy of a brother's grasp, he may kneel at any altar and pray to His father, in his manner, without disturbing his neighbor, who prays to the same God in his manner; it is no longer any difference, whether the prayers are said in English, in German, in Hebrew, or in any other language, as long as the one who prays is conversant in it—it vibrates in every heart, it is felt in every bosom.

Blessed be the Almighty, who has, after a battle of nigh two thousand years, taught men and sects to dedicate churches and temples, not as a place of worship for a certain number of believers, but to mankind; the houses of God have at last, with few exceptions, become places where mankind meet as brethren, in love and peace.

Words and thoughts now sink the scale and not the creeds, which in many instances have not been felt nor obeyed.

So far have we arrived, but with this only the first point of progress is reached; we stand united; the good men are linked together hand in hand; they stand upon the ruins of darkness and prejudice, and the flag that waves above their heads bears the inscription "Light"—"Progress." These two words have become the battle-cry of the last centuries, and following them in the future to victory, we will ere long reach also the second prophecy of our text, that—

II. The houses of God are to unite mankind in one voice.

"The time will come that I will gather all nations and tongues." Once arrived at the point that we have now reached; that the houses of God unite mankind in brotherly love—the work will not cease, but in rapid succession the barriers of forms will be torn down, so that the human family united in love, will also be gathered into one voice—form. Up to our present age, the lover of truth could not look into the kernel of religion, for the shell that surrounded it, the many forms and ceremonies into which the truth was wrapped up, concealed the spark from view; but the work of unwrapping has commenced, and also here the churches and temples, and amongst them again the temples of Israel in the first rank, took the lead, the many forms that accumulated in the course of ages are abolished, and in their place the kernel became visible, so that now within the walls of our temples mankind may unite to praise the Lord in a simple manner, which has always been the aim of Judaism, but which was marred in the course of time.

It is the temple of Israel that takes its pride in reciting the following confession: "Hear, O Israel, the Lord our God, the Lord is one; and love thy neighbor as thyself;" as the two principal features of service.

But this alone will not suffice, the different churches, temples, and places of worship must learn the truth that it is their highest duty, and must be their highest ambition to bring mankind to unite in one voice.

The road is surveyed and it needs only leveling the ground, to build some tunnels, break through the rocks and mountains of prejudice and darkness, and the tracks may be safely laid.

The dawn of a brighter day has begun—there is a movement going the rounds in every religious sect and creed that travels onward to seek the light, and the longer they seek the more will love the antique form, and clothe itself in a mantle suitable to time that wraps the human family in its fold.

From the time of that great German reformer, Martin Luther, up to this day, the church has never, never ceased sifting and sifting—the dust is kept asunder from the seed, and this is it which I consider leveling the ground; there are yet prejudices and darkness to be overcome, mankind must again manage to pass on dry land over a red sea of intolerance and hate, before they will come to the point that the temples and places of worship will unite mankind in one voice—the movement is irresistible and "ONWARD" is the watchword, churches and temples, synagogues and chapels will take the lead, and following them will be carried the standard of the united human race, bearing the words: One God, One Family, One Form.

Once united in this noble trinity, it is the time of which Jesaias speaks: "the time will come that will gather all nations and tongues." United in their temples and houses of worship like one family in brotherly love and peace they will also be united in one form, so that they may—

III. "Come to glorify the Lord." "They shall come and see my glory." This is the third part of Jesaias' prophecy, and we can easily trace the connection of these points. The basis of all is brotherly love. This established and acknowledged, the religions will move onward, with the tendency to meet at a certain point. Essence of faith, this gained, the human race will come to see the glory of God as it is written:

"And the Lord shall be king over all the earth." "On that day the Lord alone shall be one, and His name shall be one."

To see the glory of God mankind must stand united as one family; one form must be taught in all temples, churches and places of worship. The names may differ, if the contents are those which enlightened Judaism and Christianity teaches—humanity. As long as hate, prejudice, darkness yet prevail on earth, man cannot see see the glory of the Most High, for his Shechina is only visible in a ray of light, and light excludes hate, prejudice and darkness. The more these abominations will be abolished, the nearer will we come to reach our destination.

Churches, temples, and houses of worship, my friends, ought to work and teach in this light, if these places will be worthy of the name and title—Houses of God.

A true Beth El, where we invoke the blessing of the Most High, must teach to unite mankind in brotherly love; in one form, with humanity for its foundation, to invoke the glory of God.

To this end may this temple be dedicated. May brotherly love be found here and so established. May the word of God be taught here, so that all its visitors may be able to concur therein, and may it finally become the means to draw nigh the glory and the blessing of God unto us and all mankind. Amen.

The passage of Scripture commencing "Restore tranquillity, O Lord, to the many thousands of Israel," was then read, followed by the reading of I. Kings viii., 54-61, "And it was so that when Solomon had made an end of praying all this prayer and supplication unto the Lord, he arose from before the altar of the Lord, from kneeling on his knees, with his hands spread up to Heaven."

The men then took the scrolls from the desk, and being seated in the front pew, the damsels decorated the same with wreaths and flowers, placing others on the desks and stands, when, the organ symphony being ended, the men bear their scrolls up the stone steps to the ark, where they are taken by the minister and deposited in the ark, the choir singing a portion of Psalm XXVII, "Raise your heads, O ye gates! and be raised high ye everlasting doors, and let the King of glory enter," etc. The minister, standing in front of and almost in the vail, says, "We praise Thee, O God! We acknowledge Thee to be the Lord," etc. The hymn, "Durch die Welt und ihre Heere schallet," etc., was then read and sung, after which the Rev. Dr. Wise delivered a fine dedication sermon of considerable length, reviewing the history of the sanctuary, its preservation and purposes, and above all the significant preservation of the Israelites for so many ages and through so much adversity; dating their existence from almost the earliest period of history, and destined to exist, in spirit at least, as long as history shall be written.

In closing he said: "Therefore, my beloved brethren, in consecrating this beautiful building to the service of the one and eternal God; in adding this edifice to the common sanctuary of Israel, you erect an additional rock of hope to light and truth; another depository of truth, of salvation, and happiness to all mankind; you add to the glorious future of our country and the redemption of God's children, therefore let us dedicate this house to the Most High, with fervent prayer, with holy devotion, with song and psalter. Rise brethren and assist me in dedicating this house to the One, Eternal and Sole God, to the everlasting truth which He revealed to Israel, by Moses and the prophets to the blessing of Israel and the happiness of our beloved country. Rise and invoke with me the name of the Ruler of the Universe."

Dr. Wise then pronounced the invocation and dedication rites in an impressive manner, addressing the Most High by repeating the several distinctive terms and attributes appropriate to his name as Governor and Ruler over all things.

The exercises were concluded with the usual Divine service of Sabbath evening, beginning with the Sabbath Psalm 92.

Dedication of the Temple Beth El, Detroit, August 30.

The congregation Beth El, of Detroit, was established in 1850 by some ten gentlemen, some of whom, like Cohn, Schlossman, Silberman, Trounstein and others, are still members thereof. Having purchased a lot for the purpose of burying the dead, they organized for regular meetings of divine worship; first in the upper loft of Mr. Silberman's store and then opposite the market-house two stories high, until six years ago they bought a church and adjoining house and dedicated it to a synagogue. Rev. L. Adler, now of Chicago, was the first minister of note in this congregation. Rabbi Isidor Kalisch was here several years and introduced the *Minhag America.*

Meanwhile, however, this congregation has grown up to a large and influential one. The synagogue became too small and was too far out of town, so that they wanted a new temple. Happily a church offered for sale in the very heart of the city, on the corner of one of the finest and most quiet private streets—corner of Washington avenue and Cliffton street—a Baptist church, 60 by 90 feet, a good strong brick building, with a fine front yard, which makes a good appearance. The house was purchased for $17,000, and $10,000 were spent in improvement and repairs, so that it looks now beautifully painted in fine fresco, with furniture of black walnut and crimson cushions, the ark in the style of the New York temple, with the two chandeliers of seven lamps precisely as in the Cincinnati temple, pulpit, reader's table, and all surroundings in a very fine style. The building itself is high, airy, with windows on four sides, and decorated in the best taste. The seats are arranged in family pews. There is but one gallery for the organ and the choir. The house is highly respectable and an honor to the congregation. The basement is furnished for school-rooms, although it is not well constructed for the purpose, it having neither light, nor room and air enough.

The present officers of the congregation are: Rev. Mr. Eppstein, Minister; Messrs. D. J. Workum, President; Jacob Silberman, V. P.; S. Schloss, Treasurer; Simon Cohen, Secretary; S. Freedman, S. Heavenrich, M. C. Fechheimer and J. Van Baalen, Trustees.

As chairmen of the various committees are mentioned, Simon Heavenrich, chairman of the committees on building and on reception; D. J. Workum, chairman on committee of arrangements; M. C. Fechheimer and Simon Freedman, committee of printing.

A programme of divine service for the dedication was issued not exactly suiting our taste. Two German hymns without any reference to dedication are placed in the pamphlet between the Hebrew and English, and part of the 42d Psalm is introduced without any cause. The arrangement of the circuits, the ascension, and decorating the scrolls of the Law were taken from the pamphlet published at the dedication of the Cincinnati temple.

Previous to the dedication, prayers were offered up in the old place of worship; then the scrolls of the law were removed to the basement of the new building. Three o'clock P. M. the doors were opened and people holding cards of invitation were admitted. Four o'clock P. M. precisely the ceremonies commenced, and were conducted until half-past six, including the regular service of Sabbath eve. It was all done in the best style. Twelve girls dressed in white and bearing flower wreaths and boquets preceded the bearers of the Law, the rabbis and officers followed. The choir discoursed classical music in a very fine style, and Rev. Mr. Eppstein led in excellent taste, and with a splendid voice. The three circuits were conducted well, and the perpetual light was lit by Mr. Workum, the Parnass. The first discourse, published in a Detroit daily paper of Saturday last, was delivered by Rev. Mr. Eppstein, and we will re-produce it in our next number, in order to introduce the gentleman to our readers. The scrolls of the Law were carried and deposited in the ark by the oldest members of the congregation after the girls had tastefully decorated it. The reader will find our dedication sermon on the 4th page of this paper. The whole service came off in the very best style, highly honorable to all connected with the arrangement and fully satisfactory to the large congregation, among whom we noticed the citizens and clergymen of nearly all denominations in this city, the adjutants of the Governor and other officials.

The day of dedication will long be cherished in the memory of the congregation. It was a fine gala day to the glory of God and to the honor of Israel.

"At the evening, at Merrill Hall," says the *Advertiser* and *Tribune*, "a festival of the members of the congregation and invited guests was held. A fine supper was served and the occasion was one of great enjoyment." It was one of those German festivals with that pleasant social tone of hearty gladness and diverse entertainments.

In the morning, during divine service, which, with some additions, is the same as in the Cincinnati temple, the choir sang excellently, the Rev. Mr. Eppstein conducted the divine service in an impressive manner, and the congregation was very devout. We preached in German on Isaiah lxvi, 1 and 2.

Sunday, two o'clock P. M., the school was opened in the new school-house, under the tuition of Rev. Mr. Eppstein and Mr. Brown, and presided over by Mr. B. Prell. The house is somewhat too small for the pupils. The attendance was large, addresses were made, and parents and children were well pleased. In the evening we visited the Bene Berith Lodge, and saw the brethren, whom we addressed on the subject of the order, especially the proposed "Orphans' Home."

On the whole, we have to say that we were well pleased with all we saw and heard in this community. There is peace, harmony and good will there. A fine spirit of piety and progress reigns and promises a fine future. The Israelites live in the best understanding and harmony with their Christian neighbors, and are highly esteemed as men, citizens and merchants. May it always be so.

We can not conclude this account without mentioning the exertions of Mr. A. J. Franklin, who organized and, since then, conducts gratuitously the fine choir of this temple. Formerly there was an *unisono* choir in the synagogue; but Mr. Franklin introduced scientific music, nay, classical music, from the pure motive of attachment to the sacred cause and to the fine art; for he is a business man, otherwise engaged, but he cares aught for sacrifices to carry out this laudable enterprise. The choir is, indeed, excellent, as good as any in New York, Cincinnati or elsewhere. This deserves particular thanks.

XII LETTER OF ISAAC HART, A MEMBER OF BETH EL, TO RABBI ISAAC LEESER, 1867

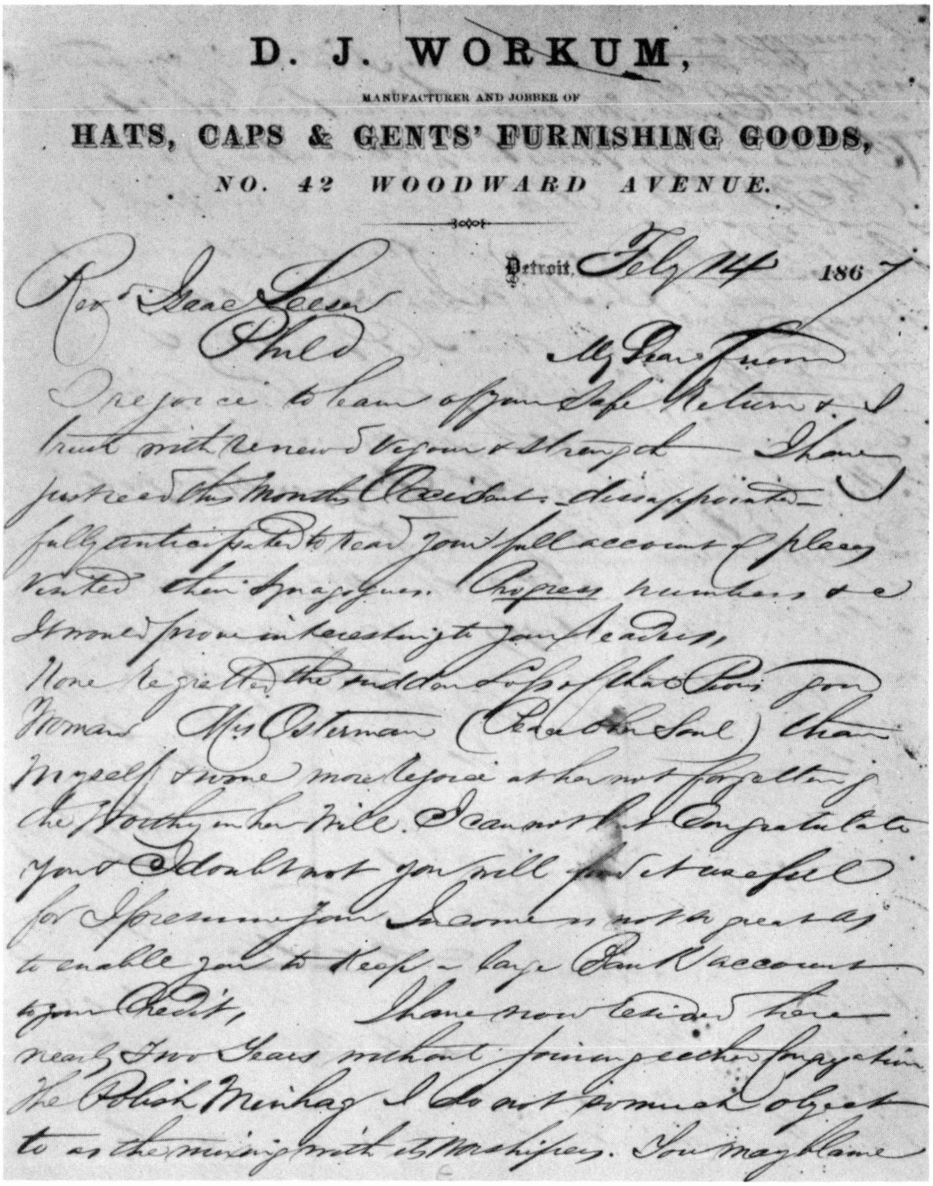

D. J. WORKUM,
MANUFACTURER AND JOBBER OF
HATS, CAPS & GENTS' FURNISHING GOODS,
NO. 42 WOODWARD AVENUE.

Detroit, Feby 14 1867

Revd Isaac Leeser
Phild

My Dear Friend

I rejoice to learn of your Safe Return & I trust with renewed Vigour & Strength. I have just read this Months Occident, disappointed. I fully anticipated to read your full account of places visited their Synagogues, Progress, numbers &c. It would prove interesting to your Readers.

None Regretted the sudden Loss of that Pious good Woman Mrs Osterman (Peace to her Soul) than Myself & none more rejoice at her not forgetting the Worthy in her Will. I cannot but Congratulate you & I doubt not you will find it useful for I presume your Income is not so great as to enable you to keep a large Bank account to your Credit. I have now resided here nearly Two Years without joining either Congregation The Polish Minhag I do not so much object to as the mixing with its Worshipers. You may blame

me but were you here in my Situation you would
& the same. My immediate kindest & best Friends
(Friends not only in Words but noble actions) are those
Connected with the Reform Synagogue my Visits &
Visitors are the same while the others I know not
& from what I see (them care not to know
I have at times visited their Synagogue & the Service
is not what I admire. Give me the Portuguese
Service above all others for Solemnity. The
Minister of the Mark St Synagogue Mr Epstein
is a very talented Man He Preaches every Sabbath
alternately English & German this Synagogue was well
attended. He has that happy oratory of making his
hearers feel his Words & frequently the whole audience
are in tears at the Strength of his inspiring Words
The Polish Synagogue is fairly attended they have a Hazan
but no Preacher, Miss Hart & family unite
with myself in kind regards
With your Friend
Isaac Hart
We have formed a Social Club of about 40 Members,
Cards, Dramatic Performances Lectures Concerts Balls
&c. In the Performances in English some in German
by the Members their Wives & Sisters was played equal to any Stage

2-14-1862

XIII RABBI'S SELECTION COMMITTEE OF CONGREGATION BETH EL WRITES TO DR. KAUFMANN KOHLER, JUNE 9, 1869

(1)

Detroit. Mich. June 9th 1869

Sr. Ehrwürden Herrn Dr K. Kohler in Fürth

Hochgeachteter Herr Dr.!

Ihre Zuschrift vom 7. Mai, an Hr. Dr. Lilienthal in C. wurde den Unterzeichneten unterbreitet, mit der praktischen Andeutung sich in direkten Briefwechsel mit Ihnen, geehrter H. Dr., zu setzen, was sowohl in semi-offizieller Weise als Committee der isr. Gemeinde Detroits, als auch in Gemässheit der Empfehlungen der HH. Drs. Lilienthal & Felsenthal, mit besonderer persönlicher Hochachtung hiermit geschieht. – Die zur Einleitung u. Erklärung einiger offenherziger Erläuterungen, die zu machen wir uns um so mehr gedrungen fühlen, als wir die Responsibilität, einen so gut empfohlenen Mann über's weite Meer zu rufen, nur dann über=nehmen möchten, wenn ein gegenseitiges Verständniss der Umstände damit als thunlich, voraussetzt würde.

Unsere Gemeinde "Beth El" (es sind noch mehrere jüd. Gemeinden hier) besteht ungefähr 19 Jahre, fing, wie die meisten älteren amerik. isr. Gemeinden, mit den geringsten Mitteln eine Fortsetzung des orthodox jüdischen Synagogen Gottesdienstes an, wie sich die, von allen Theilen Deutschlands (welches sich bis zur Weichsel erstreckt) kommenden Mitglieder eben über den „Hergebrachten" einigen konnten. Diese Verhältnisse sowohl als das gegenseitige, sich an Confessions=wesen gewöhnende Individuum, gab den fungirenden Rabbi's Gelegenheit „Reform" einzuführen, so dass unsere Congregation, die als eine Reform=

gemeinde dasteht, individuell nichts destoweniger alle Schattirü[ngen]
von rituellen Ansichten in sich schließt, die sich vom Orthodoxismus
einerseits bis zum religiösen Indifferentismus andererseits erstreck[en]
u. dennoch als Gemeinde der Reform huldigt. — Die älteren Mitg[lieder]
die orthodox, werden immer weniger oder fügen sich passiv in den Neu-
=erungen, so daß Sie zwar keine "junge emporstrebende Gemeinde
"hier fänden, die sich naturgemäß leicht mit einer ~~...~~ von frischem
"Ernst beseelten leitenden jungen Kraft verständigen würde" —
aber dennoch ein Feld hier finden dürften, welches für solch er-
habenen Ansichten, wie Sie H. Dr. sie aussprechen, wenn auch noch nicht
ganz kultivirt doch kulturfähig wäre. —

Im Verhältnisse zum Gottesdienste vor 19 Jahren zurück haben wir
Riesenfortschritte gemacht und möchten Ihnen in Folgendem die gegen-
++ wärtig übliche Weise zur Notiz bringen:

Wir haben den sog. "Minhag America v. Dr. I. M. Wise" eingeführt, solch[er]
Minhag ist ein Compromisse der Sulzbacher Thephilla mit den Forderung[en]
der jüngstvergangenen Neuzeit — die Gebete bedeutend abgekürzt,
viele ganz weggelassen, jedoch alles hebräisch, ברכו, שמע, מי כמכה & קדושה
werden vor dem Chor mit Orgelbegleitung rezitirt, ebenso wird das Aus u. [Ein-]
heben durch einen jüdischen Choral eingeleitet und die Predigt beginnt u. schließt
mit einem deutsch. resp. engl. Liede, je nachdem deutsch oder engl. ~~vorgetragen~~ gepredigt wi[rd]
Die Haftorah wird nur deutsch oder engl. vorgetragen, das Lesen der Thora
in 3 jähr. Cyclus hebräisch — Aufrufen und Mischeberachmachen findet nicht statt,
der President & vice President stehen dem Rabbi zur Seite. Für besonderen Geleg[enheiten]

heiten (den ersten Tempelbesuch von Wöchnerinnen, Neuvermählter, am Neumond etc)
sind passende deutsche oder engl. Gebete sporadisch, und dem Rabi überlassen.
Für ר"ה & י"כ wurde bis jetzt noch immer das Heidenheimsche Machsor, mit
Weglassung langer Piutim, benützt und es gibt noch immer einige Leute in unserer
Gemeinde die שחרית, מוסף &c. "ohren". die vorgenannte Gebetordnung hat
Bezug auf שבת, für י"ט (Yomtoff) sind nur unbedeutende Zusätze in der Minhag
America Thephille eingeschaltet und alle hebr. Gebete werden mehr im dekla-
matorischen Tone als im alten Singsang (Niegun) vom Rabiner vorgetragen.
der Hut ist noch auf dem Kopf – der Tallas ist herunter – Frauen u Männer sitzen
beisammen. Bis vor ungefähr 6 Monaten unter-
hielt unsere Gemeinde eine deutsch eng. hebr. Elementarschule unter dem
Rabi mit Hilfslehrer, wo auch der Religionsunterricht ertheilt wurde.
die Gemeinde ließ die Elementarschule fallen, da keine bessere Resultate erzielt
wurden als die öffentl. Schulen liefern – der Religionsunterricht für die Jugend
ist jetzt ganz dem Rabbiner übergeben und man erwartet daß Samstag
Nachmittag u. Sonntag Vormittag derselbe sich dieser Pflicht unterzieht;
die Kinder verstehen, mit sehr geringen Ausnahmen, das Deutsche; obgleich
das Englische bei vielen als ausschließliche Umgangssprache benützt wird.
Sollte dies am Anfange eine Bürde für den Religionslehrer sein, so
würde auch andrerseits dies Englischreden der Kinder demselben vielfach Gelegenheit geben, sich selbst die Landessprache bald anzueignen. Darauf
können Sie sich wohl verlassen daß jedem Gemeindeglied daran zu thun
ist, daß der Jugend eine religiös-sittliche Erziehung beigebracht wird
u. die Majorität der aus ungefähr 70 Mitgliedern bestehenden Gemeinde

zu einer freien, humanen Entwickelung des Judenthums unter der wissenschaftlichen Leitung eines Mannes, der für weitern Fortschritt auf dem Felde der Verbesserung jüdischer Zustände wissenschaftliche u. theologische Gründe beizubringen wüßte, gern die Hand bieten; jedenfalls sind eine Majorität der die Gemeinde<u>lasten</u> — tragenden Mitglied von diesem Sinne beseelt.

Die <u>finanzielle</u> Lage der Gemeinde erlaubt nicht die Besoldung eines Rabbiners zwei thousand dollars ($2000.–) zu übersteigen. — Eine drei 3 jährige Anstellung sowie Vergütung mäßiger Reisekosten würde bewilligt werden. —

Detroit ist eine hübsche Stadt v. ohngefähr 80,000 E. unser Tempel neu an einer der schönsten Straßen gelegen, u in jeder Beziehung ein anständig würdiges Gotteshaus.

Ein <u>lediger</u> Mann kann in den <u>besten</u> <u>christlichen</u>* Hotels für ca $45. pr Monat Kost & Logis bekommen, jedenfalls würde es nicht mehr, ja bedeutend weniger in einer anständigen <u>jüdischen</u> Familie kosten.

Weniger als obiges Salair reicht hin, in theuren Kriegsjahren unsern Rabbiner mit ziemlich großer Familie, anständig zu unterhalten und stehen einem tüchtigen Manne, der sich noch Privatinstruktionen widmen möchte, schöne Nebeneinkünfte offen, ebenso bringen Hochzeiten anständige Honorare.

Hochgeehrter Hr Dr. Wir fühlten uns berufen, Sie mit vorstehendem bekannt zu machen, wenn Ihnen die statuirten Verhältnisse zusagen so bitten wir uns Ihre Ansichten, resp Zustimmung <u>baldigst</u> mitzutheilen im bejahenden Falle dürfte ein Ruf zur Rabbinerstelle in Detroit die Folge sein. Da dies mehr in Ihrem Interesse als dem der Gemeinde geschrieben ist und die Stelle am 1st Sept vakant wird, wir einen Rabbiner für die Feiertage sehr zu haben wünschen, bitten wir um baldige Ant[wort]

Hochachtungsvoll

Martin Butzel
M. Cohen
H. Reman
[illegible]

Committee

Adresse: Martin Butzel
of E S Heineman & Co, Detroit Mich.
North America.

* Der Preis v. Kost & Logis in den besten christlichen Hotels würde blos deshalb angeführt, weil solche der [illegible] ist der [illegible] bemerkt wird, u bitten solches nicht zu [illegible]. —

APPENDIX

XIV LETTER OF NOTIFICATION TO DR. HENRY ZIRNDORF OF HIS ELECTION AS RABBI OF CONGREGATION BETH EL

Detroit Mich. June 9th 1876

Dr. H. Zirndorf
Münster, Westfalen

Dear Sir, it affords me much personal pleasure to inform you of your election by unanimous vote of the congregation as our spiritual guide for the term of three years, as provided in the contract herewith enclosed. On June 5th a cable dispatch was sent by me which read "Dr. Zirndorf, Münster, Prussia, Elected, Butzel." No doubt the same has come in your possession in due time. It is perhaps useless to say anything further in relation to the contract, inasmuch as you will perceive that my letter of March 22/76 and your answer thereto of April 11/76 are the basis of the engagement as part of the contract—for your information would, however, explain that our congregation owns real estate worth twenty-five thousand dollars—and being an incorporated society—consequently our engagements are considered good and collectable by law—although I cannot conceive it possible that such a state of affairs can overtake congr. Beth El. I merely mention this for your satisfaction and the same time state it would be a superfluity to have the contract signed by either the German or American Consulate—we look upon a civil contract as binding our congregation—and shall accept your own individual signature as sufficient—in point of fact we hold moral obligations as the strongest tie to any agreement—with that view we intend to carry out our part. Although the contract is silent about a yearly "two weeks" vacation, let me assure you, you will find no difficulty to obtain it inasmuch as during the hot summer months a general vacation to professional gentlemen are usually granted. In relation to travelling expenses our congregation has allowed only two hundred dollars in gold—this sum may appear insufficient to you—but in consideration of a very fair salary offered many of the members are of opinion that you will in course of time not regret to have come amongst us and find satisfactory results, nevertheless. The time fixed from October first next, we expect does meet your views (the term of the present incumbent expires on November 1st next) the same time should you intend to reach Detroit in September you will find gentlemen whose hospitality will furnish a stopping place for yourself and your good lady—until you have arranged your own household affairs. All such personal effects not needed on your journey, you can pack into cases (iron hoop strapped) and forward as freight in *care* of *any* of the *agents* appearing on the margin of the enclosed card—mark the cases with your name in care of Merchants Dispatch Transportation Company, New York *"Bonded to Detroit Mich."* The Merchants Dispatch Company will advance the ocean freight and is perfectly responsible. Detroit being a port of entry, you can get your property here, after your arrival without much trouble. I would suggest to sell furniture and all bulky articles, but retain all linens, wearing apparels, bedding and such articles which are easily packed. Your books, particularly "new ones" have either your name written or stamped on them. The route you can select via Havre, Bremen or Hamburg *to New York* is best and most direct. After landing on the dock in New York or Hoboken, there is Raabs Express, which will take care of your baggage and deliver such to any address in New York City you may please to give. I would recommend the Arlington House on 14th Street, or the Prescott House on Broadway for you to stop. Mr. Stein of the Arlington will use you & family well. From New York buy tickets to Detroit direct. Ask for New York Central via Suspension Bridge and Great Western Railroad—it only takes twenty-four (24) hours travel by cars to your destination. If you will inform me in time by which ocean line and name of steamer when leaving port in Europe &c., very likely some of our people can arrange to meet you at the steamer's arrival in New York, thereby render you such assistance as may prove acceptable to you. Our sec'y Mr. Fechheimer is absent from home and requested me to mention about your inquiry whether to bring a servant girl along or not—I would say although as a rule servants are not so good here as in Europe—yet if you should incur the trouble & expenses to bring one—she might not stay & remain any length of time with you—consequently cannot advise you to undertake the risk.

You will pardon me for calling your respectful attention to a matter concerning congregations and ministers alike, a number of Hebrew scholars in this country forming two factions, some of the Eastern gentlemen working in opposition against their Western brethren and institutions—both parties claim to be reformers and the true champions of enlightment & knowledge—but these pen and ink warriors indulge in personalities to a great extent,—not always creditable to themselves nor to the laymen. Almost every new arrival of professional gentlemen connected with Jewish institutions in this country is made aware of the advantages to belong or take sides with one or the other party by their representations. I take the liberty to caution you against either upon arrival in New York. You will have ample opportunities in future to judge for yourself upon the true merits of the pretentions or reality of their claims &c. without any undue influence brought on from motives to serve their own purposes. Again asking your pardon for my style of writing but rest assured my intentions are to convey such information as may seem best to serve your interests in all regards. My having been absent from home on business has delayed this letter a few days beyond my intention. With highest esteem for yourself & family &c.

I remain

Most respectfully yours,
Martin Butzel, Pres.
Congr Beth El

XV PROGRAM OF THE ELEVENTH COUNCIL OF UNION OF AMERICAN HEBREW CONGREGATIONS AND DELEGATE'S BADGE

July 9-11, 1889

(At this Council the Central Conference of American Rabbis was founded)

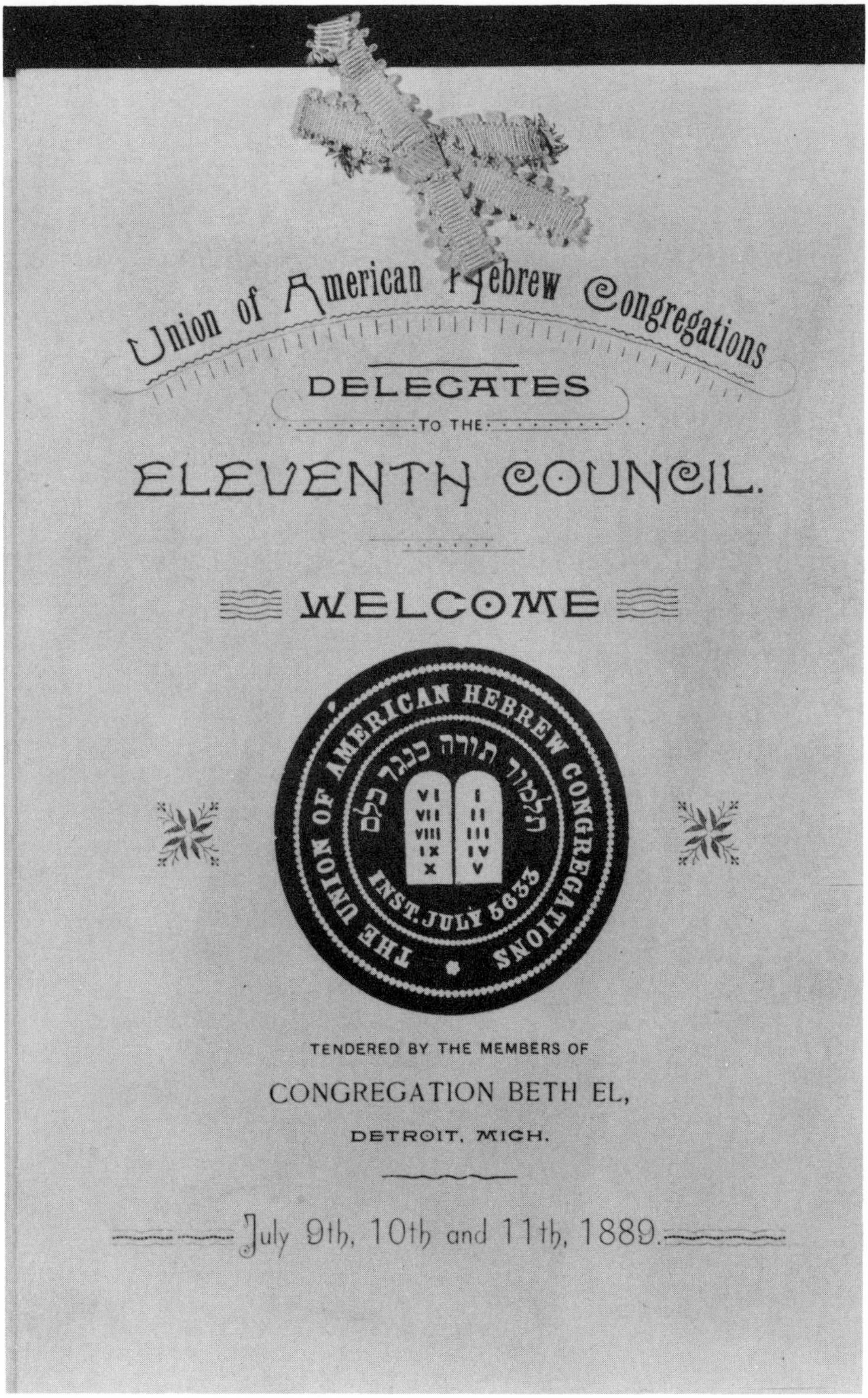

Union of American Hebrew Congregations

DELEGATES

TO THE

ELEVENTH COUNCIL.

WELCOME

THE UNION OF AMERICAN HEBREW CONGREGATIONS

תלמוד תורה כנגד כלם

INST. JULY 5633

TENDERED BY THE MEMBERS OF

CONGREGATION BETH EL,

DETROIT, MICH.

July 9th, 10th and 11th, 1889.

XVI PROGRAM OF THE SEMI-CENTENNIAL CELEBRATION OF CONGREGATION BETH EL

November 29, 1900

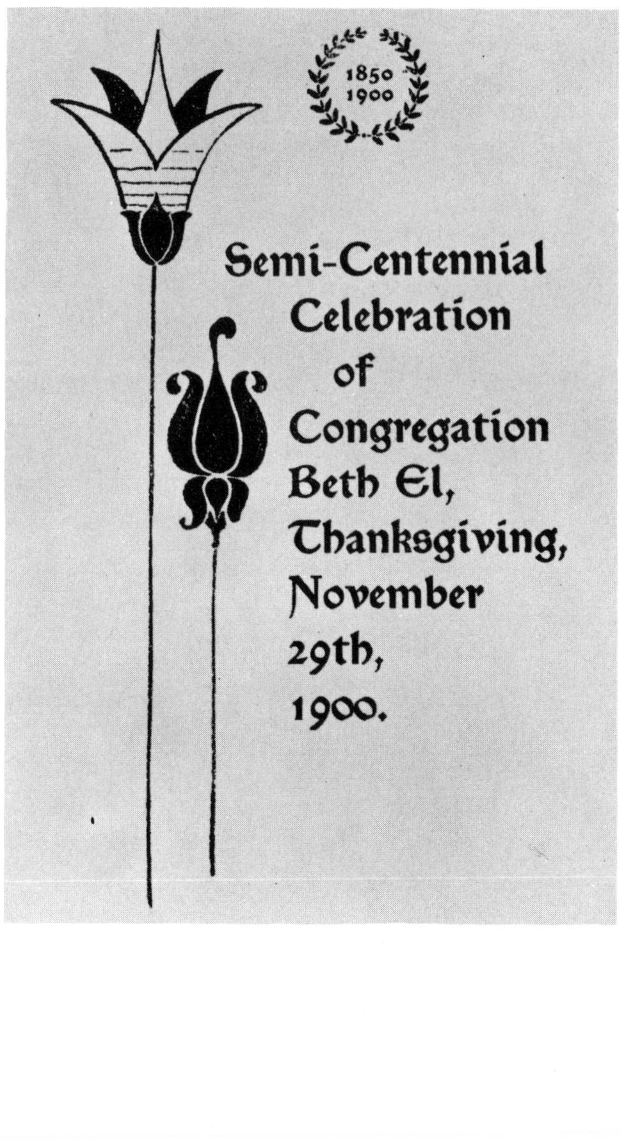

1850
1900
Semi-Centennial
Celebration
of
Congregation
Beth El,
Thanksgiving,
November
29th,
1900.

Order of Exercises.

1. ORGAN PRELUDE—"Festival Hymn," . . *Saint Saens*
MR. FREDERICK ALEXANDER

2. QUARTETTE—"I will extol Thee, O God," . . *Costa*
TEMPLE BETH EL CHOIR

3. PRAYER— . . . . . .
RABBI LEO M. FRANKLIN

4. TENOR SOLO { *a* "Du bist wie eine Blume," . *Meyer*
b "Elegie" (with 'Cello obligato), *Massenet*
MR. ELVIN SINGER

5. GREETING— . . . . . .
LOUIS BLITZ, PRESIDENT TEMPLE BETH EL

6. SOPRANO DUET—"I waited for the Lord," . *Mendelssohn*
MISSES MARIE PULCHER AND META GOEBEL

7. SCRIPTURE READING.

8. CONTRALTO SOLO—"Glorify the Lord," . *Geo. Intes*
MISS MINNIE S. WELZ

9. ADDRESS— . . . . .
DR. LOUIS GROSSMAN, CINCINNATI, OHIO.

10. 'CELLO SOLO—"Adagio," . . . *Mozart*
MR. ALFRED HOFMAN

11. ADDRESS—"Our Sabbath School," . .
MR. ADOLPH SLOMAN, CHAIRMAN S. S. BOARD

12. SOPRANO SOLO—"Midnight," (with 'Cello obligato),
MISS META GOEBEL

13. ADDRESS— . . . . . .
RABBI LEO M. FRANKLIN, MINISTER TEMPLE BETH EL

14. QUARTETTE—"Festival Anthem," . . *Verdi*
TEMPLE BETH EL CHOIR

15. BENEDICTION.

16. ORGAN POSTLUDE—"Hallelujah," . . *Handel*
MR. FREDERICK ALEXANDER

XVII RELIGIOUS SCHOOL PROGRAM OF THE SEMI-CENTENNIAL CELEBRATION OF CONGREGATION BETH EL

December 2, 1900

1850 1900

Semi-Centennial Celebration of Temple Beth El Sabbath School.

SUNDAY, DECEMBER 2, 1900.

Order of Exercises.

1.	SONG,	SCHOOL
2.	OUR SCHOOL,	JOS. M. WELT
3.	OUR NEW SABBATH SCHOOL,	IDA HART
4.	SONG,	SABBATH SCHOOL CHOIR
5.	OUR TEACHERS,	FRANK BLITZ
6.	OUR S. S. BOARD,	MARGUERITE SLOMAN
7.	PIANO SOLO,	LOTTIE MARYMONT
8.	OUR BOYS,	PEARL TANNENHOLZ
9.	OUR GIRLS,	IRA GREENBAUM
10.	VOCAL DUET,	MAUDE AND HAZEL BARLOW
11.	OUR POST CONFIRMATION CLASS,	HERBERT SLOMAN
12.	OUR SELF-SACRIFICE FUND,	RETTA FRANK
13.	SONG,	HENRY BROWN
14.	OUR CHOIR,	JESSIE GRABOWSKY
15.	SONG,	S. S. CHOIR
16.	OUR LIBRARY,	ELOISE AMBERG
17.	PIANO SOLO,	STELLA SPATER
18.	SONG—"America,"	SCHOOL

JULIAN H. KROLIK, Toastmaster.

XVIII PROGRAM OF THE DEDICATION OF THE TEMPLE ON WOODWARD NEAR ELIOT

September 18, 1903

"Unless the Lord build a house in vain do they labor who build it."—Psalm 127, 1.

1850. 1903.

DEDICATION SERVICES

"Thy gates shall stand open continually"

TEMPLE BETH EL

Friday Evening, September Eighteenth,

at half after seven,

Sabbath Morning, September Nineteenth,

at ten o'clock,

Nineteen hundred and three,

Detroit, Mich.

XIX SERVICES OF DEDICATION OF PRESENT TEMPLE AT WOODWARD AND GLADSTONE

November 10-12, 1922

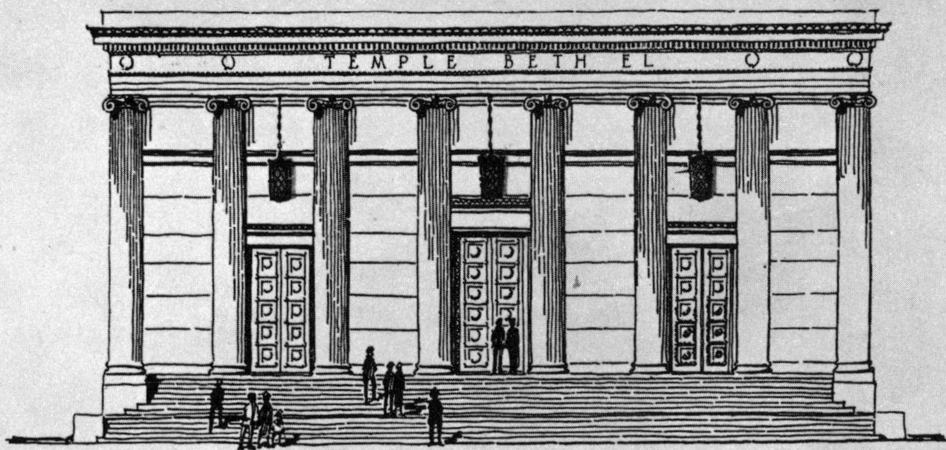

"Thy Gates Shall Stand Open Continually."

Congregation Beth El

[FOUNDED SEPTEMBER, 1850]

Rabbi, LEO M. FRANKLIN   *Assistant Rabbi*, HENRY J. BERKOWITZ

Officers

President, ISAAC GOLDBERG   *Treasurer*, LOUIS SIMON
Vice-President, ADOLPH FINSTERWALD   *Secretary*, MAGNUS A. HIRSCHFELD
Honorary Warden, EMANUEL WODIC

Executive Board

MILTON M. ALEXANDER
DAVID A. BROWN
LEO M. BUTZEL
ISRAEL COHEN
BERNARD GINSBURG
SAMUEL HEAVENRICH
ALBERT KAHN
DAY KROLIK
MILFORD STERN
LOUIS WELT

The Architect of the building is Mr. Albert Kahn.

The planning and construction of the new Temple was in charge of a Building Committee consisting of the Officers of the Congregation and the Rabbis in consultation with the Executive Board.

Special committees have had charge of arrangements for the details of the Dedication Services. To every hand and every heart whose labor and whose love have contributed to making this great day possible, the thanks and the appreciation of the Officers and Members of Congregation Beth El are herewith extended.

Friday Evening, November Tenth, at 7:30

Organ Preludes:
(*a*) Improvisation on Schlesinger's "Etz Chayim" ...... *Tyler*
(*b*) C-Sharp Minor .... *Rachmaninoff*

Introduction: "Open Ye Portals" .... WILLIAM HOWLAND
(*Especially written for this Dedication Service*)

"Great and Marvelous Are Thy Works" .... *Gaul*
CHOIR AND CHORUS

Invocation .... RABBI LEO M. FRANKLIN

S'u Sh'orim .... CHOIR

Scrolls are Placed in the Ark

Sh'ma Yisroel .... CHOIR

Lighting of the Perpetual Light .... EMANUEL WODIC

Tenor Solo: "The Lord is my Light" .... *Allitsen*
MR. GEORGE BECKER

Presentation of the Key .... SAMUEL HEAVENRICH

Acceptance of the Key .... ISAAC GOLDBERG
President, Congregation Beth El

Address .... RABBI LEO M. FRANKLIN

Sabbath Eve Service .... RABBI HENRY J. BERKOWITZ
(*U. P. B. pages 4-18*)

Dedication Hymn .... MR. WILLIAM HOWLAND
(*Especially written for this Service by Edith Ella Davis*)

Dedication Sermon .... RABBI EDWARD N. CALISCH
President, Central Conference of American Rabbis
Richmond, Va.

Conclusion of Ritual Service .... RABBI SAMUEL S. MAYERBERG
Dayton, Ohio

Anthem: "Great Is Jehovah the Lord" .... *Schubert*
CHOIR AND CHORUS

Prayer and Benediction .... RABBI DAVID PHILIPSON
Cincinnati, Ohio

Organ Postlude: "Hallel" .... *Tyler*

Saturday Morning, November Eleventh, at 10:00

Organ Prelude: "Sonata I" .... *Borowski*

Anthem: "The Lord Is in His Holy Temple" .... *Hawley*

DOUBLE QUARTET

Invocation .... RABBI PHILIP F. WATERMAN
Grand Rapids, Mich.

Sabbath Service (U. P. B., pages 67–112) ...... RABBI HENRY J. BERKOWITZ

The Scroll Service (Gen. 18, 1–33) .... RABBI LEO M. FRANKLIN

Scripture Lesson (First Kings VIII) .... RABBI PHILIP F. WATERMAN

Etz Chayim .... CHOIR

Address .... RABBI SAMUEL S. MAYERBERG

Alto Solo: "Awake, Put on Strength" .... *Rogers*

MISS IRENE TRAUB

Sermon .... RABBI DAVID PHILIPSON

Concluding Service and Kaddish .... RABBI LEO M. FRANKLIN

Anthem: "How Lovely Are Thy Dwellings" .... *Wolcott*

Closing Prayer and Benediction .... RABBI EDWARD N. CALISCH

Organ Postlude: "Improvisatore" .... *Tyler*

Sunday Morning, November Twelfth, at 10:30

Organ Prelude: "Andante—Fifth Symphony" .... *Beethoven*

Dedication Anthem: "Sing Hosanna in the Highest" .... *Dudley Buck*

DOUBLE QUARTET

Invocation .... RABBI HENRY J. BERKOWITZ

Greetings from Sister Congregations .... RABBI A. M. HERSHMAN
Congregation Shaarey Zedek, Detroit

Ritual Responses .... RABBI HENRY J. BERKOWITZ

Address .... RABBI ABRAM SIMON

Soprano Solo: "The Earth Is the Lord's" .... *Stephens*

MRS. CHARLES WELKER

Sermon .... RABBI LOUIS WOLSEY
Cleveland, Ohio

Anthem: "Praise the Lord" .... *Randegger*

DOUBLE QUARTET

Concluding Words .... RABBI LEO M. FRANKLIN

Benediction

Postlude: "Fugue E Major" .... *Bach*

XX PROGRAM OF SEVENTY-FIFTH ANNIVERSARY CELEBRATION OF CONGREGATION BETH EL

December 13, 1925

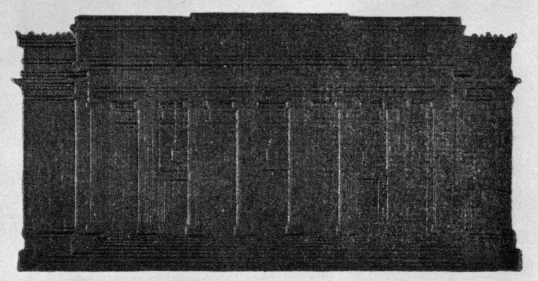

"Thy Gates Shall Stand Open Continually"

1850 1925

Seventy-Fifth Anniversary

Temple Beth El

Detroit

Divine Services

SUNDAY, DECEMBER THIRTEENTH
NINETEEN TWENTY FIVE

XXI PERPETUAL ARTICLES OF INCORPORATION OF CONGREGATION BETH EL

December 2, 1930

(ECCLESIASTICAL CORPORATIONS)

ARTICLES OF ASSOCIATION

of the

CONGREGATION BETH EL

We, the undersigned, desiring to become incorporated under the provisions of Act No. 84, P.A. 1921, do hereby make, execute and adopt the following articles of association, to-wit:

FIRST: The name assumed by this corporation and by which it shall be known in law, is Congregation Beth El;

SECOND: The location of said congregation shall be in the City of Detroit, County of Wayne and State of Michigan;

THIRD: The time for which said corporation shall be created shall be perpetual;

FOURTH: Its purpose shall be to perpetuate Judaism and uphold the belief in and worship of the One God;

FIFTH: This corporation shall proceed under section five, Chapter 1, Part 1, of the above named act.

SIXTH: This corporation shall have all of the powers, benefits and privileges accruing by virtue of any and all of the provisions of Chapter 3, Part 4, of Act No. 84 of the Public Acts of 1921 of the State of Michigan, as the said act may be amended from time to time.

IN WITNESS WHEREOF, we, the parties hereby associating for the purpose of giving legal effect to these articles, hereunto sign our names and places of residence:

Done at the City of Detroit, County of Wayne and State of Michigan, this 2nd day of December 1930.

(Signatures)	(Residences)
Herman J. Brachman	Detroit, Michigan.
Maurice J. Kaplan	Detroit, Michigan. 2905 Webb.
Clarence H. Enggass.	Detroit, Mich.
Adolph Finsterwald	Detroit Mich. (7410 La Salle Blvd.,
Joseph Hackman	Detroit Michigan
Morris Garvett	Detroit, Michigan.
Blanche Gilbert	Detroit, Michigan.
Alvin W. Hersch	Detroit Michigan.
Walter S. Heavenrich	Detroit, Michigan.
Israel Himelhoch	Detroit, Mich.
Day Krolik	Detroit, Mich.
Jacob Mazer	Detroit, Mich.
Harry R. Solomon	Detroit, Michigan.
Milford Stern	Detroit, Michigan.
Elsie K. Sulzberger	Detroit, Mich.
Mervin S. Welt	Detroit, Mich.

APPENDIX

XXII PROGRAM OF THE THIRTY-SEVENTH COUNCIL OF THE UNION OF AMERICAN HEBREW CONGREGATIONS

April 26–May 1, 1941

PROGRAM

★

Thirty-Seventh Council

of the

UNION OF AMERICAN HEBREW CONGREGATIONS

NATIONAL FEDERATION OF TEMPLE SISTERHOODS

Fourteenth Biennial Assembly

NATIONAL FEDERATION OF TEMPLE BROTHERHOODS

Ninth Biennial Convention

NATIONAL FEDERATION OF TEMPLE YOUTH

Second Biennial Convention

★

APRIL 26, 27, 28, 29, 30, and MAY 1, 1941

HEADQUARTERS

STATLER HOTEL

DETROIT

XXIII EXCERPTS FROM ADDRESSES AT THE CENTENNIAL ANNIVERSARY BANQUET OF CONGREGATION BETH EL

March 25, 1950

MR. NATE S. SHAPERO

One hundred years is a long time. Yet, in this world of revolutionary changes and fast-moving events, time, of itself, is unimportant unless it is measured in terms of progress and achievement, with which our Temple abounds. These are the reasons for our celebration tonight.

The history of our Temple illuminates many basic lessons and truths that challenge us today as we build for the future of our congregation. They are as fundamental today as they were one hundred years ago. Time has merely added to their lustre and significance.

That small band of Jews who founded Temple Beth El in 1850 were inspired by a positive desire to remain loyal to the faith of their fathers in a new land which recognized freedom of worship as a basic right of all Americans. With their wisdom and devotion they knew that by practicing the teachings of Judaism they could make a signal contribution as citizens to the democratic life of Detroit and to the United States. Since 1850 Temple Beth El through its lay and rabbinical leadership has been a major force of moral and spiritual truth and practice in the state of Michigan. Our congregation has enriched this community which has grown from a population of approximately 21,000 in 1850 to well over 2,000,000. Under the dynamic spiritual leadership of Dr. Glazer, our Temple has grown from 900 families in 1941 to 1600 families in 1950 and is today the fourth largest Jewish congregation in the United States.

We pay homage tonight to the founders of our Temple and to their successors. With their vision and understanding they realized that in order to survive on the American scene Judaism must be constantly adjusted to changing needs and circumstances without surrendering its basic ideals. For one hundred years Temple Beth El has been in the front rank of progressive Judaism. In 1862 it adopted a liberal platform involving many reforms in ritual and in worship. It was one of the first Temples to join in the organization of the Union of American Hebrew Congregations in 1873. It was one of the founders of the Hebrew Union College; and here in Detroit the Central Conference of American Rabbis was organized.

Temple Beth El shall always strive to achieve new levels of accomplishment in making Judaism more vital and more meaningful.

We are proud of our democratic traditions which have been exemplified throughout the years. This was best expressed when the unassigned pew system was introduced for the first time in the United States at Temple Beth El by Dr. Franklin in 1903.

For one hundred years Temple Beth El has emphasized religious education for children and adults and has firmly clung to the conviction that only through loyalty to Judaism can a Jewish community survive and flourish in America. These high standards of dignity and learning have influenced every Jewish organization in the community. We shall continue to add to the prestige and effectiveness of Jewish religious life by preserving and extending these high standards.

With a community awareness, Temple Beth El has been identified with the leadership of every social, civic, or philanthropic movement in our great city. Our Temple was the first to pioneer in establishing a common ground where Jews and Christians could come together as Americans, and has been a leading force and influence in establishing better human relationships amongst all groups in the community. We shall continue this work of cooperation and reconciliation with our fellow citizens for the safety and advance of our American democracy.

Throughout the many years Temple Beth El has been responsible for the establishment of the principal Jewish organizations in this city and state and we shall continue to inspire and strengthen all of them.

These are but a few of the accomplishments and teachings of our rich and glorious past. They are the guide posts on our road of the future. They will point the way in seeking even higher levels of attainment in our spiritual, cultural, and educational program.

We can best pay our respects to the past and our gratitude for this priceless heritage by rededicating ourselves to the sacred tasks and responsibilities which lie immediately ahead of us; to further strengthen our Temple and build an even better and stronger community as Jews and as Americans.

DR. NELSON GLUECK

In the translation of the ideals of Judaism into all the avenues of our lives as Jews and as Americans, this congregation has long played an important role. Temple Beth El, with its magnificent traditions, and its spirited and devoted rabbis and officers and members, is bound to play an increasingly important role not only in matters which affect the individual congregant, but which influence our community and country as a whole. History has given us a spiritual inheritance which we find inseparable from the American promise.

We Americans, Jews and Christians, are partners in the noblest social experiment that has ever taken place on such a vast scale in the history of civilization—an experiment based upon the Bill of Rights, even as that Bill of Rights is based upon the ethical injunctions of the Bible. We have guaranteed the opportunities of freedom and the freedom of opportunity to all the citizens of our country, and we must be on the watch and prepared to battle both in times of war and peace for both the spirit and letter of that guarantee. We must remember that there are dangers which confront us not only from abroad, but which threaten our liberties also here at home. The voice of America will sound clear and true and serve as the clarion call to human freedom, against which no tyranny or armament, however terrifying, can ultimately prevail, as long as it echoes the instruction of the message of Sinai.

We Jews know through historical memory that not by bread alone can we live, nor even by alms,—and especially we the descendants of the People of the Book. We have learned that the sturdiest foundations of a healthy Jewish life are to be found above all in the house of worship, and what that house of worship, such as Temple Beth El, stands for.

The sense and hope of survival for us and mankind bespeak and demand on our part an all-enveloping passion for the fundamentals of Judaism—a Judaism adaptable, changeable, interpretable, unshakable, a Judaism alert to life and progress, rich in promise to the faithful, open to all mankind—an American Judaism, strengthening and being strengthened by the aims of the America of Washington and Jefferson and Lincoln and Walt Whitman—a Reform Judaism, concerned not so much with the forms of approaching as with the facts of seeking and finding, in company with our fellows of all faiths, the blessed unity of the all-embracing love of one God, the God of Israel, the God of Mankind, the God of the Universe.

To that unity, to that Judaism, to that God, this congregation is consecrated. Upon Temple Beth El and all those connected with it, upon Rabbi Glazer, and all who labor in the army of the Lord, upon all Israel, upon America and all of mankind, we invoke God's blessing, repeating the words of the inscription on the ancient synagogue: *Peace, Peace upon all Israel, Amen, Amen, Selah!*

DR. SOLOMON B. FREEHOF

Evidently something very strange is going on in our world. It is a problem, a tremendous increased convenience, a tremendous increased discontent. Why, this discontent is a problem in itself. Our concern is to record the bewildering fact: a vast increase in the actual conveniences that save toil, a tremendous amount of discontent. In some mysterious way the great effort of technology to take the heavy burden of physical toil off our shoulders, that which broke the spirit of hundreds of previous generations, for some reason that effort has not made us happy. Our discontent has kept pace with the increase of conveniences. It is a remarkable situation and it is perfectly clear that the next advance towards happiness will not have to be done in the laboratory except in the laboratory of the human heart.

Now you see what is wrong with us. We have the freedom and we have not the *faith.* We have the freedom to express anything and we do not have anything to express. We do not believe in religion very strongly these days. We are not so ardent for culture. We are not sure about democracy. We have freedom for nothing. When you have no great cause to develop with your liberty, then you waste your liberty on trivial things; so it becomes the liberty to misbehavior, the liberty to hang around taverns, the liberty to waste life and forget responsibilities. There is great freedom in this age, freedom without a great faith. Until faith is recovered there will never be happiness in the freest of eras.

So the future of ourselves and our descendants in the next half century depends not so much any more upon the laboratory and the plant. You can improve the radio a million times, you can have the television colored or not colored, you can make five hundred improvements in washing machines and the like, and people will still be miserable. It is evident now that the change must come elsewhere. The next progress will have to be in the home, in the church, and in the schools. We will have to build up in human beings a certain contentment with the blessings of life; they have more with which to be content than any previous generation, a certain world feeling that will add to world stability and affect the statesmen, and a certain rebirth of faith in exalted things for which freedom can be used. When we will add the personal, moral qualities to the grand industrial and technological achievements, when the home and the church and the school will do their part in the laboratory and the factory, there is a good chance that the coming generation can be the happiest in the history of humanity.

DR. B. BENEDICT GLAZER

At the very outset, let me say that the glorious history and present position of eminence occupied by Temple Beth El is a tribute to the lay and spiritual leaders who have guided its destinies so well throughout the successive generations of its growth and achievement. However, in the fateful times through which we are passing, when great issues are at stake, when the future of our civilization is being weighed in the balance, the present and the future of Temple Beth El are in a sense far more important than its past.

To me the presence of Temple Beth El in this community represents a flaming symbol of the Jewish will to survive. For it is in the synagogue that we find the basic and indispensable program for Jewish survival, and this program is built primarily upon the moral and spiritual heritage bequeathed to us from our ancient past, a program which has acquired new meanings and new directions in the face of modern conditions and requirements. It is through the synagogue that we, as Jews, become whole and integrated personalities, and the best type of citizen.

It is eminently appropriate, therefore, on an occasion such as this to rehearse briefly what I consider to be the three-fold program of the synagogue, which has never lost its validity and which is needed now more than ever before. In the first place, the synagogue has always fostered the ideal of learning. It has encouraged its adherents to study Jewish sources; to become familiar with Jewish law and traditions; to teach their children the fundamentals of Judaism. This ideal of learning was definitive in shaping the lives of our ancestors as a literate people. The Jewish generations of today are the beneficiaries of this intellectual tradition, so carefully nurtured by the Jewish emphasis upon the value of the educational process. However, learning was never an end, in itself, for the Jew. It was always associated with moral ends and spiritual purposes, with the acceptance of social responsibility. "The fear of the Lord is the beginning of wisdom," says the writer of the Book of Proverbs. Our tradition does not glorify men who are merely intellectuals, who regarded their proficiency in art, literature or science as an end in itself. Our tradition did not nurture a strain of "irresponsibles," to use a term coined by Archibald McLeish, or passive barbarians, to employ a figure minted by Louis Mumford, to describe those who divorce knowledge from conscience.

The second ideal which has ever been fostered by the program of the synagogue is the ideal of character. The most magnificent expression of Jewish character is to be found in the teachings of the Prophets of Israel. It is no accident that the millennial concern of Israel with the demands of the moral law has provided the Western World with its only alternative to chaos. Pity, mercy, love, justice, righteousness and peace, are at the very heart of the vocabulary of Judaism. And these expressions of Jewish character are not the product of academic speculation in the realm of ethical choices. They flow from our own bitter and tragic experiences throughout our history, with bondage, suffering, persecution, exile and death. We are exhorted by the writers of the Old Testament not to oppress the stranger, the widow or the orphan, because we have known what it was to be among the weak and disadvantaged members of human society. It will be a sorry day in Jewish life if our people lose this acute moral sensitivity to oppression and injustice, as these evils exist in the total context of human society and not merely within our own household.

And finally, the synagogue inspires and cultivates the ideal of piety. Piety has been defined as man's reverential attachment to the sources of his being and the steadying and controlling of his life by that attachment. Thus, in this sense, the cultivation of piety represents at the very outset man's quest for the Infinite God, the eternal guarantor of the principles of value, meaning and truth. On a more personal level, piety symbolizes the whole series of Jewish loyalties as they are practiced in the home, in the community and in the synagogue. It is, in fact, the emotional expression of our loyalty to our home, to our country, to our fellow-men, to our God. It is the pious person who is willing to assume the moral disciplines antecedent to the realization of the Messianic dream of one God, one world and one humanity.

APPENDIX

XXIV PRESIDENTS OF THE SISTERHOOD OF TEMPLE BETH EL

1901–1954

*Mrs. Adolph Sloman	1901–1908
*Mrs. Abe I. Wolf	1908–1912
Mrs. David J. Epston	1912–1914
*Mrs. Abe I. Wolf	1914–1916
Mrs. Isaac Gilbert	1916–1919
*Mrs. Adolph Sloman	1919–1920
Mrs. Mayer B. Sulzberger	1920–1921
Mrs. Wallace Rosenheim	1921–1922
Mrs. Mayer B. Sulzberger	1922–1923
Mrs. Wallace Rosenheim	1923–1926
Mrs. Oscar C. Robinson	1926–1929
Mrs. Sol A. Wolff	1929–1932
*Mrs. Samuel L. Van Noorden	1932–1934
*Mrs. Herman Lewis	1934
Mrs. Maier B. Finsterwald	1934–1935
Mrs. Harry Krohn	1935–1937
Mrs. Philip Bloomgarden	1937–1939
Mrs. Lawrence Freedman	1939–1941
*Mrs. Henry Meyers	1941–1943
Mrs. John C. Hopp	1943–1946
Mrs. Maurice Klein	1946–1948
Mrs. M. George Wayburn	1948–1951
Mrs. Arthur H. Rice	1951–1953
Mrs. Sanford R. Klein	1953–

*Deceased

XXV PRESIDENTS OF THE MEN'S CLUB OF CONGREGATION BETH EL 1919–1954

*Walter S. Heavenrich	1919–1921
Melville S. Welt	1921–1923
*Jacob Nathan	1923–1924
*Harry R. Solomon	1924–1926
Morris Garvett	1926–1928
*Edwin A. Wolf	1928–1929
A. C. Lappin	1929–1930
*Sidney M. Fecheimer	1931–1933
Joseph Magidsohn	1933–1935
*Irving L. Hirschman	1935–1937
Saul H. Rose	1937–1938
Leo I. Franklin	1938–1939
Harry C. Markle	1939–1940
Benjamin Wilk	1940–1942
Dr. Nathan H. Schlafer	1942–1943
Nathan M. Lerner	1943–1944
Theodore D. Birnkrant	1944–1945
Leon S. Wayburn	1945–1947
Arthur L. Goulson	1947–1948
Arthur H. Rice	1948–1949
Walter Schmier	1949–1950
Dr. Max B. Winslow	1950–1951
Dr. Hilliard Goldstick	1951–1952
Raymond K. Rubiner	1952–1953
William C. Sloman	1953–1954
Dr. Leo A. Greenblatt	1954–

*Deceased

APPENDIX

XXVI MEMBERSHIP STATISTICS OF CONGREGATION BETH EL

1850–1954

1850	12
1855	25
1860	40
1865	60
1870	70
1875	80
1880	102
1885	84
1890	117
1895	138
1900	181
1905	352
1910	422
1915	576
1920	889
1925	1,246
1930	1,150
1940	1,013
1945	1,182
1950	1,500
1954	1,663

Index

I. INDEX OF NAMES

Y

Z

II. LIST OF ILLUSTRATIONS

(exclusive of Appendix)

LIST OF ILLUSTRATIONS

PROPOSED DEVELOPMENT PLAN FOR T